My Two Years in Russia

An American Anarchist's
Disillusionment, and the Betrayal of the
Russian Revolution by Lenin's Soviet
Union

Emma Goldman

Red and Black Publishers, St Petersburg, Florida

Originally published in two volumes, 1923 and 1924

Library of Congress Cataloging-in-Publication Data

Goldman, Emma, 1869-1940.
    My two years in Russia : an American anarchist's disillusionment, and the betrayal
of the Russian Revolution by Lenin's Soviet Union / Emma Goldman.
        p. cm.
    "Originally published in two volumes, 1923 and 1924."
    ISBN 978-1-934941-24-9
 1. Soviet Union--History--Revolution, 1917-1921--Personal narratives. 2.
Communism--Soviet Union. 3. Goldman, Emma, 1869-1940--Travel--Soviet Union. I.
Title.
    DK265.7.G58 2008
    947.084'1092--dc22
    [B]

                                                                        2008021855

Red and Black Publishers, PO Box 7542, St Petersburg, Florida, 33734

Contact us at: info@RedandBlackPublishers.com

            Printed and manufactured in the United States of America

Contents

Preface

To First Volume of American Edition

The decision to record my experiences, observations, and reactions during my stay in Russia I had made long before I thought of leaving that country. In fact, that was my main reason for departing from that tragically heroic land.

The strongest of us are loath to give up a long-cherished dream. I had come to Russia possessed by the hope that I should find a new-born country, with its people wholly consecrated to the great, though very difficult, task of revolutionary reconstruction. And I had fervently hoped that I might become an active part of the inspiring work.

I found reality in Russia grotesque, totally unlike the great ideal that had borne me upon the crest of high hope to the land of promise. It required fifteen long months before I could get my bearings. Each day, each week, each month added new links to the fatal chain that pulled down my cherished edifice. I fought desperately against the disillusionment. For a long time I strove against the still voice within me which urged me to face the overpowering facts. I would not and could not give up.

Then came Kronstadt. It was the final wrench. It completed the terrible realization that the Russian Revolution was no more.

I saw before me the Bolshevik State, formidable, crushing every constructive revolutionary effort, suppressing, debasing, and disintegrating everything. Unable and unwilling to become a cog in that sinister machine, and aware that I could be of no practical use to Russia and her people, I decided to leave the country. Once out of it, I would relate honestly, frankly, and as objectively as humanly possible to me the story of my two years' stay in Russia.

I left in December, 1921. I could have written then, fresh under the influence of the ghastly experience. But I waited four months before I could bring myself to write a series of articles. I delayed another four months before beginning the present volume.

I do not pretend to write a history. Removed by fifty or a hundred years from the events he is describing, the historian may seem to be objective. But real history is not a compilation of mere data. It is valueless without the human element which the historian necessarily gets from the writings of the contemporaries of the events in question. It is the personal reactions of the participants and observers which lend vitality to all history and make it vivid and alive. Thus, numerous histories have been written of the French Revolution; yet there are only a very few that stand out true and convincing, illuminative in the degree in which the historian has felt his subject through the medium of human documents left by the contemporaries of the period.

I myself — and I believe, most students of history — have felt and visualized the Great French Revolution much more vitally from the letters and diaries of contemporaries, such as Mme. Roland, Mirabeau, and other eye witnesses, than from the so-called objective historians. By a strange coincidence a volume of letters written during the French Revolution and compiled by the able German anarchist publicist, Gustav Landauer, came into my hands during the most critical period of my Russian experience. I was actually reading them while hearing the Bolshevik artillery begin the bombardment of the Kronstadt rebels. Those letters gave me a most vivid insight into the events of the French Revolution. As never before they brought home to me the realization that the Bolshevik régime in Russia was, on the whole, a significant replica of what had happened in France more than a century before.

Great interpreters of the French Revolution, like Thomas Carlyle and Peter Kropotkin, drew their understanding and inspiration from the human records of the period. Similarly will the future historians of the Great Russian Revolution — if they are to write real history and not a mere compilation of facts — draw from the impressions and reactions of those who have lived through the Russian Revolution, who have shared the misery and travail of the people, and who actually participated in or witnessed the tragic panorama in its daily unfoldment.

While in Russia I had no clear idea how much had already been written on the subject of the Russian Revolution. But the few books which reached me occasionally impressed me as most inadequate. They were written by people with no first-hand knowledge of the situation and were sadly superficial. Some of the writers had spent from two weeks to two months in Russia, did not know the language of the country, and in most instances were chaperoned by official guides and interpreters. I do not refer here to the writers who, in and out of Russia, play the role of Bolshevik court functionaries. They are a class apart. With them I deal in the chapter on the "Travelling Salesmen of the Revolution." Here I have in mind the sincere friends of the Russian Revolution. The work of most of them has resulted in incalculable confusion and mischief. They have helped to perpetuate the myth that the Bolsheviki and the Revolution are synonymous. Yet nothing is further from the truth.

The actual Russian Revolution took place in the summer months of 1917. During that period the peasants possessed themselves of the land, the workers of the factories, thus demonstrating that they knew well the meaning of social revolution. The October change was the finishing touch to the work begun six months previously. In the great uprising the Bolsheviki assumed the voice of the people. They clothed themselves with the agrarian programme of the Social Revolutionists and the industrial tactics of the Anarchists. But after the high tide of revolutionary enthusiasm had carried them into power, the Bolsheviki discarded their false plumes. It was then that began the spiritual separation between the Bolsheviki and the Russian Revolution. With each succeeding day the gap grew wider, their interests more conflicting. To-day it is no exaggeration to state that the Bolsheviki stand as the arch enemies of the Russian Revolution.

Superstitions die hard. In the case of this modern superstition the process is doubly hard because various factors have combined to administer artificial respiration. International intervention, the blockade, and the very efficient world propaganda of the Communist Party have kept the Bolshevik myth alive. Even the terrible famine is being exploited to that end.

How powerful a hold that superstition wields I realize from my own experience. I had always known that the Bolsheviki are Marxists. For thirty years I fought the Marxian theory as a cold, mechanistic, enslaving formula. In pamphlets, lectures and debates I argued against it. I was therefore not unaware of what might be expected from the Bolsheviki. But the Allied attack upon them made them the symbol of the Russian Revolution, and brought me to their defence.

From November, 1917, until February, 1918, while out on bail for my attitude against the war, I toured America in defence of the Bolsheviki. I published a pamphlet in elucidation of the Russian Revolution and in justification of the Bolsheviki. I defended them as embodying in practice the spirit of the revolution, in spite of their theoretic Marxism. My attitude toward them at that time is characterized in the following passages from my pamphlet, "The Truth About the Bolsheviki:"(in Mother Earth Publishing Association, New York, February, 1917.)

"The Russian Revolution is a miracle in more than one respect. Among other extraordinary paradoxes it presents the phenomenon of the Marxian Social Democrats, Lenin and Trotsky, adopting Anarchist revolutionary tactics, while the Anarchists Kropotkin, Tcherkessov, Tschaikovsky are denying these tactics and falling into Marxian reasoning, which they had all their lives repudiated as 'German metaphysics.' "

The Bolsheviki of 1903, though revolutionists, adhered to the Marxian doctrine concerning the industrialization of Russia and the historic mission of the bourgeoisie as a necessary evolutionary process before the Russian masses could come into their own. The Bolsheviki of 1917 no longer believe in the predestined function of the bourgeoisie. They have been swept forward on the waves of Bakunin; namely, that once the masses become conscious of their economic power, they make their own history and need not be bound by traditions and processes of a dead past which, like secret treaties, are made at a round table and are not dictated by life itself.

In 1918, Madame Breshkovsky visited the United States and began her campaign against the Bolsheviki. I was then in the Missouri Penitentiary. Grieved and shocked by the work of the "Little Grandmother of the Russian Revolution," I wrote imploring her to bethink herself and not betray the cause she had given her life to. On that occasion I emphasized the fact that while neither of us agreed with the Bolsheviki in theory, we should yet be one with them in defending the Revolution.

When the Courts of the State of New York upheld the fraudulent methods by which I was disfranchised and my American citizenship of thirty-two years denied me, I waived my right of appeal in order that I might return to Russia and help in the great work. I believed fervently that the Bolsheviki were furthering the Revolution and exerting themselves in behalf of the people. I clung to my faith and belief for more than a year after my coming to Russia.

Observation and study, extensive travel through various parts of the country, meeting with every shade of political opinion and every variety of friend and enemy of the Bolsheviki—all convinced me of the ghastly delusion which had been foisted upon the world.

I refer to these circumstances to indicate that my change of mind and heart was a painful and difficult process, and that my final decision to speak out is for the sole reason that the people everywhere may learn to differentiate between the Bolsheviki and the Russian Revolution.

The conventional conception of gratitude is that one must not be critical of those who have shown him kindness. Thanks to this notion parents enslave their children more effectively than by brutal treatment; and by it friends tyrannize over one another. In fact, all human relationships are to-day vitiated by this noxious idea.

Some people have upbraided me for my critical attitude toward the Bolsheviki. "How ungrateful to attack the Communist Government after the hospitality and kindness she enjoyed in Russia!" they indignantly exclaim. I do not mean to gainsay that I have received advantages while I was in Russia. I could have received many more had I been willing to serve the powers that be. It is that very circumstance which has made it bitterly hard for me to speak out against the evils as I saw them day by day. But finally I realized that silence is indeed a sign of consent. Not to cry out against the betrayal of the Russian Revolution would have made me a party to that betrayal. The Revolution and the welfare of the masses in and out of Russia are by far too important to me to allow any personal consideration for the Communists I have met and learned to respect to obscure my sense of justice and to cause me to refrain from giving to the world my two years' experience in Russia.

In certain quarters objections will no doubt be raised because I have given no names of the persons I am quoting. Some may even exploit the fact to discredit my veracity. But I prefer to face that rather than to turn any one over to the tender mercies of the Tcheka, which would inevitably result were I to divulge the names of the Communists or non-Communists who felt free to speak to me. Those familiar with the real situation in Russia and who are not under the mesmeric influence of the Bolshevik superstition or in the employ of the Communists will bear me out that I have given a true picture. The rest of the world will learn in due time.

Friends whose opinion I value have been good enough to suggest that my quarrel with the Bolsheviki is due to my social philosophy rather than to the failure of the Bolshevik régime. As an Anarchist, they claim, I would naturally insist on the importance of the individual and of personal liberty, but in the revolutionary period both must be subordinated to the good of the whole. Other friends point out that destruction, violence, and terrorism are inevitable factors in a revolution. As a revolutionist, they say, I cannot consistently object to the violence practised by the Bolsheviki.

Both these criticisms would be justified had I come to Russia expecting to find Anarchism realized, or if I were to maintain that revolutions can be made peacefully. Anarchism to me never was a mechanistic arrangement of social relationships to be imposed upon man by political scene-shifting or by a transfer of power from one social class to another. Anarchism to me was and is the child, not of destruction, but of construction—the result of growth and development of the conscious creative social efforts of a regenerated people. I do not therefore expect Anarchism to follow in the immediate footsteps of centuries of despotism and submission. And I certainly did not expect to see it ushered in by the Marxian theory.

I did, however, hope to find in Russia at least the beginnings of the social changes for which the Revolution had been fought. Not the fate of the individual was my main concern as a revolutionist. I should have been content if the Russian workers and peasants as a whole had derived essential social betterment as a result of the Bolshevik régime.

Two years of earnest study, investigation, and research convinced me that the great benefits brought to the Russian people by Bolshevism exist only on paper, painted in glowing colours to the masses of Europe and America by efficient Bolshevik propaganda. As advertising wizards the Bolsheviki excel anything the world had ever known before. But in reality the Russian people have gained nothing from the Bolshevik experiment. To be sure, the peasants have the land; not by the grace of the Bolsheviki, but through their own direct efforts, set in motion long before the October change. That the peasants were able to retain the land is due mostly to the static Slav tenacity; owing to the circumstance that they form by far the largest part of the population and are deeply rooted in the soil, they could not as easily be torn away from it as the workers from their means of production.

The Russian workers, like the peasants, also employed direct action. They possessed themselves of the factories, organized their own shop committees, and were virtually in control of the economic life of Russia. But soon they were stripped of their power and placed under the industrial yoke of the Bolshevik State. Chattel slavery became the lot of the Russian proletariat. It was suppressed and exploited in the name of something which was later to bring it comfort, light, and warmth. Try as I might I could find nowhere any evidence of benefits received either by the workers or the peasants from the Bolshevik régime.

On the other hand, I did find the revolutionary faith of the people broken, the spirit of solidarity crushed, the meaning of comradeship and mutual helpfulness distorted. One must have lived in Russia, close to the everyday affairs of the people; one must have seen and felt their utter disillusionment and despair to appreciate fully the disintegrating effect of the Bolshevik principle and methods — disintegrating all that was once the pride and the glory of revolutionary Russia.

The argument that destruction and terror are part of revolution I do not dispute. I know that in the past every great political and social change necessitated violence. America might still be under the British yoke but for the heroic colonists who dared to oppose British tyranny by force of arms. Black slavery might still be a legalized institution in the United States but for the militant spirit of the John Browns. I have never denied that violence is inevitable, nor do I gainsay it now. Yet it is one thing to employ violence in combat, as a means of defence. It is quite another thing to make a principle of terrorism, to institutionalize it, to assign it the most vital place in the social struggle. Such terrorism begets counter-revolution and in turn itself becomes counter-revolutionary.

Rarely has a revolution been fought with as little violence as the Russian Revolution. Nor would have Red Terror followed had the people and the cultural forces remained in control of the Revolution. This was demonstrated by the spirit of fellowship and solidarity which prevailed throughout Russia during the first months after the October revolution. But an insignificant minority bent on creating an absolute State is necessarily driven to oppression and terrorism.

There is another objection to my criticism on the part of the Communists. Russia is on strike, they say, and it is unethical for a revolutionist to side against the workers when they are striking against their masters. That is pure demagoguery practised by the Bolsheviki to silence criticism.

It is not true that the Russian people are on strike. On the contrary, the truth of the matter is that the Russian people have been locked out and that the Bolshevik State—even as the bourgeois industrial master—uses the sword and the gun to keep the people out. In the case of the Bolsheviki this tyranny is masked by a world-stirring slogan: thus they have succeeded in blinding the masses. Just because I am a revolutionist I refuse to side with the master class, which in Russia is called the Communist Party.

Till the end of my days my place shall be with the disinherited and oppressed. It is immaterial to me whether Tyranny rules in the Kremlin or in any other seat of the mighty. I could do nothing for suffering Russia while in that country. Perhaps I can do something now by pointing out the lessons of the Russian experience. Not my concern for the Russian people only has prompted the writing of this volume: it is my interest in the masses everywhere.

Emma Goldman.

Berlin, July, 1922.

Preface

To Second Volume of American Edition

The annals of literature tell of books expurgated, of whole chapters eliminated or changed beyond recognition. But I believe it has rarely happened that a work should be published with more than a third of it left out and—without the reviewers being aware of the fact. This doubtful distinction has fallen to the lot of my work on Russia.

The story of that painful experience might well make another chapter, but for the present it is sufficient to give the bare facts of the case.

My manuscript was sent to the original purchaser in two parts, at different times. Subsequently the publishing house of Doubleday, Page Co. bought the rights to my work, but when the first printed copies reached me I discovered to my dismay that not only had my original title, "My Two Years in Russia," been changed to "My Disillusionment in Russia," but that the last twelve chapters were entirely missing, including my Afterword which is, at least to myself, the most vital part.

There followed an exchange of cables and letters, which gradually elicited the fact that Doubleday, Page Co. had secured my manuscript from a literary agency in the good faith that it was complete. By some conspiracy of circumstances the second installment of my work either failed to reach the original purchaser or was lost in his office. At any rate, the book was published without anyone suspecting its incompleteness.

The present volume contains the chapters missing from the American edition, and I deeply appreciate the devotion of my friends who made the appearance of an additional volume possible in America and this complete edition possible in England — in justice to myself and to my readers.

The adventures of my manuscript are not without their humorous side, which throws a peculiar light on the critics. Of almost a hundred American reviewers of my work only two sensed its incompleteness. And, incidentally, one of them is not a "regular" critic but a librarian. Rather a reflection on professional acumen or conscientiousness.

It was a waste of time to notice the "criticism" of those who have either not read the book or lacked the wit to realize that it was unfinished. Of all the alleged "reviews" only two deserve consideration as written by earnest and able men.

One of them thought that the published title of my book was more appropriate to its contents than the name I had chosen. My disillusionment, he asserted, is not only with the Bolsheviki but with the Revolution itself. In support of this contention he cited Bukharin's statement to the effect that "a revolution cannot be accomplished without terror, disorganization, and even wanton destruction, any more than an omelette can be made without breaking the eggs." But it seems not to have occurred to my critic that, though the breaking of the eggs is necessary, no omelette can be made if the yolk be thrown away. And that is precisely what the Communist Party did to the Russian Revolution. For the yolk they substituted Bolshevism, more specifically Leninism, with the result shown in my book — a result that is gradually being realized as an entire failure by the world at large.

The reviewer referred to also believes that it was "grim necessity, the driving need to preserve not the Revolution but the remnants of civilization, which forced the Bolsheviki to lay hands on every available weapon, the Terror, the Tcheka, suppression of free speech and press, censorship, military conscription, conscription of labour, requisitioning of peasants' crops, even bribery and corruption." He evidently agrees with me that the Communists employed all these methods; and that, as he himself states, "the 'means' largely determines the 'end'"—a conclusion the proof and demonstration of which are contained in my book. The only mistake in this viewpoint, however—a most vital one—is the assumption that the Bolsheviki were forced to resort to the methods referred to in order to "preserve the remnants of civilization." Such a view is based on an entire misconception of the philosophy and practice of Bolshevism. Nothing can be further from the desire or intention of Leninism than the "preservation of the remnants of civilization." Had my critic said instead, "the preservation of the Communist dictatorship, of the political absolutism of the Party," he would have come nearer the truth, and we should have no quarrel on the matter. We must not fail to consider the Bolsheviki continue to employ exactly the same methods to-day as they did in what the reviewer calls "the moments of grim necessity, in 1919, 1920, and 1921."

We are in 1925. The military fronts have long ago been liquidated; internal counter-revolution is suppressed; the old bourgeoisie is eliminated; the "moments of grim necessity" are past. In fact, Russia is being politically recognized by various governments of Europe and Asia, and the Bolsheviki are inviting international capital to come to their country whose natural wealth, as Tchicherin assures the world capitalists, is "waiting to be exploited." The "moments of grim necessity" are gone, but the Terror, the Tchecka, suppression of free speech and press, and all the other Communist methods of former years still remain in force. Indeed, they are being applied even more brutally and barbarously since the death of Lenin. Is it to "preserve the remnants of civilization" or to strengthen the weakening Party dictatorship?

My critic further charged me with believing that "had the Russians made the Revolution à la Bakunin instead of à la Marx" the result would have been different and more satisfactory. I plead guilty to the charge. In truth, I not only believe so; I am certain of it. The Russian Revolution—more correctly, the Bolshevik methods—conclusively demonstrated how a revolution should not be made. The Russian experiment has proven the fatality of a political party usurping the functions of the revolutionary people, of an omnipotent State seeking to impose its will upon the country, of a dictatorship attempting to "organize" the new life. But I need not repeat here the reflections summed up in my concluding chapter.

A second critic believes me a "prejudiced witness," because I — an Anarchist — am opposed to government, whatever its forms. Yet the whole first part of my book entirely disproves the assumption of my prejudice. I defended the Bolsheviki while still in America, and for long months in Russia I sought every opportunity to cooperate with them and to aid in the great task of revolutionary upbuilding. Though an Anarchist and an anti-governmentalist, I had not come to Russia expecting to find my ideal realized. I saw in the Bolsheviki the symbol of the Revolution and I was eager to work with them in spite of our differences. However, if lack of aloofness from the actualities of life means that one cannot judge things fairly, then my critic is right. One could not have lived through two years of Communist terror, of a régime involving the enslavement of the whole people, the annihilation of the most fundamental values, human and revolutionary, of corruption and mismanagement and yet have remained aloof or "impartial" in the critic's sense. I doubt whether the latter, though not an Anarchist, would have done so. Could he, being human?

In conclusion, the present publication of the chapters missing in the first edition comes at a very significant period in the life of Russia. When the "NEP," Lenin's new economic policy, was introduced, there rose the hope of a better day, of a gradual abolition of the policies of terror and persecution. The Communist dictatorship seemed inclined to relax its strangle-hold upon the thoughts and lives of the people. But the hope was short-lived. Since the death of Lenin the Bolsheviki have returned to the terror of the worst days of their régime. Despotism, fearing for its power, seeks safety in blood-shed. As timely as in 1922 is my book to-day.

When the first series of my articles on Russia appeared, in 1922, and later when my book was published in America, I was bitterly attacked and denounced by American radicals of almost every camp. But I felt confident that the time would come when the mask would be torn from the false face of Bolshevism and the great delusion exposed. The time has come even sooner than I anticipated. In most civilized lands — in France, England, Germany, in the Scandinavian and Latin countries, even in America the fog of blind faith is gradually lifting. The reactionary character of the Bolshevik régime is being realized by the masses, its terrorism and persecution of non-Communist opinion condemned. The torture of the political victims of the dictatorship in the prisons of Russia, in the concentration camps of the frozen North and in Siberian exile, is rousing the conscience of the more progressive elements the world over. In almost every country societies for the defence and aid of the politicals imprisoned in Russia have been formed, with the object of securing their liberation and the establishment of freedom of opinion and expression in Russia.

If my work will help in these efforts to throw light upon the real situation in Russia and to awaken the world to the true character of Bolshevism and the fatality of dictatorship—be it Fascist or Communist—I shall bear with equanimity the misunderstanding and misrepresentation of foe or friend. And I shall not regret the travail and struggle of spirit that produced this work, which now, after many vicissitudes, is at last complete in print.

Emma Goldman.

August, 1925.

Chapter 1: Deportation to Russia

On the night of December 21, 1919, together with two hundred and forty-eight other political prisoners, I was deported from America. Although it was generally known we were to be deported, few really believed that the United States would so completely deny her past as an asylum for political refugees, some of whom had lived and worked in America for more than thirty years.

In my own case, the decision to eliminate me first became known when, in 1909, the Federal authorities went out of their way to disfranchise the man whose name gave me citizenship. That Washington waited till 1917 was due to the circumstance that the psychologic moment for the finale was lacking. Perhaps I should have contested my case at that time. With the then-prevalent public opinion, the Courts would probably not have sustained the fraudulent proceedings which robbed me of citizenship. But it did not seem credible then that America would stoop to the Tsaristic method of deportation.

Our anti-war agitation added fuel to the war hysteria of 1917, and thus furnished the Federal authorities with the desired opportunity to complete the conspiracy begun against me in Rochester, N. Y., 1909.

It was on December 5, 1919, while in Chicago lecturing, that I was telegraphically apprised of the fact that the order for my deportation was final. The question of my citizenship was then raised in court, but was of course decided adversely. I had intended to take the case to a higher tribunal, but finally I decided to carry the matter no further: Soviet Russia was luring me.

Ludicrously secretive were the authorities about our deportation. To the very last moment we were kept in ignorance as to the time. Then, unexpectedly, in the wee small hours of December 21st we were spirited away. The scene set for this performance was most thrilling. It was six o'clock Sunday morning, December 21, 1919, when under heavy military convoy we stepped aboard the *Buford*.

For twenty-eight days we were prisoners. Sentries at our cabin doors day and night, sentries on deck during the hour we were daily permitted to breathe the fresh air. Our men comrades were cooped up in dark, damp quarters, wretchedly fed, all of us in complete ignorance of the direction we were to take. Yet our spirits were high — Russia, free, new Russia was before US.

All my life Russia's heroic struggle for freedom was as a beacon to me. The revolutionary zeal of her martyred men and women, which neither fortress nor *katorga* could suppress, was my inspiration in the darkest hours. When the news of the February Revolution flashed across the world, I longed to hasten to the land which had performed the miracle and had freed her people from the age-old yoke of Tsarism. But America held me. The thought of thirty years of struggle for my ideals, of my friends and associates, made it impossible to tear myself away. I would go to Russia later, I thought.

Then came America's entry into the war and the need of remaining true to the American people who were swept into the hurricane against their will. After all, I owed a great debt, I owed my growth and development to what was finest and best in America, to her fighters for liberty, to the sons and daughters of the revolution to come. I would be true to them. But the frenzied militarists soon terminated my work.

At last I was bound for Russia and all else was almost blotted out. I would behold with mine own eyes *matushka Rossiya*, the land freed from political and economic masters; the Russian *dubinushka*, as the peasant was called, raised from the dust; the Russian worker, the modern Samson, who with a sweep of his mighty arm had pulled down the pillars of decaying society. The twenty-eight days on our floating prison passed in a sort of trance. I was hardly conscious of my surroundings.

Finally we reached Finland, across which we were forced to journey in sealed cars. On the Russian border we were met by a committee of the Soviet Government, headed by Zorin. They had come to greet the first political refugees driven from America for opinion's sake.

It was a cold day, with the earth a sheet of white, but spring was in our hearts. Soon we were to behold revolutionary Russia. I preferred to be alone when I touched the sacred soil: my exaltation was too great, and I feared I might not be able to control my emotion. When I reached Beloostrov the first enthusiastic reception tendered the refugees was over, but the place was still surcharged with intensity of feeling. I could sense the awe and humility of our group who, treated like felons in the United States, were here received as dear brothers and comrades and welcomed by the Red soldiers, the liberators of Russia.

From Beloostrov we were driven to the village where another reception had been prepared: A dark hall filled to suffocation, the platform lit up by tallow candles, a huge red flag, on the stage a group of women in black nuns' attire. I stood as in a dream in the breathless silence. Suddenly a voice rang out. It beat like metal on my ears and seemed uninspired, but it spoke of the great suffering of the Russian people and of the enemies of the Revolution. Others addressed the audience, but I was held by the women in black, their faces ghastly in the yellow light. Were these really nuns? Had the Revolution penetrated even the walls of superstition? Had the Red Dawn broken into the narrow lives of these ascetics? It all seemed strange, fascinating.

Somehow I found myself on the platform. I could only blurt out that like my comrades I had not come to Russia to teach: I had come to learn, to draw sustenance and hope from her, to lay down my life on the altar of the Revolution.

After the meeting we were escorted to the waiting Petrograd train, the women in the black hood intoning the "Internationale," the whole audience joining in. I was in the car with our host, Zorin, who had lived in America and spoke English fluently. He talked enthusiastically about the Soviet Government and its marvellous achievements. His conversation was illuminative, but one phrase struck me as discordant. Speaking of the political organization of his Party, he remarked: "Tammany Hall has nothing on us, and as to Boss Murphy, we could teach him a thing or two." I thought the man was jesting. What relation could there be between Tammany Hall, Boss Murphy, and the Soviet Government?

I inquired about our comrades who had hastened from America at the first news of the Revolution. Many of them had died at the front, Zorin informed me, others were working with the Soviet Government. And Shatov? William Shatov, a brilliant speaker and able organizer, was a well-known figure in America, frequently associated with us in our work. We had sent him a telegram from Finland and were much surprised at his failure to reply. Why did not Shatov come to meet us? "Shatov had to leave for Siberia, where he is to take the post of Minister of Railways," said Zorin.

In Petrograd our group again received an ovation. Then the deportees were taken to the famous Tauride Palace, where they were to be fed and housed for the night. Zorin asked Alexander Berkman and myself to accept his hospitality. We entered the waiting automobile. The city was dark and deserted; not a living soul to be seen anywhere. We had not gone very far when the car was suddenly halted, and an electric light flashed into our eyes. It was the militia, demanding the password. Petrograd had recently fought back the Yudenitch attack and was still under martial law. The process was repeated frequently along the route. Shortly before we reached our destination we passed a well-lighted building. "It is our station house," Zorin explained, "but we have few prisoners there now. Capital punishment is abolished and we have recently proclaimed a general political amnesty."

Presently the automobile came to a halt. "The First House of the Soviets," said Zorin, "the living place of the most active members of our Party." Zorin and his wife occupied two rooms, simply but comfortably furnished. Tea and refreshments were served, and our hosts entertained us with the absorbing story of the marvellous defence the Petrograd workers had organized against the Yudenitch forces. How heroically the men and women, even the children, had rushed to the defence of the Red City! What wonderful self-discipline and cooperation the proletariat demonstrated. The evening passed in these reminiscences, and I was about to retire to the room secured for me when a young woman arrived who introduced herself as the sister-in-law of "Bill" Shatov. She greeted us warmly and asked us to come up to see her sister who lived on the floor above. When we reached their apartment I found myself embraced by big jovial Bill himself. How strange of Zorin to tell me that Shatov had left for Siberia! What did it mean? Shatov explained that he had been ordered not to meet us at the border, to prevent his giving us our first impressions of Soviet Russia. He had fallen into disfavour with the Government and was being sent to Siberia into virtual exile. His trip had been delayed and therefore we still happened to find him.

We spent much time with Shatov before he left Petrograd. For whole days I listened to his story of the Revolution, with its light and shadows, and the developing tendency of the Bolsheviki toward the right. Shatov, however, insisted that it was necessary for all the revolutionary elements to work with the Bolsheviki Government. Of course, the Communists had made many mistakes, but what they did was inevitable, imposed upon them by Allied interference and the blockade.

A few days after our arrival Zorin asked Alexander Berkman and myself to accompany him to Smolny. Smolny, the erstwhile boarding school for the daughters of the aristocracy, had been the centre of revolutionary events. Almost every stone had played its part. Now it was the seat of the Petrograd Government. I found the place heavily guarded and giving the impression of a beehive of officials and government employees. The Department of the Third International was particularly interesting. It was the domain of Zinoviev. I was much impressed by the magnitude of it all.

After showing us about, Zorin invited us to the Smolny dining room. The meal consisted of good soup, meat and potatoes, bread and tea. Rather a good meal in starving Russia, I thought.

Our group of deportees was quartered in Smolny. I was anxious about my travelling companions, the two girls who had shared my cabin on the Buford. I wished to take them back with me to the First House of the Soviet. Zorin sent for them. They arrived greatly excited and told us that the whole group of deportees had been placed under military guard. The news was startling. The people who had been driven out of America for their political opinions, now in Revolutionary Russia again prisoners — three days after their arrival. What had happened?

We turned to Zorin. He seemed embarrassed. "Some mistake," he said, and immediately began to make inquiries. It developed that four ordinary criminals had been found among the politicals deported by the United States Government, and therefore a guard was placed over the whole group. The proceeding seemed to me unjust and uncalled for. It was my first lesson in Bolshevik methods.

Chapter 2: Petrograd

My parents had moved to St. Petersburg when I was thirteen. Under the discipline of a German school in Königsberg and the Prussian attitude toward everything Russian, I had grown up in the atmosphere of hatred to that country. I dreaded especially the terrible Nihilists [*Narodniki* – anarchists] who had killed Tsar Alexander II, so good and kind, as I had been taught. St. Petersburg was to me an evil thing. But the gayety of the city, its vivacity and brilliancy, soon dispelled my childish fancies and made the city appear like a fairy dream. Then my curiosity was aroused by the revolutionary mystery which seemed to hang over everyone, and of which no one dared to speak. When four years later I left with my sister for America I was no longer the German Gretchen to whom Russia spelt evil. My whole soul had been transformed and the seed planted for what was to be my life's work. Especially did St. Petersburg remain in my memory a vivid picture, full of life and mystery.

I found Petrograd of 1920 quite a different place. It was almost in ruins, as if a hurricane had swept over it. The houses looked like broken old tombs upon neglected and forgotten cemeteries. The streets were dirty and deserted; all life had gone from them. The population of Petrograd before the war was almost two million; in 1920 it had dwindled to five hundred thousand. The people walked about like living corpses; the shortage of food and fuel was slowly sapping the city; grim death was clutching at its heart. Emaciated and frostbitten men, women, and children were being whipped by the common lash, the search for a piece of bread or a stick of wood. It was a heart-rending sight by day, an oppressive weight at night. Especially were the nights of the first month in Petrograd dreadful. The utter stillness of the large city was paralysing. It fairly haunted me, this awful oppressive silence broken only by occasional shots. I would lay awake trying to pierce the mystery. Did not Zorin say that capital punishment had been abolished? Why this shooting? [The Civil War was still raging near Petrograd.] Doubts disturbed my mind, but I tried to wave them aside. I had come to learn.

Much of my first knowledge and impressions of the October Revolution and the events that followed I received from the Zorins. As already mentioned, both had lived in America, spoke English, and were eager to enlighten me upon the history of the Revolution. They were devoted to the cause and worked very hard; he, especially, who was secretary of the Petrograd committee of his party, besides editing the daily *Krasnaya Gazetta*, and participating in other activities.

It was from Zorin that I first learned about that legendary figure, Makhno. The latter was an Anarchist, I was informed, who under the Tsar had been sentenced to *katorga*. Liberated by the general political amnesty of the February revolution, he became the leader of a peasant army in the Ukraina, proving himself extremely able and daring and doing splendid work in the defence of the Revolution. For some time Makhno worked in harmony with the Bolsheviki, fighting the counter-revolutionary forces. Then he became antagonistic, and now his army, recruited from bandit elements, was fighting the Bolsheviki. Zorin related that he had been one of a committee sent to Makhno to bring about an understanding. But Makhno would not listen to reason. He continued his warfare against the Soviets and was considered a dangerous counter-revolutionist.

I had no means of verifying the story, and I was far from disbelieving the Zorins. Both appeared most sincere and dedicated to their work, types of religious zealots ready to burn the heretic, but equally ready to sacrifice their own lives for their cause. I was much impressed by the simplicity of their lives. Holding a responsible position, Zorin could have received special rations, but they lived very poorly, their supper often consisting only of herring, black bread, and tea. I thought it especially admirable because Lisa Zorin was with child at the time.

Two weeks after my arrival in Russia I was invited to attend the Alexander Herzen commemoration in the Winter Palace. The white marble hall where the gathering took place seemed to intensify the bitter frost, but the people present were unmindful of the penetrating cold. I also was conscious only of the unique situation: Alexander Herzen, one of the most hated revolutionists of his time, honoured in the Winter Palace! Frequently before the spirit of Herzen had found its way into the house of the Romanovs. It was when the *Kolokol*, published abroad and sparkling with the brilliancy of Herzen and Turgenev, would in some mysterious manner be discovered on the desk of the Tsar. Now the Tsars were no more, but the spirit of Herzen had risen again and was witnessing the realization of the dream of one of Russia's great men.

One evening I was informed that Zinoviev had returned from Moscow and would see me. He arrived about midnight. He looked very tired and was constantly disturbed by urgent messages. Our talk was of a general nature, of the grave situation in Russia, the shortage of food and fuel then particularly poignant, and about the labour situation in America. He was anxious to know "how soon the revolution could be expected in the United States." He left upon me no definite impression, but I was conscious of something lacking in the man, though I could not determine at the time just what it was.

Another Communist I saw much of the first weeks was John Reed. I had known him in America. He was living in the Astoria, working hard and preparing for his return to the United States. He was to journey through Latvia and he seemed apprehensive of the outcome. He had been in Russia during the October days and this was his second visit. Like Shatov he also insisted that the dark sides of the Bolshevik regime were inevitable. He believed fervently that the Soviet Government would emerge from its narrow party lines and that it would presently establish the Communistic Commonwealth. We spent much time together, discussing the various phases of the situation.

So far I had met none of the Anarchists and their failure to call rather surprised me. One day a friend I had known in the States came to inquire whether I would see several members of an Anarchist organization. I readily assented. From them I learned a version of the

Russian Revolution and the Bolshevik regime utterly different from what I had heard before. It was so startling, so terrible that I could not believe it. They invited me to attend a small gathering they had called to present to me their views.

The following Sunday I went to their conference. Passing Nevsky Prospekt, near Liteiny Street, I came upon a group of women huddled together to protect themselves from the cold. They were surrounded by soldiers, talking and gesticulating. Those women, I learned, were prostitutes who were selling themselves for a pound of bread, a piece of soap or chocolate. The soldiers were the only ones who could afford to buy them because of their extra rations. Prostitution in revolutionary Russia. I wondered. What is the Communist Government doing for these unfortunates? What are the Workers' and Peasants' Soviets doing? My escort smiled sadly. The Soviet Government had closed the houses of prostitution and was now trying to drive the women off the streets, but hunger and cold drove them back again; besides, the soldiers had to be humoured. It was too ghastly, too incredible to be real, yet there they were, those shivering creatures for sale and their buyers, the red defenders of the Revolution. "The cursed interventionists, the blockade — they are responsible," said my escort. Why, yes, the counter-revolutionists and the blockade are responsible, I reassured myself. I tried to dismiss the thought of that huddled group, but it clung to me. I felt something snap within me.

At last we reached the Anarchist quarters, in a dilapidated house in a filthy backyard. I was ushered into a small room crowded with men and women. The sight recalled pictures of thirty years ago when, persecuted and hunted from place to place, the Anarchists in America were compelled to meet in a dingy hall on Orchard Street, New York, or in the dark rear room of a saloon. That was in capitalistic America. But this is revolutionary Russia, which the Anarchists had helped to free. Why should they have to gather in secret and in such a place?

That evening and the following day I listened to a recital of the betrayal of the Revolution by the Bolsheviki. Workers from the Baltic factories spoke of their enslavement, Kronstadt sailors voiced their bitterness and indignation against the people they had helped to power and who had become their masters. One of the speakers had been condemned to death by the Bolsheviki for his Anarchist ideas, but had escaped and was now living illegally. He related how the sailors had been robbed of the freedom of their Soviets, how every breath of life was being censored. Others spoke of the Red Terror and repression in Moscow, which resulted in the throwing of a bomb into the gathering of the Moscow section of the Communist Party in September, 1919. They told me of the over-filled prisons, of the violence practised on the workers and peasants. I listened rather impatiently, for everything in me cried out against this indictment. It sounded impossible; it could not be. Someone was surely at fault, but probably it was they, my comrades, I thought. They were unreasonable, impatient for immediate results. Was not violence inevitable in a revolution, and was it not imposed upon the Bolsheviki by the Interventionists? My comrades were indignant! "Disguise yourself so the Bolsheviki do not recognize you; take a pamphlet of Kropotkin and try to distribute it in a Soviet meeting. You will soon see whether we told you the truth. "Above all, get out of the First House of the Soviet. Live among the people and you will have all the proofs you need."

How childish and thrilling it all seemed in the face of the world event that was taking place in Russia! No, I could not credit their stories. I would wait and study conditions. But my mind was in a turmoil, and the nights became more oppressive than ever.

The day arrived when I was given a chance to attend the meeting of the Petro-Soviet. It was to be a double celebration in honour of the return of Karl Radek to Russia and Joffe's report on the peace treaty with Esthonia. As usual I went with the Zorins. The gathering was in the Tauride Palace, the former meeting place of the Russian Duma. Every entrance to the hall was guarded by soldiers, the platform surrounded by them holding their guns at attention. The hall was crowded to the very doors. I was on the platform overlooking the sea of faces below. Starved and wretched they looked, these sons and daughters of the people, the heroes of Red Petrograd. How they had suffered and endured for the Revolution! I felt very humble before them.

Zinoviev presided. After the "Internationale" had been sung by the audience standing, Zinoviev opened the meeting. He spoke at length. His voice is high pitched, without depth. The moment I heard him I realized what I had missed in him at our first meeting-depth, strength of character. Next came Radek. He was clever, witty, sarcastic, and he paid his respects to the counter-revolutionists and to the White Guards. Altogether an interesting man and an interesting address.

Joffe looked the diplomat. Well fed and groomed, he seemed rather out of place in that assembly. He spoke of the peace conditions with Esthonia, which were received with enthusiasm by the audience. Certainly these people wanted peace. Would it ever come to Russia?

Last spoke Zorin, by far the ablest and most convincing that evening. Then the meeting was thrown open to discussion. A Menshevik asked for the floor. Immediately pandemonium broke loose. Yells of "Traitor!" "Kolchak!" "Counter-Revolutionist!" came from all parts of the audience and even from the platform. It looked to me like an unworthy proceeding for a revolutionary assembly. [Lenin explained a year previous in 1919, in the thesis he delivered at the First Communist International: "At first, when the Mensheviks had a majority in the Soviets, they were in favor of the Soviets. All we heard then was: 'Long live the Soviets!', 'For the Soviets!', 'The Soviets are revolutionary democracy!' When, however, we Bolsheviks secured a majority in the Soviets, they changed their tune; they said: 'the Soviets must not exist side-by-side with the Constituent Assembly.' In complaining of persecution by the Bolsheviks, the Russian Mensheviks and Socialist revolutionaries try to conceal the fact that they are persecuted for participating in the Civil War on the side of the bourgeoisie against the proletariat . . . The majority of the Mensheviks went over to the bourgeoisie and fought against us during the Civil War. We, of course, persecute Mensheviks, we even shoot them, when they wage war against us, fight against our Red Army and shoot our Red commanders."]

On the way home I spoke to Zorin about it. He laughed. "Free speech is a bourgeois superstition," he said; "during a revolutionary period there can be no free speech." I was rather dubious about the sweeping statement, but I felt that l had no right to judge. I was a newcomer, while the people at the Tauride Palace had sacrificed and suffered so much for the Revolution. I had no right to judge.

Chapter 3: Disturbing Thoughts

Life went on. Each day brought new conflicting thoughts and emotions. The feature which affected me most was the inequality I witnessed in my immediate environment. I learned that the rations issued to the tenants of the First House of the Soviet (Astoria) were much superior to those received by the workers in the factories. To be sure, they were not sufficient to sustain life—but no one in the Astoria lived from these rations alone. The members of the Communist Party, quartered in the Astoria, worked in Smolny, and the rations in Smolny were the best in Petrograd. Moreover, trade was not entirely suppressed at that time. The markets were doing a lucrative business, though no one seemed able or willing to explain to me where the purchasing capacity came from. The workers could not afford to buy butter which was then 2,000 rubles a pound, sugar at 3,000, or meat at 1,000. The inequality was most apparent in the Astoria kitchen. I went there frequently, though it was torture to prepare a meal: the savage scramble for an inch of space on the stove, the greedy watching of the women lest any one have something extra in the saucepan, the quarrels and screams when someone fished out a piece of meat from the pot of a neighbor! But there was one redeeming feature in the picture—it was the resentment of the servants who worked in the Astoria. They were servants, though called comrades, and they felt keenly the inequality: the Revolution to them was not a mere theory to be realized in years to come. It was a living thing. I was made aware of it one day.

The rations were distributed at the Commissary, but one had to fetch them himself. One day, while waiting my turn in the long line, a peasant girl came in and asked for vinegar. "Vinegar! Who is it calls for such a luxury?" cried several women. It appeared that the girl was Zinoviev's servant. She spoke of him as her master, who worked very hard and was surely entitled to something extra. At once a storm of indignation broke loose. "Master! Is that what we made the Revolution for, or was it to do away with masters? Zinoviev is no more than we, and he is not entitled to more."

These working women were crude, even brutal, but their sense of justice was instinctive. The Revolution to them was something fundamentally vital. They saw the inequality at every step and bitterly resented it. I was disturbed. I sought to reassure myself that Zinoviev and the other leaders of the Communists would not use their power for selfish benefit. It was the shortage of food and the lack of efficient organization which made it impossible to feed all alike, and of course the blockade and not the Bolsheviki was responsible for it. The Allied Interventionists, who were trying to get at Russia's throat, were the cause.

Every Communist I met reiterated this thought; even some of the Anarchists insisted on it. The little group antagonistic to the Soviet Government was not convincing. But how reconcile the explanation given to me with some of the stories I learned every day—stories of systematic terrorism, of relentless persecution, and suppression of other revolutionary elements?

Another circumstance which perplexed me was that, the markets were stacked with meat, fish, soap, potatoes, even shoes, every time that the rations were given out. How did these things get to the markets? Everyone spoke about it, but no one seemed to know. One day I was in a watchmaker's shop when a soldier entered. He conversed with the proprietor in Yiddish, relating that he had just returned from Siberia with a shipment of tea. Would the watchmaker take fifty pounds? Tea was sold at a premium at the time—no one but the privileged few could permit themselves such a luxury. Of course the watchmaker would take the tea. When the soldier left I asked the shopkeeper if he did not think it rather risky to transact such illegal business so openly. I happen to understand Yiddish, I told him. Did he not fear I would report him? "That's nothing," the man replied nonchalantly, "the Tcheka knows all about it—it draws its percentage from the soldier and myself."

I began to suspect that the reason for much of the evil was also within Russia, not only outside of it. But then, I argued, police officials and detectives graft everywhere. That is the common disease of the breed. In Russia, where scarcity of food and three years of starvation must needs turn most people into grafters, theft is inevitable. The Bolsheviki are trying to suppress it with an iron hand. How can they be blamed? But try as I might I could not silence my doubts. I groped for some moral support, for a dependable word, for someone to shed light on the disturbing questions.

It occurred to me to write to Maxim Gorki. He might help. I called his attention to his own dismay and disappointment while visiting America. He had come believing in her democracy and liberalism, and found bigotry and lack of hospitality instead. I felt sure Gorki would understand the struggle going on within me, though the cause was not the same. Would he see me? Two days later I received a short note asking me to call.

I had admired Gorki for many years. He was the living affirmation of my belief that the creative artist cannot be suppressed. Gorki, the child of the people, the pariah, had by his genius become one of the world's greatest, one who by his pen and deep human sympathy made the social outcast our kin. For years I toured America interpreting Gorki's genious to the American people, elucidating the greatness, beauty, and humanity of the man and his works. Now I was to see him and through him get a glimpse into the complex soul of Russia.

I found the main entrance of his house nailed up, and there seemed to be no way of getting in. I almost gave up in despair when a woman pointed to a dingy staircase. I climbed to the very top and knocked on the first door I saw. It was thrown open, momentarily blinding me with a flood of light and steam from an overheated kitchen. Then I was ushered into a large dining room. It was dimly lit, chilly and cheerless in spite of a fire and a large collection of Dutch china on the walls. One of the three women I had noticed in the kitchen sat down at the table with me, pretending to read a book but all the while watching me out of the corner of her eye. It was an awkward half-hour of waiting.

Presently Gorki arrived. Tall, gaunt, and coughing, he looked ill and weary. He took me to his study, semi-dark and of depressing effect. No sooner had we seated ourselves than the door flew open and another young woman, whom I had not observed before, brought him a glass of dark fluid, medicine evidently. Then the telephone began to ring; a few minutes later Gorki was called out of the room. I realized that I would not be able to talk with him. Returning, he must have noticed my disappointment. We agreed to postpone our talk till some less disturbed opportunity presented itself. He escorted me to the door, remarking, "You ought to visit the Baltflot [Baltic Fleet]. The Kronstadt sailors are nearly all instinctive Anarchists. You would find a field there." I smiled. "Instinctive Anarchists?" I said, "that means they are unspoiled by preconceived notions, unsophisticated, and receptive. Is that what you mean?"

"Yes, that is what I mean," he replied.

The interview with Gorki left me depressed. Nor was our second meeting more satisfactory on the occasion of my first trip to Moscow. By the same train travelled Radek, Demyan Bedny the popular Bolshevik versifier, and Zipperovitch, then the president of the Petrograd unions. We found ourselves in the same car, the one reserved for Bolshevik officials and State dignitaries, comfortable and roomy. On the other hand, the "common" man, the non-Communist without influence, had literally to fight his way into the always overcrowded railway carriages, provided he had a propusk to travel — a most difficult thing to procure.

I spent the time of the journey discussing Russian conditions with Zipperovitch, a kindly man of deep convictions, and with Demyan Bedny, a big coarse-looking man. Radek held forth at length on his experiences in Germany and German prisons.

I learned that Gorki was also on the train, and I was glad of another opportunity for a chat with him when he called to see me. The one thing uppermost in my mind at the moment was an article which had appeared in the Petrograd *Pravda* a few days before my departure. It treated of morally defective children, the writer urging prison for them. Nothing I had heard or seen during my six weeks in Russia so outraged me as this brutal and antiquated attitude toward the child. I was eager to know what Gorki thought of the matter. Of course, he was opposed to prisons for the morally defective, he would advocate reformatories instead. "What do you mean by morally defective?" I asked. "Our young are the result of alcoholism rampant during the Russian-Japanese War, and of syphilis. What except moral defection could result from such a heritage?" he replied. I argued that morality changes with conditions and climate, and that unless one believed in the theory of free will one cannot consider morality a fixed matter. As to children, their sense of responsibility is primitive, and they lack the spirit of social adherence. But Gorki insisted that there was a fearful spread of moral defection among children and that such cases should be isolated.

I then broached the problem that was troubling me most. What about persecution and terror—were all the horrors inevitable, or was there some fault in Bolshevism itself? The Bolsheviki were making mistakes, but they were doing the best they knew how, Gorki said drily. Nothing more could be expected, he thought.

I recalled a certain article by Gorki, published in his paper, *New Life*, which I had read in the Missouri Penitentiary. It was a scathing arraignment of the Bolsheviki. There must have been powerful reasons to change Gorki's point of view so completely. Perhaps he is right. I must wait. I must study the situation; I must get at the facts. Above all, I must see for myself Bolshevism at work.

We spoke of the drama. On my first visit, by way of introduction, I had shown Gorki an announcement card of the dramatic course I had given in America. John Galsworthy was among the playwrights I had discussed then. Gorki expressed surprise that I considered Galsworthy an artist. In his opinion Galsworthy could not be compared with Bernard Shaw. I had to differ. I did not underestimate Shaw, but considered Galsworthy the greater artist. I detected irritation in Gorki, and as his hacking cough continued, I broke off the discussion. He soon left. I remained dejected from the interview. It gave me nothing.

When we pulled into the Moscow station my chaperon, Demyan Bedny, had vanished and I was left on the platform with all my traps. Radek came to my rescue. He called a porter, took me and my baggage to his waiting automobile and insisted that I come to his apartments in the Kremlin. There I was graciously received by his wife and invited to dinner served by their maid. After that Radek began the difficult task of getting me quartered in the Hotel National, known as the First House of the Moscow Soviet. With all his influence it required hours to secure a room for me.

Radek's luxurious apartment, the maidservant, the splendid dinner seemed strange in Russia. But the comradely concern of Radek and the hospitality of his wife were grateful to me. Except at the Zorins and the Shatovs I had not met with anything like it. I felt that kindliness, sympathy, and solidarity were still alive in Russia.

Chapter 4: Moscow: First Impressions

Coming from Petrograd to Moscow is like being suddenly transferred from a desert to active life, so great is the contrast. On reaching the large open square in front of the main Moscow station I was amazed at the sight of busy crowds, cabbies, and porters. The same picture presented itself all the way from the station to the Kremlin. The streets were alive with men, women, and children. Almost everybody carried a bundle, or dragged a loaded sleigh. There was life, motion, and movement, quite different from the stillness that oppressed me in Petrograd.

I noticed considerable display of the military in the city, and scores of men dressed in leather suits with guns in their belts. "Tcheka men, our Extraordinary Commission," explained Radek. I had heard of the Tcheka before: Petrograd talked of it with dread and hatred. However, the soldiers and Tchekists were never much in evidence in the city on the Neva. Here in Moscow they seemed everywhere. Their presence reminded me of a remark Jack [John] Reed had made: "Moscow is a military encampment," he had said; "spies everywhere, the bureaucracy most autocratic. I always feel relieved when I get out of Moscow." But, then, Petrograd is a proletarian city and is permeated with the spirit of the Revolution. Moscow always was hierarchical. Still the life was intense, varied, and interesting. What struck me most forcible, besides the display of militarism, was the preoccupation of the people. There seemed to be no common interest between them. Everyone rushed about as a detached unit in quest of his own, pushing and knocking against everyone else. Repeatedly I saw women or children fall from exhaustion without any one stopping to lend assistance. People stared at me when I would bend over the heap on the slippery pavement or gather up the bundles that had fallen into the street. I spoke to friends about what looked to me like a strange lack of fellow-feeling. They explained it as a result partly of the general distrust and suspicion created by the Tcheka, and partly due to the absorbing task of getting the day's food. One had neither vitality nor feeling left to think of others. Yet there did not seem to be such a scarcity of food as in Petrograd, and the people were warmer and better dressed.

I spent much time on the streets and in the market places. Most of the latter, as also the famous Soukharevka, were in full operation. Occasionally soldiers would raid the markets; but as a rule they were suffered to continue. They presented the most vital and interesting part of the city's life. Here gathered proletarian and aristocrat, Communist and bourgeois, peasant and intellectual. Here they were bound by the common desire to sell and buy, to trade and bargain. Here one could find for sale a rusty iron pot alongside of an exquisite ikon; an old pair of shoes and intricately worked lace; a few yards of cheap calico and a beautiful old Persian shawl. The rich of yesterday, hungry and emaciated, denuding themselves of their last glories; the rich of to-day buying—it was indeed an amazing picture in revolutionary Russia.

Who was buying the finery of the past, and where did the purchasing power come from? The buyers were numerous. In Moscow one was not so limited as to sources of information as in Petrograd; the very streets furnished that source.

The Russian people even after four years of war and three years of revolution remained unsophisticated. They were suspicious of strangers and reticent at first. But when they learned that one had come from America and did not belong to the governing political party, they gradually lost their reserve. Much information I gathered from them and some explanation of the things that perplexed me since my arrival. I talked frequently with the workers and peasants and the women on the markets.

The forces which had led up to the Russian Revolution had remained terra incognito to these simple folk, but the Revolution itself had struck deep into their souls. They knew nothing of theories, but they believed that there was to be no more of the hated *barin* (master) and now the *barin* was again upon them. "The *barin* has everything," they would say, "white bread, clothing, even chocolate, while we have nothing." "Communism, equality, freedom," they jeered, "lies and deception."

I would return to the National bruised and battered, my illusions gradually shattered, my foundations crumbling. But I would not let go. After all, I thought, the common people could not understand the tremendous difficulties confronting the Soviet Government: the imperialist forces arraigned against Russia, the many attacks which drained her of her men who otherwise would be employed in productive labour, the blockade which was relentlessly slaying Russia's young and weak. Of course, the people could not understand these things, and I must not be misled by their bitterness born of suffering. I must be patient. I must get to the source of the evils confronting me.

The National, like the Petrograd Astoria, was a former hotel but not nearly in as good condition. No rations were given out there except three quarters of a pound of bread every two days. Instead there was a common dining room where dinners and suppers were served. The meals consisted of soup and a little meat, sometimes fish or pancakes, and tea. In the evening we usually had kasha and tea. The food was not too plentiful, but one could exist on it were it not so abominably prepared.

I saw no reason for this spoiling of provisions. Visiting the kitchen I discovered an array of servants controlled by a number of officials, commandants, and inspectors. The kitchen staff were poorly paid; moreover, they were not given the same food served to us. They resented this discrimination and their interest was not in their work. This situation resulted in much graft and waste, criminal in the face of the general scarcity of food. Few of the tenants of the National, I learned, took their meals in the common dining room. They prepared or had their meals prepared by servants in a separate kitchen set aside for that purpose. There, as in the Astoria, I found the same scramble for a place on the stove, the same bickering and quarrelling, the same greedy, envious watching of each other. Was that Communism in action, I wondered. I heard the usual explanation: Yudenitch, Deniken, Kolchak, the blockade—but the stereotyped phrases no longer satisfied me.

Before I left Petrograd Jack Reed said to me: "When you reach Moscow, look up Angelica Balabanova. She will receive you gladly and will put you up should you be unable to find a room." I had heard of Balabanova before, knew of her work, and was naturally anxious to meet her.

A few days after reaching Moscow I called her up. Would she see me? Yes, at once, though she was not feeling well. I found Balabanova in a small cheerless room, lying huddled up on the sofa. She was not prepossessing but for her eyes, large and luminous, radiating sympathy and kindness. She received me most graciously, like an old friend, and immediately ordered the inevitable samovar. Over our tea we talked of America, the labour movement there, our deportation, and finally about Russia. I put to her the questions I had asked many Communists regarding the contrasts and discrepancies which confronted me at every step. She surprised me by not giving the usual excuses; she was the first who did not repeat the old refrain. She did refer to the scarcity of food, fuel, and clothing which was responsible for much of the graft and corruption; but on the whole she thought life itself mean and limited. "A rock on which the highest hopes are shattered. Life thwarts the best intentions and breaks the finest spirits," she said. Rather an unusual view for a Marxian, a Communist, and one in the thick of the battle. I knew she was then secretary of the Third International. Here was a personality, one who was not a mere echo, one who felt deeply the complexity of the Russian situation. I went away profoundly impressed, and attracted by her sad, luminous eyes.

I soon discovered that Balabanova—or Balabanoff, as she preferred to be called—was at the beck and call of everybody. Though poor in health and engaged in many functions, she yet found time to minister to the needs of her legion callers. Often she went without necessaries herself, giving away her own rations, always busy trying to secure medicine or some little delicacy for the sick and suffering. Her special concern were the stranded Italians of whom there were quite a number in Petrograd and Moscow. Balabanova had lived and worked in Italy for many years until she almost became Italian herself. She felt deeply with them, who were as far away from their native soil as from events in Russia. She was their friend, their advisor, their main support in a world of strife and struggle. Not only the Italians but almost everyone else was the concern of this remarkable little woman: no one needed a Communist membership card to Angelica's heart. No wonder some of her comrades considered her a "sentimentalist who wasted her precious time in philanthropy." Many verbal battles I had on this score with the type of Communist who had become callous and hard, altogether barren of the qualities which characterized the Russian idealist of the past.

Similar criticism as of Balabanova I heard expressed of another leading Communist, Lunacharsky. Already in Petrograd I was told sneeringly, "Lunacharsky is a scatterbrain who wastes millions on foolish ventures." But I was eager to meet the man who was the Commissar of one of the important departments in Russia, that of education. Presently an opportunity presented itself.

The Kremlin, the old citadel of Tsardom, I found heavily guarded and inaccessible to the "common" man. But I had come by appointment and in the company of a man who had an admission card, and therefore passed the guard without trouble. We soon reached the Lunacharsky apartments, situated in an old quaint building within the walls. Though the reception room was crowded with people waiting to be admitted, Lunacharsky called me in as soon as I was announced.

His greeting was very cordial. Did I "intend to remain a free bird" was one of his first questions, or would I be willing to join him in his work? I was rather surprised. Why should one have to give up his freedom, especially in educational work? Were not initiative and freedom essential? However, I had come to learn from Lunacharsky about the revolutionary system of education in Russia, of which we had heard so much in America. I was especially interested in the care the children were receiving. The Moscow *Pravda*, like the Petrograd newspapers, had been agitated by a controversy about the treatment of the morally defective. I expressed surprise at such an attitude in Soviet Russia. "Of course, it is all barbarous and antiquated," Lunacharsky said, "and I am fighting it tooth and nail. The sponsors of prisons for children are old criminal jurists, still imbued with Tsarist methods. I have organized a commission of physicians, pedagogues, and psychologists to deal with this question. Of course, those children must not be punished." I felt tremendously relieved. Here at last was a man who had gotten away from the cruel old methods of punishment. I told him of the splendid work done in capitalist America by Judge Lindsay and of some of the experimental schools for backward children. Lunacharsky was much interested. "Yes, that is just what we want here, the American system of education," he exclaimed. "You surely do not mean the American public school system?" I asked. "You know of the insurgent movement in America against our public school method of education, the work done by Professor Dewey and others?" Lunacharsky had heard little about it. Russia had been so long cut off from the western world and there was great lack of books on modern education. He was eager to learn of the new ideas and methods. I sensed in Lunacharsky a personality full of faith and devotion to the Revolution, one who was carrying on the great work of education in a physically and spiritually difficult environment.

He suggested the calling of a conference of teachers if I would talk to them about the new tendencies in education in America, to which I readily consented. Schools and other institutions in his charge were to be visited later. I left Lunacharsky filled with new hope. I would join him in his work, I thought. What greater service could one render the Russian people?

During my visit to Moscow I saw Lunacharsky several times. He was always the same kindly gracious man, but I soon began to notice that he was being handicapped in his work by forces within his own party: most of his good intentions and decisions never saw the light. Evidently Lunacharsky was caught in the same machine that apparently held everything in its iron grip. What was that machine? Who directed its movements?

Although the control of visitors at the National was very strict, no one being able to go in or out without a special *propusk* (permit), men and women of different political factions managed to call on me: Anarchists, Left Social Revolutionists, Coöperators, and people I had known in America and who had returned to Russia to play their part in the Revolution. They had come with deep faith and high hope, but I found almost all of them discouraged, some even embittered. Though widely differing in their political views, nearly all of my callers related an identical story, the story of the high tide of the Revolution, of the wonderful spirit that led the people forward, of the possibilities of the masses, the role of the Bolsheviki as the spokesmen of the most extreme revolutionary slogans and their betrayal of the Revolution after they had secured power. All spoke of the Brest

Litovsk peace as the beginning of the downward march. The Left Social Revolutionists especially, men of culture and earnestness, who had suffered much under the Tsar and now saw their hopes and aspirations thwarted, were most emphatic in their condemnation. They supported their statements by evidence of the havoc wrought by the methods of forcible requisition and the punitive expeditions to the villages, of the abyss created between town and country, the hatred engendered between peasant and worker. They told of the persecution of their comrades, the shooting of innocent men and women, the criminal inefficiency, waste, and destruction.

How, then, could the Bolsheviki maintain themselves in power? After all, they were only a small minority, about five hundred thousand members as an exaggerated estimate. The Russian masses, I was told, were exhausted by hunger and cowed by terrorism. Moreover, they had lost faith in all parties and ideas. Nevertheless, there were frequent peasant uprisings in various parts of Russia, but these were ruthlessly quelled. There were also constant strikes in Moscow, Petrograd, and other industrial centres, but the censorship was so rigid little ever became known to the masses at large.

I sounded my visitors on intervention. "We want none of outside interference," was the uniform sentiment. They held that it merely strengthened the hands of the Bolsheviki. They felt that they could not publicly even speak out against them so long as Russia was being attacked, much less fight their régime. "Have not their tactics and methods been imposed on the Bolsheviki by intervention and blockade?" I argued. "Only partly so," was the reply. "Most of their methods spring from their lack of understanding of the character and the needs of the Russian people and the mad obsession of dictatorship, which is not even the dictatorship of the proletariat but the dictatorship of a small group over the proletariat."

When I broached the subject of the People's Soviets and the elections my visitors smiled. "Elections! There are no such things in Russia, unless you call threats and terrorism elections. It is by these alone that the Bolsheviki secure a majority. A few Mensheviki, Social Revolutionists, or Anarchists are permitted to slip into the Soviets, but they have not the shadow of a chance to be heard."

The picture painted looked black and dismal. Still I clung to my faith.

Chapter 5: Meeting People

At a conference of the Moscow Anarchists in March I first learned of the part some Anarchists had played in the Russian Revolution. In the July uprising of 1917 the Kronstadt sailors were led by the Anarchist Yarchuck; the Constituent Assembly was dispersed by Zhelezniakov; the Anarchists had participated on every front and helped to drive back the Allied attacks. It was the consensus of opinion that the Anarchists were always among the first to face fire, as they were also the most active in the reconstructive work. One of the biggest factories near Moscow, which did not stop work during the entire period of the Revolution, was managed by an Anarchist. Anarchists were doing important work in the Foreign Office and in all other departments. I learned that the Anarchists had virtually helped the Bolsheviki into power. Five months later, in April, 1918, machine guns were used to destroy the Moscow Anarchist Club and to suppress their Press. That was before Mirbach arrived in Moscow. The field had to be "cleared of disturbing elements," and the Anarchists were the first to suffer. Since then the persecution of the Anarchists has never ceased.

The Moscow Anarchist Conference was critical not only toward the existing régime, but toward its own comrades as well. It spoke frankly of the negative sides of the movement, and of its lack of unity and coöperation during the revolutionary period. Later I was to learn more of the internal dissensions in the Anarchist movement. Before closing, the Conference decided to call on the Soviet Government to release the imprisoned Anarchists and to legalize Anarchist educational work. The Conference asked Alexander Berkman and myself to sign the resolution to that effect. It was a shock to me that Anarchists should ask any government to legalize their efforts, but I still believed the Soviet Government to be at least to some extent expressive of the Revolution. I signed the resolution, and as I was to see Lenin in a few days I promised to take the matter up with him.

The interview with Lenin was arranged by Balabanova. "You must see Ilitch, talk to him about the things that are disturbing you and the work you would like to do," she had said. But some time passed before the opportunity came. At last one day Balabanova called up to ask whether I could go at once. Lenin had sent his car and we were quickly driven over to the Kremlin, passed without question by the guards, and at last ushered into the workroom of the all-powerful president of the People's Commissars.

When we entered Lenin held a copy of the brochure Trial and Speeches in his hands. I had given my only copy to Balabanova, who had evidently sent the booklet on ahead of us to Lenin. One of his first questions was, "When could the Social Revolution be expected in America?" I had been asked the question repeatedly before, but I was astounded to hear it from Lenin. It seemed incredible that a man of his information should know so little about conditions in America.

My Russian at this time was halting, but Lenin declared that though he had lived in Europe for many years he had not learned to speak foreign languages: the conversation would therefore have to be carried on in Russian. At once he launched into a eulogy of our speeches in court. "What a splendid opportunity for propaganda," he said; "it is worth going to prison, if the courts can so successfully be turned into a forum." I felt his steady cold gaze upon me, penetrating my very being, as if he were reflecting upon the use I might be put to. Presently he asked what I would want to do. I told him I would like to repay America what it had done for Russia. I spoke of the Society of the Friends of Russian Freedom, organized thirty years ago by George Kennan and later reorganized by Alice Stone Blackwell and other liberal Americans. I briefly sketched the splendid work they had done to arouse interest in the struggle for Russian freedom, and the great moral and financial aid the Society had given through all those years.

To organize a Russian society for American freedom was my plan. Lenin appeared enthusiastic. "That is a great idea, and you shall have all the help you want. But, of course, it will be under the auspices of the Third International. Prepare your plan in writing and send it to me."

I broached the subject of the Anarchists in Russia. I showed him a letter I had received from Martens, the Soviet representative in America, shortly before my deportation. Martens asserted that the Anarchists in Russia enjoyed full freedom of speech and Press. Since my arrival I found scores of Anarchists in prison and their Press suppressed. I explained that I could not think of working with the Soviet Government so long as my comrades were in prison for opinion's sake. I also told him of the resolutions of the Moscow Anarchist Conference. He listened patiently and promised to bring the matter to the attention of his party. "But as to free speech," he remarked, "that is, of course, a bourgeois notion. There can be no free speech in a revolutionary period. We have the peasantry against us because we can give them nothing in return for their bread. We will have them on our side when we have something to exchange. Then you can have all the free speech you want—but not now. Recently we needed peasants to cart some wood into the city. They demanded salt. We thought we had no salt, but then we discovered seventy poods in Moscow in one of our warehouses. At once the peasants were willing to cart the wood. Your comrades must wait until we can meet the needs of the peasants. Meanwhile, they should work with us. Look at William Shatov, for instance, who has helped save Petrograd from Yudenitch. He works with us and we appreciate his services. Shatov was among the first to receive the order of the Red Banner."

Free speech, free Press, the spiritual achievements of centuries, what were they to this man? A Puritan, he was sure his scheme alone could redeem Russia. Those who served his plans were right, the others could not be tolerated.

A shrewd Asiatic, this Lenin. He knows how to play on the weak sides of men by flattery, rewards, medals. I left convinced that his approach to people was purely utilitarian, for the use he could get out of them for his scheme. And his scheme—was it the Revolution?

I prepared the plan for the Society of the Russian Friends of American Freedom and elaborated the details of the work I had in mind, but refused to place myself under the protecting wing of the

Third International. I explained to Lenin that the American people had little faith in politics, and would certainly consider it an imposition to be directed and guided by a political machine from Moscow. I could not consistently align myself with the Third International.

Some time later I saw Tchicherin. I believe it was 4 A.M. when our interview took place. He also asked about the possibilities of a revolution in America, and seemed to doubt my judgment when I informed him that there was no hope of it in the near future. We spoke of the I.W.W., which had evidently been misrepresented to him. I assured Tchicherin that while I am not an I.W.W. I must state that they represented the only conscious and effective revolutionary proletarian organization in the United States, and were sure to play an important role in the future labour history of the country.

Next to Balabanova, Tchicherin impressed me as the most simple and unassuming of the leading Communists in Moscow. But all were equally naïve in their estimate of the world outside of Russia. Was their judgment so faulty because they had been cut off from Europe and America so long? Or was their great need of European help father to their wish? At any rate, they all clung to the idea of approaching revolutions in the western countries, forgetful that revolutions are not made to order, and apparently unconscious that their own revolution had been twisted out of shape and semblance and was gradually being done to death.

The editor of the London *Daily Herald*, accompanied by one of his reporters, had preceded me to Moscow. They wanted to visit Kropotkin, and they had been given a special car. Together with Alexander Berkman and A. Shapiro, I was able to join Mr. Lansbury.

The Kropotkin cottage stood back in the garden away from the street. Only a faint ray from a kerosene lamp lit up the path to the house. Kropotkin received us with his characteristic graciousness, evidently glad at our visit. But I was shocked at his altered appearance. The last time I had seen him was in 1907, in Paris, which I visited after the Anarchist Congress in Amsterdam. Kropotkin, barred from France for many years, had just been given the right to return. He was then sixty-five years of age, but still so full of life and energy that he seemed much younger. Now he looked old and worn.

I was eager to get some light from Kropotkin on the problems that were troubling me, particularly on the relation of the Bolsheviki to the Revolution. What was his opinion? Why had he been silent so long?

I took no notes and therefore I can give only the gist of what Kropotkin said. He stated that the Revolution had carried the people to great spiritual heights and had paved the way for profound social changes. If the people had been permitted to apply their released energies, Russia would not be in her present condition of ruin. The Bolsheviki, who had been carried to the top by the revolutionary wave, first caught the popular ear by extreme revolutionary slogans, thereby gaining the confidence of the masses and the support of militant revolutionists.

He continued to narrate that early in the October period the Bolsheviki began to subordinate the interests of the Revolution to the establishment of their dictatorship, which coerced and paralysed every social activity. He stated that the coöperatives were the main medium that could have bridged the interests of the peasants and the workers. The coöperatives were among the first to be crushed. He spoke with much feeling of the oppression, the persecution, the hounding of every shade of opinion, and cited numerous instances of the misery and distress of the people. He emphasized that the Bolsheviki had discredited Socialism and Communism in the eyes of the Russian people.

"Why haven't you raised your voice against these evils, against this machine that is sapping the life blood of the Revolution?" I asked. He gave two reasons. As long as Russia was being attacked by the combined Imperialists, and Russian women and children were dying from the effects of the blockade, he could not join the shrieking chorus of the ex-revolutionists in the cry of "Crucify!" He preferred silence. Secondly, there was no medium of expression in Russia itself. To protest to the Government was useless. Its concern was to maintain itself in power. It could not stop at such "trifles" as human rights or human lives. Then he added: "We have always pointed out the effects of Marxism in action. Why be surprised now?"

I asked Kropotkin whether he was noting down his impressions and observations. Surely he must see the importance of such a record to his comrades and to the workers; in fact, to the whole world. "No," he said; "it is impossible to write when one is in the midst of great human suffering, when every hour brings new tragedies. Then there may be a raid at any moment. The Tcheka comes swooping inside out, and marches off with every scrap of paper. Under such constant stress it is impossible to keep records. But besides these considerations there is my book on Ethics. I can only work a few hours a day, and I must concentrate on that to the exclusion of everything else."

After a tender embrace which Peter never failed to give those he loved, we returned to our car. My heart was heavy, my spirit confused and troubled by what I had heard. I was also distressed by the poor state of health of our comrade: I feared he could not survive till spring. The thought that Peter Kropotkin might go to his grave and that the world might never know what he thought of the Russian Revolution was appalling.

Chapter 6: Preparing For American Deportees

Events in Moscow, quickly following each other, were full of interest. I wanted to remain in that vital city, but as I had left all my effects in Petrograd I decided to return there and then come back to Moscow to join Lunacharsky in his work. A few days before my departure a young woman, an Anarchist, came to visit me. She was from the Petrograd Museum of the Revolution and she called to inquire whether I would take charge of the Museum branch work in Moscow. She explained that the original idea of the Museum was due to the famous old revolutionist Vera Nikolaievna Figner, and that it had recently been organized by non-partisan elements. The majority of the men and women who worked in the Museum were not Communists, she said; but they were devoted to the Revolution and anxious to create something which could in the future serve as a source of information and inspiration to earnest students of the great Russian Revolution. When my caller was informed that I was about to return to Petrograd, she invited me to visit the Museum and to become acquainted with its work.

Upon my arrival in Petrograd I found unexpected work awaiting me. Zorin informed me that he had been notified by Tchicherin that a thousand Russians had been deported from America and were on their way to Russia. They were to be met at the border and quarters were to be immediately prepared for them in Petrograd. Zorin asked me to join the Commission about to be organized for that purpose.

The plan of such a commission for American deportees had been broached to Zorin soon after our arrival in Russia. At that time Zorin directed us to talk the matter over with Tchicherin, which we did. But three months passed without anything having been done about it. Meanwhile, our comrades of the *Buford* were still walking from department to department, trying to be placed where they might do some good. They were a sorry lot, those men who had come to Russia with such high hopes, eager to render service to the revolutionary people. Most of them were skilled workers, mechanics — men Russia needed badly; but the cumbersome Bolshevik machine and general inefficiency made it a very complex matter to put them to work. Some had tried independently to secure jobs, but they could accomplish very little. Moreover, those who found employment were soon made to feel that the Russian workers resented the eagerness and intensity of their brothers from America. "Wait till you have starved as long as we," they would say, "wait till you have tasted the blessings of Commissarship, and we will see if you are still so eager." In every way the deportees were discouraged and their enthusiasm dampened.

To avoid this unnecessary waste of energy and suffering the Commission was at last organized in Petrograd. It consisted of Ravitch, the then Minister of Internal Affairs for the Northern District; her secretary, Kaplun; two members of the Bureau of War Prisoners; Alexander Berkman and myself. The new deportees were due in two weeks, and much work was to be done to prepare for their reception. It was unfortunate that no active participation could be expected from Ravitch because her time was too much occupied. Besides holding the post of Minister of the Interior she was Chief of the Petrograd Militia, and she also represented the Moscow Foreign Office in Petrograd. Her regular working hours were from 8 A.M. to 2 A.M. Kaplun, a very able administrator, had charge of the entire internal work of the Department and could therefore give us very little of his time. There remained only four persons to accomplish within a short time the big task of preparing living quarters for a thousand deportees in starved and ruined Russia. Moreover, Alexander Berkman, heading the Reception Committee, had to leave for the Latvian border to meet the exiles.

It was an almost impossible task for one person, but I was very anxious to save the second group of deportees the bitter experiences and the disappointments of my fellow companions of the Buford. I could undertake the work only by making the condition that I be given the right of entry to the various government departments, for I had learned by that time how paralysing was the effect of the bureaucratic red tape which delayed and often frustrated the most earnest and energetic efforts. Kaplun consented. "Call on me at any time for anything you may require," he said; "I will give orders that you be admitted everywhere and supplied with everything you need. If that should not help, call on the Tcheka," he added. I had never called upon the police before, I informed him; why should I do so in revolutionary Russia? "In bourgeois countries that is a different matter," explained Kaplun; "with us the Tcheka defends the Revolution and fights sabotage." I started on my work determined to do without the Tcheka. Surely there must be other methods, I thought.

Then began a chase over Petrograd. Materials were very scarce and it was most difficult to procure them owing to the unbelievably centralized Bolshevik methods. Thus to get a pound of nails one had to file applications in about ten or fifteen bureaus; to secure some bed linen or ordinary dishes one wasted days. Everywhere in the offices crowds of Government employees stood about smoking cigarettes, awaiting the hour when the tedious task of the day would be over. My co-workers of the War Prisoners' Bureau fumed at the irritating and unnecessary delays, but to no purpose. They threatened with the Tcheka, with the concentration camp, even with raztrel (shooting). The latter was the most favourite argument. Whenever any difficulty arose one immediately heard raztreliat—to be shot. But the expression, so terrible in its significance, was gradually losing its effect upon the people: man gets used to everything.

I decided to try other methods. I would talk to the employees in the departments about the vital interest the conscious American workers felt in the great Russian Revolution, and of their faith and hope in the Russian proletariat. The people would become interested immediately, but the questions they would ask were as strange as they were pitiful: "Have the people enough to eat in America? How soon will the Revolution be there? Why did you come to starving Russia?" They were eager for information and news, these mentally and physically starved people, cut off by the barbarous blockade from all touch with the western world. Things American were something wonderful to them. A piece of chocolate or a cracker were unheard-of dainties — they proved the key to everybody's heart.

Within two weeks I succeeded in procuring most of the things needed for the expected deportees, including furniture, linen, and dishes. A miracle, everybody said.

However, the renovation of the houses that were to serve as living quarters for the exiles was not accomplished so easily. I inspected what, as I was told, had once been first-class hotels. I found them located in the former prostitute district; cheap dives they were, until the Bolsheviki closed all brothels. They were germ-eaten, ill-smelling, and filthy. It was no small problem to turn those dark holes into a fit habitation within two weeks. A coat of paint was a luxury not to be thought of. There was nothing else to do but to strip the rooms of furniture and draperies, and have them thoroughly cleaned and disinfected.

One morning a group of forlorn-looking creatures, in charge of two militiamen, were brought to my temporary office. They came to work, I was informed. The group consisted of a one-armed old man, a consumptive woman, and eight boys and girls, mere children, pale, starved, and in rags. "Where do these unfortunates come from?" "They are speculators," one of the militiamen replied; "we rounded them up on the market." The prisoners began to weep. They were no speculators, they protested; they were starving, they had received no bread in two days. They were compelled to go out to the market to sell matches or thread to secure a little bread. In the midst of this scene the old man fainted from exhaustion, demonstrating better than words that he had speculated only in hunger. I had seen such "speculators" before, driven in groups through the streets of Moscow and Petrograd by convoys with loaded guns pointed at the backs of the prisoners.

I could not think of having the work done by these starved creatures. But the militiamen insisted that they would not let them go; they had orders to make them work. I called up Kaplun and informed him that I considered it out of the question to have quarters for American deportees prepared by Russian convicts whose only crime was hunger. Thereupon Kaplun ordered the group set free and consented that I give them of the bread sent for the workers' rations. But a valuable day was lost.

The next morning a group of boys and girls came singing along the Nevski Prospekt. They were *kursanti* from the Tauride Palace who were sent to my office to work. On my first visit to the palace I had been shown the quarters of the *kursanti*, the students of the Bolshevik academy. They were mostly village boys and girls housed, fed, clothed, and educated by the Government, later to be placed in responsible positions in the Soviet régime. At the time I was impressed by the institutions, but by April I had looked somewhat beneath the surface. I recalled what a young woman, a Communist, had told me in Moscow about these students. "They are the special caste now being reared in Russia," she had said. "Like the church which maintains and educates its religious priesthood, our Government trains a military and civic priesthood. They are a favoured lot." I had more than one occasion to convince myself of the truth of it. The *kursanti* were being given every advantage and many special privileges. They knew their importance and they behaved accordingly.

Their first demand when they came to me was for the extra rations of bread they had been promised. This demand satisfied, they stood about and seemed to have no idea of work. It was evident that whatever else the *kursanti* might be taught, it was not to labour. But, then, few people in Russia know how to work. The situation looked hopeless. Only ten days remained till the arrival of the deportees, and the "hotels" assigned for their use were still in as uninhabitable a condition as before. It was no use to threaten with the Tcheka, as my co-workers did. I appealed to the boys and girls in the spirit of the American deportees who were about to arrive in Russia full of enthusiasm for the Revolution and eager to join in the great work of reconstruction. The *kursanti* were the pampered charges of the Government, but they were not long from the villages, and they had had no time to become corrupt. My appeal was effective. They took up the work with a will, and at the end of ten days the three famous hotels were as ready as far as willingness to work and hot water without soap could make them. We were very proud of our achievement and we eagerly awaited the arrival of the deportees.

At last they came, but to our great surprise they proved to be no deportees at all. They were Russian war prisoners from Germany. The misunderstanding was due to the blunder of some official in Tchicherin's office who misread the radio information about the party due at the border. The prepared hotels were locked and sealed; they were not to be used for the returned war prisoners because "they were prepared for American deportees who still might come." All the efforts and labour had been in vain.

Chapter 7: Rest Homes For Workers

Since my return from Moscow I noticed a change in Zorin's attitude: he was reserved, distant, and not as friendly as when we first met. I ascribed it to the fact that he was overworked and fatigued, and not wishing to waste his valuable time I ceased visiting the Zorins as frequently as before. One day, however, he called up to ask if Alexander Berkman and myself would join him in certain work he was planning, and which was to be done in hurry-up American style, as he put it. On calling to see him we found him rather excited – an unusual thing for Zorin who was generally quiet and reserved. He was full of a new scheme to build "rest homes" for workers. He explained that on Kameniy Ostrov were the magnificent mansions of the Stolypins, the Polovtsovs, and others of the aristocracy and bourgeoisie, and that he was planning to turn them into recreation centres for workers. Would we join in the work? Of course, we consented eagerly, and the next morning we went over to inspect the island. It was indeed an ideal spot, dotted with magnificent mansions, some of them veritable museums, containing rare gems of painting, tapestry, and furniture. The man in charge of buildings called our attention to the art treasures, protesting that they would be injured or entirely destroyed if put to the planned use. But Zorin was set on his scheme. "Recreation homes for workers are more important than art," he said.

We returned to the Astoria determined to devote ourselves to the work and to go at it intensively, as the houses were to be ready for the First of May. We prepared detailed plans for dining rooms, sleeping chambers, reading rooms, theatre and lecture halls, and recreation places for the workers. As the first and most necessary step we proposed the organization of a dining room to feed the workers who were to be employed in preparing the place for their comrades. I had learned from my previous experience with the hotels that much valuable time was lost because of the failure to provide for those actually employed on such work. Zorin consented and promised that we were to take charge within a few days. But a week passed and nothing further was heard about what was to be a rush job. Some time later Zorin called up to ask us to accompany him to the island. On our arrival there we found half-a-dozen Commissars already in charge, with scores of people idling about. Zorin reassured us that matters would arrange themselves and that we should have an opportunity to organize the work as planned. However, we soon realized that the newly fledged officialdom was as hard to cope with as the old bureaucracy.

Every Commissar had his favourites whom he managed to list as employed on the job, thereby entitling them to bread rations and a meal. Thus almost before any actual workers appeared on the scene, eighty alleged "technicians" were already in possession of dinner tickets and bread cards. The men actually mobilized for the work received hardly anything. The result was general sabotage. Most of the men sent over to prepare the rest homes for the workers came from concentration camps: they were convicts and military deserters. I had often watched them at work, and in justice to them it must be said that they did not over exert themselves. "Why should we?" they would say. "We are fed on Sovietkis soup; dirty dishwater it is, and we receive only what is left over from the idlers who order us about. And who will rest in these homes? Not we or our brothers in the factories. Only those who belong to the party or who have a pull will enjoy this place. Besides, the spring is near; we are needed at home on the farm. Why are we kept here?" Indeed, they did not exert themselves, those stalwart sons of Russia's soil. There was no incentive: they had no point of contact with the life about them, and there was no one who could translate to them the meaning of work in revolutionary Russia. They were dazed by war, revolution, and hunger—nothing could rouse them out of their stupor.

Many of the buildings on Kameniy Ostrov had been taken up for boarding schools and homes for defectives; some were occupied by old professors, teachers, and other intellectuals. Since the Revolution these people lived there unmolested, but now orders came to vacate, to make room for the rest homes. As almost no provision had been made to supply the dispossessed ones with other quarters, they were practically forced into the streets. Those friendly with Zinoviev, Gorki, or other influential Communists took their troubles to them, but persons lacking "pull" found no redress. The scenes of misery which I was compelled to witness daily exhausted my energies. It was all unnecessarily cruel, impractical, without any bearing on the Revolution. Added to this was the chaos and confusion which prevailed. The bureaucratic officials seemed to take particular delight in countermanding each other's orders. Houses already in the process of renovation, and on which much work and material were spent, would suddenly be left unfinished and some other work begun. Mansions filled with art treasures were turned into night lodgings, and dirty iron cots put among antique furniture and oil paintings—an incongruous, stupid waste of time and energy. Zorin would frequently hold consultations by the hour with the staff of artists and engineers making plans for theatres, lecture halls, and amusement places, while the Commissars sabotaged the work. I stood the painful and ridiculous situation for two weeks, then gave up the matter in despair.

Early in May the workers' rest homes on Kameniy Ostrov were opened with much pomp, music, and speeches. Glowing accounts were sent broadcast of the marvellous things done for the workers in Russia. In reality, it was Coney Island transferred to the environs of Petrograd, a gaudy showplace for credulous visitors. From that time on Zorin's demeanour to me changed. He became cold, even antagonistic. No doubt he began to sense the struggle which was going on within me, and the break which was bound to come. I did, however, see much of Lisa Zorin, who had just become a mother. I nursed her and the baby, glad of the opportunity thus to express my gratitude for the warm friendship the Zorins had shown me during my first months in Russia. I appreciated their sterling honesty and devotion. Both were so favourably placed politically that they could be supplied with everything they wanted, yet Lisa Zorin lacked the simplest garments for her baby. "Thousands of Russian working women have no more, and why should I?" Lisa would say. When she was so weak that she could not nurse her baby, Zorin could not be induced to ask for special rations. I had to conspire against them by buying eggs and butter on the market to save the lives of mother and child. But their fine quality of character made my inner struggle the more difficult. Reason urged me to look the social facts in the face. My personal attachment to the Communists I had learned to know and esteem refused to accept the facts. Never mind the evils—I would say to myself—as long as there are such as the Zorins and the Balabanovas, there must be something vital in the ideas they represent. I held on tenaciously to the phantom I had myself created.

Chapter 8: The First Of May In Petrograd

In 1890 the First of May was for the first time celebrated in America as Labour's international holiday. May Day became to me a great, inspiring event. To witness the celebration of the First of May in a free country — it was something to dream of, to long for, but perhaps never to be realized. And now, in 1920, the dream of many years was about to become real in revolutionary Russia. I could hardly await the morning of May First. It was a glorious day, with the warm sun melting away the last crust of the hard winter. Early in the morning strains of music greeted me: groups of workers and soldiers were marching through the streets, singing revolutionary songs. The city was gaily decorated: the Uritski Square, facing the Winter Palace, was a mass of red, the streets near by a veritable riot of colour. Great crowds were about, all wending their way to the Field of Mars where the heroes of the Revolution were buried.

Though I had an admission card to the reviewing stand I preferred to remain among the people, to feel myself a part of the great hosts that had brought about the world event. This was their day — the day of their making. Yet they seemed peculiarly quiet, oppressively silent. There was no joy in their singing, no mirth in their laughter. Mechanically they marched, automatically they responded to the claqueurs on the reviewing stand shouting "Hurrah" as the columns passed.

In the evening a pageant was to take place. Long before the appointed hour the Uritski Square down to the palace and to the banks of the Neva was crowded with people gathered to witness the open-air performance symbolizing the triumph of the people. The play consisted of three parts, the first portraying the conditions which led up to the war and the role of the German Socialists in it; the second reproduced the February Revolution, with Kerensky in power; the last — the October Revolution. It was a play beautifully set and powerfully acted, a play vivid, real, fascinating. It was given on the steps of the former Stock Exchange, facing the Square. On the highest step sat kings and queens with their courtiers, attended by soldiery in gay uniforms. The scene represents a gala court affair: the announcement is made that a monument is to be built in honour of world capitalism. There is much rejoicing, and a wild orgy of music and dance ensues. Then from the depths there emerge the enslaved and toiling masses, their chains ringing mournfully to the music above. They are responding to the command to build the monument for their masters: some are seen carrying hammers and anvils; others stagger under the weight of huge blocks of stone and loads of brick. The workers are toiling in their world of misery and darkness, lashed to greater effort by the whip of the slave drivers, while above there is light and joy, and the masters are feasting. The completion of the monument is signalled by large yellow disks hoisted on high amidst the rejoicing of the world on top.

At this moment a little red flag is seen waving below, and a small figure is haranguing the people. Angry fists are raised and then flag and figure disappear, only to reappear again in different parts of the underworld. Again the red flag waves, now here, now there. The people slowly gain confidence and presently become threatening. Indignation and anger grow — the kings and queens become alarmed. They fly to the safety of the citadels, and the army prepares to defend the stronghold of capitalism.

It is August, 1914. The rulers are again feasting, and the workers are slaving. The members of the Second International attend the confab of the mighty. They remain deaf to the plea of the workers to save them from the horrors of war. Then the strains of "God Save the King " announce the arrival of the English army. It is followed by Russian soldiers with machine guns and artillery, and a procession of nurses and cripples, the tribute to the Moloch of war.

The next act pictures the February Revolution. Red flags appear everywhere, armed motor cars dash about. The people storm the Winter Palace and haul down the emblem of Tsardom. The Kerensky Government assumes control, and the people are driven back to war. Then comes the marvellous scene of the October Revolution, with soldiers and sailors galloping along the open space before the white marble building. They dash up the steps into the palace, there is a brief struggle, and the victors are hailed by the masses in wild jubilation. The "Internationale" floats upon the air; it mounts higher and higher into exultant peals of joy. Russia is free — the workers, sailors, and soldiers usher in the new era, the beginning of the world commune!

Tremendously stirring was the picture. But the vast mass remained silent. Only a faint applause was heard from the great throng. I was dumbfounded. How explain this astonishing lack of response? When I spoke to Lisa Zorin about it she said that the people had actually lived through the October Revolution, and that the performance necessarily fell flat by comparison with the reality of 1917. But my little Communist neighbour gave a different version. "The people had suffered so many disappointments since October, 1917," she said, "that the Revolution has lost all meaning to them. The play had the effect of making their disappointment more poignant."

Chapter 9: Industrial Militarization

The Ninth Congress of the All-Russian Communist Party, held in March, 1920, was characterized by a number of measures which meant a complete turn to the right. Foremost among them was the militarization of labour and the establishment of one-man management of industry, as against the collegiate shop system. Obligatory labour had long been a law upon the statutes of the Socialist Republic, but it was carried out, as Trotsky said, "only in a small private way." Now the law was to be made effective in earnest. Russia was to have a militarized industrial army to fight economic disorganization, even as the Red Army had conquered on the various fronts. Such an army could be whipped into line only by rigid discipline, it was claimed. The factory collegiate system had to make place for military industrial management.

The measure was bitterly fought at the Congress by the Communist minority, but party discipline prevailed. However, the excitement did not abate: discussion of the subject continued long after the congress adjourned. Many of the younger Communists agreed that the measure indicated a step to the right, but they defended the decision of their party. "The collegiate system has proven a failure," they said. "The workers will not work voluntarily, and our industry must be revived if we are to survive another year."

Jack Reed also held this view. He had just returned after a futile attempt to reach America through Latvia, and for days we argued about the new policy. Jack insisted it was unavoidable so long as Russia was being attacked and blockaded. "We have been compelled to mobilize an army to fight our external enemies why not an army to fight our worst internal enemy, hunger? We can do it only by putting our industry on its feet." I pointed out the danger of the military method and questioned whether the workers could be expected to become efficient or to work intensively under compulsion. Still, Jack thought mobilization of labour unavoidable. "It must be tried, anyhow," he said.

Petrograd at the time was filled with rumours of strikes. The story made the rounds that Zinoviev and his staff, while visiting the factories to explain the new policies, were driven by the workers from the premises. To learn about the situation at first hand I decided to visit the factories. Already during my first months in Russia I had asked Zorin for permission to see them. Lisa Zorin had requested me to address some labour meetings, but I declined because I felt that it would be presumptuous on my part to undertake to teach those who had made the revolution. Besides, I was not quite at home with the Russian language then. But when I asked Zorin to let me visit some factories, he was evasive. After I had become acquainted with Ravitch I approached her on the subject, and she willingly consented.

The first works to be visited were the Putilov, the largest and most important engine and car manufacturing establishment. Forty thousand workers had been employed there before the war. Now I was informed that only 7,000 were at work. I had heard much of the Putilovtsi: they had played a heroic part in the revolutionary days and in the defence of Petrograd against Yudenitch.

At the Putilov office we were cordially received, shown about the various departments, and then turned over to a guide. There were four of us in the party, of whom only two could speak Russian. I lagged behind to question a group working at a bench. At first I was met with the usual suspicion, which I overcame by telling the men that I was bringing the greetings of their brothers in America. "And the revolution there?" I was immediately asked. It seemed to have become a national obsession, this idea of a near revolution in Europe and America. Everybody in Russia clung to that hope. It was hard to rob those misinformed people of their naïve faith. "The American revolution is not yet," I told them, "but the Russian Revolution has found an echo among the proletariat in America." I inquired about their work, their lives, and their attitude toward the new decrees. "As if we had not been driven enough before," complained one of the men. "Now we are to work under the military *nagaika* [whip]. Of course, we will have to be in the shop or they will punish us as industrial deserters. But how can they get more work out of us? We are suffering hunger and cold. We have no strength to give more. I suggested that the Government was probably compelled to introduce such methods, and that if Russian industry were not revived the condition of the workers would grow even worse. Besides, the Putilov men were receiving the preferred *payok*. "We understand the great misfortune that has befallen Russia," one of the workers replied, "but we cannot squeeze more out of ourselves. Even the two pounds of bread we are getting is not enough. Look at the bread," he said, holding up a black crust; "can we live on that? And our children? If not for our people in the country or some trading on the market we would die altogether. Now comes the new measure which is tearing us away from our people, sending us to the other end of Russia while our brothers from there are going to be dragged here, away from their soil. It's a crazy measure and it won't work."

"But what can the Government do in the face of the food shortage?" I asked. "Food shortage!" the man exclaimed; "look at the markets. Did you see any shortage of food there? Speculation and the new bourgeoisie, that's what's the matter. The one-man management is our new slave driver. First the bourgeoisie sabotaged us, and now they are again in control. But just let them try to boss us! They'll find out. Just let them try!"

The men were bitter and resentful. Presently the guide returned to see what had become of me. He took great pains to explain that industrial conditions in the mill had improved considerably since the militarization of labour went into effect. The men were more content and many more cars had been renovated and engines repaired than within an equal period under the previous management. There were 7,000 productively employed in the works, he assured me. I learned, however, that the real figure was less than 5,000 and that of these only about 2,000 were actual workers. The others were Government officials and clerks.

After the Putilov works we visited the Treugolnik, the great rubber factory of Russia. The place was clean and the machinery in good order—a well-equipped modern plant. When we reached the main workroom we were met by the superintendent, who had been in charge for twenty-five years. He would show us around himself, he said. He seemed to take great pride in the factory, as if it were his own. It rather surprised me that they had managed to keep everything in such fine shape. The guide explained that it was because nearly the whole of the old staff had been left in charge. They felt that whatever might happen they must not let the place go to ruin. It was certainly very commendable, I thought, but soon I had occasion to change my mind. At one of the tables, cutting rubber, was an old worker with kindly eyes looking out of a sad, spiritual face. He reminded me of the pilgrim Lucca in Gorki's "Night Lodgings." Our guide kept a sharp vigil, but I managed to slip away while the superintendent was explaining some machinery to the other members of our group.

"Well, *balyushka*, how is it with you?" I greeted the old worker. "Bad, *matushka*," he replied; "times are very hard for us old people." I told him how impressed I was to find everything in such good condition in the shop. "That is so," commented the old worker, "but it is because the superintendent and his staff are hoping from day to day that there may be a change again, and that the Treugolnik will go back to its former owners. I know them. I have worked here long before the German master of this plant put in the new machinery."

Passing through the various rooms of the factory I saw the women and girls look up in evident dread. It seemed strange in a country where the proletarians were the masters. Apparently the machines were not the only things that had been carefully watched over—the old discipline, too, had been preserved: the employees thought us Bolshevik inspectors.

The great flour mill of Petrograd, visited next, looked as if it were in a state of siege, with armed soldiers everywhere even inside the workrooms. The explanation given was that large quantities of precious flour had been vanishing. The soldiers watched the millmen as if they were galley slaves, and the workers naturally resented such humiliating treatment. They hardly dared to speak. One young chap, a fine-looking fellow, complained to me of the conditions. "We are here virtual prisoners," he said; "we cannot make a step without permission. We are kept hard at work eight hours with only ten minutes for our *kipyatok* [boiled water] and we are searched on leaving the mill." "Is not the theft of flour the cause of the strict surveillance?" I asked. "Not at all," replied the boy; "the Commissars of the mill and the soldiers know quite well where it goes to." I suggested that the workers might protest against such a state of affairs. "Protest, to whom?" the boy exclaimed; "we'd be called speculators and counter-revolutionists and we'd be arrested." "Has the Revolution given you nothing?" I asked. "Ah, the Revolution! But that is no more. Finished," he said bitterly.

The following morning we visited the Laferm tobacco factory. The place was in full operation. We were conducted through the plant and the whole process was explained to us, beginning with the sorting of the raw material and ending with the finished cigarettes packed for sale or shipment. The air in the workrooms was stifling, nauseating. "The women are used to this atmosphere," said the guide; "they don't mind." There were some pregnant women at work and girls no older than fourteen. They looked haggard, their chests sunken, black rings under their eyes. Some of them coughed and the hectic flush of consumption showed on their faces. "Is there a recreation room, a place where they can eat or drink their tea and inhale a bit of fresh air?" There was no such thing, I was informed. The women remained at work eight consecutive hours; they had their tea and black bread at their benches. The system was that of piece work, the employees receiving twenty-five cigarettes daily above their pay with permission to sell or exchange them.

I spoke to some of the women. They did not complain except about being compelled to live far away from the factory. In most cases it required more than two hours to go to and from work. They had asked to be quartered near the Laferm and they received a promise to that effect, but nothing more was heard of it.

Life certainly has a way of playing peculiar pranks. In America I should have scorned the use of social welfare work: I should have considered it a cheap palliative. But in Socialist Russia the sight of pregnant women working in suffocating tobacco air and saturating themselves and their unborn with the poison impressed me as a fundamental evil. I spoke to Lisa Zorin to see whether something could not be done to ameliorate the evil. Lisa claimed that piece work was the only way to induce the girls to work. As to rest rooms, the women themselves had already made a fight for them, but so far nothing could be done because no space could be spared in the factory. "But if even such small improvements had not resulted from the Revolution," I argued, "what purpose has it served?" "The workers have achieved control," Lisa replied; "they are now in power, power, and they have more important things to attend to than rest rooms—they have the Revolution to defend." Lisa Zorin had remained very much the proletarian, but she reasoned like a nun dedicated to the service of the Church.

The thought oppressed me that what she called the "defence of the Revolution" was really only the defence of her party in power. At any rate, nothing came of my attempt at social welfare work.

Chapter 10: The British Labour Mission

I was glad to learn that Angelica Balabanova arrived in Petrograd to prepare quarters for the British Labour Mission. During my stay in Moscow I had come to know and appreciate the fine spirit of Angelica. She was very devoted to me and when I fell ill she gave much time to my care, procured medicine which could be obtained only in the Kremlin drug store, and got special sick rations for me. Her friendship was generous and touching, and she endeared herself very much to me.

The Narishkin Palace was to be prepared for the Mission, and Angelica invited me to accompany her there. I noticed that she looked more worn and distressed than when I had seen her in Moscow. Our conversation made it clear to me that she suffered keenly from the reality which was so unlike her ideal. But she insisted that what seemed failure to me was conditioned in life itself, itself the greatest failure.

Narishkin Palace is situated on the southern bank of the Neva, almost opposite the Peter-and-Paul Fortress. The place was prepared for the expected guests and a number of servants and cooks installed to minister to their needs. Soon the Mission arrived—most of them typical workingmen delegates—and with them a staff of newspaper men and Mrs. Snowden. The most outstanding figure among them was Bertrand Russell, who quickly demonstrated his independence and determination to be free to investigate and learn at first hand.

In honour of the Mission the Bolsheviki organized a great demonstration on the Uritski Square. Thousands of people, among them women and children, came to show their gratitude to the English labour representatives for venturing into revolutionary Russia. The ceremony consisted of the singing of the "Internationale," followed by music and speeches, the latter translated by Balabanova in masterly fashion. Then came the military exercises. I heard Mrs. Snowden say disapprovingly, "What a display of military!" I could not resist the temptation of remarking: "Madame, remember that the big Russian army is largely the making of your own country. Had England not helped to finance the invasions into Russia, the latter could put its soldiers to useful labour."

The British Mission was entertained royally with theatres, operas, ballets, and excursions. Luxury was heaped upon them while the people slaved and went hungry. The Soviet Government left nothing undone to create a good impression and everything of a disturbing nature was kept from the visitors. Angelica hated the display and sham, and suffered keenly under the rigid watch placed upon every movement of the Mission. "Why should they not see the true state of Russia? Why should they not learn how the Russian people live?" she would lament. "Yet I am so impractical," she would correct herself; "perhaps it is all necessary." At the end of two weeks a farewell banquet was given to the visitors. Angelica insisted that I must attend. Again there were speeches and toasts, as is the custom at such functions. The speeches which seemed to ring most sincere were those of Balabanova and Madame Ravitch. The latter asked me to interpret her address, which I did. She spoke in behalf of the Russian women proletarians and praised their fortitude and devotion to the Revolution. "May the English proletarians learn the quality of their heroic Russian sisters," concluded Madame Ravitch. Mrs. Snowden, the erstwhile suffragette, had not a word in reply. She preserved a "dignified" aloofness. However, the lady became enlivened when the speeches were over and she got busy collecting autographs.

Chapter 11: A Visit From The Ukraina

Early in May two young men from the Ukraina arrived in Petrograd. Both had lived in America for a number of years and had been active in the Yiddish Labour and Anarchist movements. One of them had also been editor of an English weekly Anarchist paper, *The Alarm*, published in Chicago. In 1917, at the outbreak of the Revolution, they left for Russia together with other emigrants. Arriving in their native country, they joined the Anarchist activities there which had gained tremendous impetus through the Revolution. Their main field was the Ukraina. In 1918 they aided in the organization of the Anarchist Federation *Nabat* ["Alarm"], and began the publication of a paper with that name. Theoretically, they were at variance with the Bolsheviki; practically the Federation Anarchists, even as the Anarchists throughout Russia, worked with the Bolsheviki and also fought on every front against the counter-revolutionary forces.

When the two Ukrainian comrades learned of our arrival in Russia they repeatedly tried to reach us, but owing to the political conditions and the practical impossibility of travelling, they could not come north. Subsequently they had been arrested and imprisoned by the Bolsheviki. Immediately upon their release they started for Petrograd, travelling illegally. They knew the dangers confronting them—arrest and possible shooting for the possession and use of false documents—but they were willing to risk anything because they were determined that we should learn the facts about the *povstantsi* [revolutionary peasants] movements led by that extraordinary figure, Nestor Makhno. They wanted to acquaint us with the history of the Anarchist activities in Russia and relate how the iron hand of the Bolsheviki had crushed them.

During two weeks, in the stillness of the Petrograd nights, the two Ukrainian Anarchists unrolled before us the panorama of the struggle in the Ukraina. Dispassionately, quietly, and with almost uncanny detachment the young men told their story.

Thirteen different governments had "ruled" Ukraina. Each of them had robbed and murdered the peasantry, made ghastly pogroms, and left death and ruin in its way. The Ukrainian peasants, a more independent and spirited race than their northern brothers, had come to hate all governments and every measure which threatened their land and freedom. They banded together and fought back their oppressors all through the long years of the revolutionary period. The peasants had no theories; they could not be classed in any political party. Theirs was an instinctive hatred of tyranny, and practically the whole of Ukraina soon became a rebel camp. Into this seething cauldron there came, in 1917, Nestor Makhno.

Makhno was a Ukrainian born. A natural rebel, he became interested in Anarchism at an early age. At seventeen he attempted the life of a Tsarist spy and was sentenced to death, but owing to his extreme youth his sentence was commuted to *katorga* for life [severe imprisonment, one third of the term in chains]. The February Revolution opened the prison doors for all political prisoners, Makhno among them. He had then spent ten years in the Butirky prison, in Moscow. He had but a limited schooling when first arrested, but in prison he had used his leisure to good advantage. By the time of his release he had acquired considerable knowledge of history, political economy, and literature. Shortly after his liberation Makhno returned to his native village, Gulyai-Poleh, where he organized a trade union and the local Soviet. Then he threw himself in the revolutionary movement and during all of 1917 he was the spiritual teacher and leader of the rebel peasants, who had risen against the landed proprietors.

In 1918, when the Brest Peace opened Ukraina to German and Austrian occupation, Makhno organized the rebel peasant bands in defence against the foreign armies. He fought against Skoropadski, the Ukrainian Hetman, who was supported by German bayonets. He waged successful guerilla warfare against Petlura, Kaledin, Grigoriev, and Denikin. A conscious Anarchist, he laboured to give the instinctive rebellion of the peasantry definite aim and purpose. It was the Makhno idea that the social revolution was to be defended against all enemies, against every counter-revolutionary or reactionary attempt from right and left. At the same time educational and cultural work was carried on among the peasants to develop them along anarchist-communist lines with the aim of establishing free peasant communes.

In February, 1919, Makhno entered into an agreement with the Red Army. He was to continue to hold the southern front against Denikin and to receive from the Bolsheviki the necessary arms and ammunition. Makhno was to remain in charge of the *povstantsi*, now grown into an army, the latter to have autonomy in its local organizations, the revolutionary Soviets of the district, which covered several provinces. It was agreed that the *povstantsi* should have the right to hold conferences, freely discuss their affairs, and take action upon them. Three such conferences were held in February, March, and April. But the Bolsheviki failed to live up to the agreement. The supplies which had been promised Makhno, and which he needed desperately, would arrive after long delays or failed to come altogether. It was charged that this situation was due to the orders of Trotsky who did not look favourably upon the independent rebel army. However it be, Makhno was hampered at every step, while Denikin was gaining ground constantly. Presently the Bolsheviki began to object to the free peasant Soviets, and in May, 1919, the Commander-in-Chief of the southern armies, Kamenev, accompanied by members of the Kharkov Government, arrived at the Makhno headquarters to settle the disputed matters. In the end the Bolshevik military representatives demanded that the *povstantsi* dissolve. The latter refused, charging the Bolsheviki with a breach of their revolutionary agreement.

Meanwhile, the Denikin advance was becoming more threatening, and Makhno still received no support from the Bolsheviki. The peasant army then decided to call a special session of the Soviet for June 15th. Definite plans and methods were to be decided upon to check the growing menace of Denikin. But on June 4th Trotsky issued an order prohibiting the holding of the Conference and declaring Makhno an outlaw. In a public meeting in Kharkov, Trotsky announced that it were better to permit the Whites to remain in the Ukraina than to suffer Makhno. The presence of the Whites, he said, would influence the Ukrainian peasantry in favour of the Soviet Government, whereas Makhno and his *povstantsi* would never make peace with the Bolsheviki; they would attempt to possess themselves of some territory and to practice their ideas, which would be a constant menace to the Communist Government. It was practically a declaration of war against Makhno and his army. Soon the latter found itself attacked on two sides at once — by the Bolsheviki and Denikin. The *povstantsi* were poorly equipped and lacked the most necessary supplies for warfare, yet the peasant army for a considerable time succeeded in holding its own by the sheer military genius of its leader and the reckless courage of his devoted rebels.

At the same time the Bolsheviki began a campaign of denunciation against Makhno and his *povstantsi*. The Communist press accused him of having treacherously opened the southern front to Denikin, and branded Makhno's army a bandit gang and its leader a counter-revolutionist who must be destroyed at all cost. But this "counter-revolutionist" fully realized the Denikin menace to the Revolution. He gathered new forces and support among the peasants and in the months of September and October, 1919, his campaign against Denikin gave the latter its death blow on the Ukraina. Makhno captured Denikin's artillery base at Mariopol, annihilated the rear of the enemy's army, and succeeded in separating the main body from its base of supply. This brilliant maneuver of Makhno and the heroic fighting of the rebel army again brought about friendly contact with the Bolsheviki. The ban was lifted from the *povstantsi* and the Communist press now began to eulogize Makhno as a great military genius and brave defender of the Revolution in the Ukraina. But the differences between Makhno and the Bolsheviki were deeprooted: he strove to establish free peasant communes in the Ukraina, while the Communists were bent on imposing the Moscow rule. Ultimately a clash was inevitable, and it came early in January, 1920.

At that period a new enemy was threatening the Revolution. Grigoriev, formerly of the Tsarist army, later friend of the Bolsheviki, now turned against them. Having gained considerable support in the south because of his slogans of freedom and free Soviets, Grigoriev proposed to Makhno that they join forces against the Communist regime. Makhno called a meeting of the two armies and there publicly accused Grigoriev of counter-revolution and produced evidence of numerous pogroms organized by him against the Jews. Declaring Grigoriev an enemy of the people and of the Revolution, Makhno and his staff condemned him and his aides to death, executing them on the spot. Part of Grigoriev's army joined Makhno.

Meanwhile, Denikin kept pressing Makhno, finally forcing him to withdraw from his position. Not of course without bitter fighting all along the line of nine hundred *versts*, the retreat lasting four months, Makhno marching toward Galicia. Denikin advanced upon Kharkov, then farther north, capturing Orel and Kursk, and finally reached the gates of Tula, in the immediate neighbourhood of Moscow.

The Red Army seemed powerless to check the advance of Denikin, but meanwhile Makhno had gathered new forces and attacked Denikin in the rear. The unexpectedness of this new turn and the extraordinary military exploits of Makhno's men in this campaign disorganized the plans of Denikin, demoralized his army, and gave the Red Army the opportunity of taking the offense against the counter-revolutionary enemy in the neighbourhood of Tula.

When the Red Army reached Alexandrovsk, after having finally beaten the Denikin forces, Trotsky again demanded of Makhno that he disarm his men and place himself under the discipline of the Red Army. The *povstantsi* refused, whereupon an organized military campaign against the rebels was inaugurated, the Bolsheviki taking many prisoners and killing scores of others. Makhno, who managed to escape the Bolshevik net, was again declared an outlaw and bandit. Since then Makhno had been uninterruptedly waging guerilla warfare against the Bolshevik regime.

The story of the Ukrainian friends, which I have related here in very condensed form, sounded as romantic as the exploits of Stenka Rasin, the famous Cossack rebel immortalized by Gogol. Romantic and picturesque, but what bearing did the activities of Makhno and his men have upon Anarchism, I questioned the two comrades. Makhno, my informants explained, was himself an Anarchist seeking to free Ukraina from all oppression and striving to develop and organize the peasants' latent anarchistic tendencies. To this end Makhno had repeatedly called upon the Anarchists of the Ukraina and of Russia to aid him. He offered them the widest opportunity for propagandistic and educational work, supplied them with printing outfits and meeting places, and gave them the fullest liberty of action. Whenever Makhno captured a city, freedom of speech and press for

Anarchists and Left Social Revolutionists was established. Makhno often said: " I am a military man and I have no time for educational work. But you who are writers and speakers, you can do that work. Join me and together we shall be able to prepare the field for a real Anarchist experiment." But the chief value of the Makhno movement lay in the peasants themselves, my comrades thought. It was a spontaneous, elemental movement, the peasants' opposition to all governments being the result not of theories but of bitter experience and of instinctive love of liberty. They were fertile ground for Anarchist ideas. For this reason a number of Anarchists joined Makhno. They were with him in most of his military campaigns and energetically carried on Anarchist propaganda during that time.

I have been told by Zorin and other Communists that Makhno was a Jew-baiter and that his *povstantsi* were responsible for numerous brutal pogroms. My visitors emphatically denied the charges. Makhno bitterly fought pogroms, they stated; he had often issued proclamations against such outrages, and he had even with his own hand punished some of those guilty of assault on Jews. Hatred of the Hebrew was of course common in the Ukraina; it was not eradicated even among the Red soldiers. They, too, have assaulted, robbed, and outraged Jews; yet no one holds the Bolsheviki responsible for such isolated instances. The Ukraina is infested with armed bands who are often mistaken for Makhnovtsi and who have made pogroms. The Bolsheviki, aware of this, have exploited the confusion to discredit Makhno and his followers. However, the Anarchists of the Ukraina—I was informed—did not idealize the Makhno movement. They knew that the *povstantsi* were not conscious Anarchists. Their paper *Nabat* had repeatedly emphasized this fact. On the other hand, the Anarchists could not overlook the importance of popular movement which was instinctively rebellious, anarchistically inclined, and successful in driving back the enemies of the Revolution, which the better organized and equipped Bolshevik army could not accomplish. For this reason many Anarchists considered it their duty to work with Makhno. But the bulk remained away; they had their larger cultural, educational, and organizing work to do.

The invading counter-revolutionary forces, though differing in character and purpose, all agreed in their relentless persecution of the Anarchists. The latter were made to suffer, whatever the new regime. The Bolsheviki were no better in this regard than Denikin or any other

White element. Anarchists filled Bolshevik prisons; many had been shot and all legal Anarchist activities were suppressed. The Tcheka especially was doing ghastly work, having resurrected the old Tsarist methods, including even torture.

My young visitors spoke from experience: they had repeatedly been in Bolshevik prisons themselves.

Chapter 12: Beneath The Surface

The terrible story I had been listening to for two weeks broke over me like a storm. Was this the Revolution I had believed in all my life, yearned for, and strove to interest others in, or was it a caricature—a hideous monster that had come to jeer and mock me? The Communists I had met daily during six months—self-sacrificing, hard-working men and women imbued with a high ideal—were such people capable of the treachery and horrors charged against them? Zinoviev, Radek, Zorin, Ravitch, and many others I had learned to know—could they in the name of an ideal lie, defame, torture, kill? But, then—had not Zorin told me that capital punishment had been abolished in Russia? Yet I learned shortly after my arrival that hundreds of people had been shot on the very eve of the day when the new decree went into effect, and that as a matter of fact shooting by the Tcheka had never ceased.

That my friends were not exaggerating when they spoke of tortures by the Tcheka, I also learned from other sources. Complaints about the fearful conditions in Petrograd prisons had become so numerous that Moscow was apprised of the situation. A Tcheka inspector came to investigate. The prisoners being afraid to speak, immunity was promised them. But no sooner had the inspector left than one of the inmates, a young boy, who had been very outspoken about the brutalities practiced by the Tcheka, was dragged out of his cell and cruelly beaten.

Why did Zorin resort to lies? Surely he must have known that I would not remain in the dark very long. And then, was not Lenin also guilty of the same methods? "Anarchists of ideas [*ideyni*] are not in our prisons," he had assured me. Yet at that very moment numerous Anarchists filled the jails of Moscow and Petrograd and of many other cities in Russia. In May, 1920, scores of them had been arrested in Petrograd, among them two girls of seventeen and nineteen years of age. None of the prisoners were charged with counter-revolutionary activities: they were "Anarchists of ideas," to use Lenin's expression. Several of them had issued a manifesto for the First of May, calling attention to the appalling conditions in the factories of the Socialist Republic. The two young girls who had circulated a handbill against the "labour book," which had then just gone into effect, were also arrested.

The labour book was heralded by the Bolsheviki as one of the great Communist achievements. It would establish equality and abolish parasitism, it was claimed. As a matter of fact, the labour book was somewhat character of the yellow ticket issued to prostitutes under the Tsarist regime. It was a record of every step one made, and without it no step could be made. It bound its holder to his job, to the city he lived in, and to the room he occupied. It recorded one's political faith and party adherence, and the number of times arrested. In short, a yellow ticket. Even some Communists resented the degrading innovation. The Anarchists who protested against it were arrested by the Tcheka. When certain leading Communists were approached in the matter they repeated what Lenin had said: "Anarchists of ideas are not in our prisons."

The aura was falling from the Communists. All of them seemed to believe that the end justified the means. I recalled the statements of Radek at the first anniversary of the Third International, when he related to his audience the "marvelous spread of Communism" in America. "Fifty thousand Communists are in American prisons," he exclaimed. Molly Stimer, a girl of eighteen, and her male companions, all Communists, had been deported from America for their Communist activities." I thought at the time that Radek was misinformed. Yet it seemed strange that he did not make sure of his facts before making such assertions. They were dishonest and an insult to Molly Stimer and her Anarchist comrades, added to the injustice they had suffered at the hands of the American plutocracy.

During the past several months I had seen and heard enough to become somewhat conversant with the Communist psychology, as well as with the theories and methods of the Bolsheviki. I was no longer surprised at the story of their double-dealing with Makhno, the brutalities practiced by the Tcheka, the lies of Zorin. I had come to realize that the Communists believed implicitly in the Jesuitic formula that the end justifies all means. In fact, they gloried in that formula. Any suggestion of the value of human life, quality of character, the importance of revolutionary integrity as the basis of a new social order, was repudiated as "bourgeois sentimentality," which had no place in the revolutionary scheme of things. For the Bolsheviki the end to be achieved was the Communist State, or the so-called Dictatorship of the Proletariat. Everything which advanced that end was justifiable and revolutionary. The Lenins, Radeks, and Zorins were therefore quite consistent. Obsessed by the infallibility of their creed, giving of themselves to the fullest, they could be both heroic and despicable at the same time. They could work twenty hours a day, live on herring and tea, and order the slaughter of innocent men and women. Occasionally they sought to mask their killings by pretending a "misunderstanding," for doesn't the end justify all means? They could employ torture and deny the inquisition, they could lie and defame, and call themselves idealists. In short, they could make themselves and others believe that everything was legitimate and right from the revolutionary viewpoint; any other policy was weak, sentimental, or a betrayal of the Revolution.

On a certain occasion, when I passed criticism on the brutal way delicate women were driven into the streets to shovel snow, insisting that even if they had belonged to the bourgeoisie they were human, and that physical fitness should be taken into consideration, a Communist said to me: "You should be ashamed of yourself; you, an old revolutionist, and yet so sentimental." It was the same attitude that some Communists assumed toward Angelica Balabanova, because she was always solicitous and eager to help wherever possible. In short, I had come to see that the Bolsheviki were social puritans who sincerely believed that they alone were ordained to save mankind. My relations with the Bolsheviki became more strained, my attitude toward the Revolution as I found it more critical.

One thing grew quite clear to me: I could not affiliate myself with the Soviet Government; I could not accept any work which would place me under the control of the Communist machine. The Commissariat of Education was so thoroughly dominated by that machine that it was hopeless to expect anything but routine work. In fact, unless one was a Communist one could accomplish almost nothing. I had been eager to join Lunacharsky, whom I considered one of the most cultivated and least dogmatic of the Communists in high position. But I became convinced that Lunacharsky himself was a helpless cog in the machine, his best efforts constantly curtailed and checked. I had also learned a great deal about the system of favouratism and graft that prevailed in the management of the schools and the treatment of children. Some schools were in splendid condition, the children well fed and well clad, enjoying concerts, theatricals, dances, and other amusements. But the majority of the school children's homes were squalid, dirty, and neglected. Those in charge of the "preferred schools had little difficulty in procuring thing needed for their changes, often having an over-supply. But the caretakers of the common schools would waste their time and energies by the week going about from one department to another, discouraged and faint with endless waiting before they could obtain the merest necessities.

At first I ascribed this condition of affairs to the scarcity of food and materials. I heard it said often enough that the blockade and intervention were responsible. To a large extent that was true. Had Russia not been so starved, mismanagement and graft would not have had such fatal results. But added to the prevalent scarcity of things was the dominant notion of Communist propaganda. Even the children had to serve that end. The well-kept schools were for show, for the foreign missions and delegates who were visiting Russia. Everything was lavished on these show schools at the cost of the others.

I remembered how everybody was startled in Petrograd by an article in the Petrograd *Pravda* of May, disclosing appalling conditions in the schools. A committee of the Young Communist organizations investigated some of the institutions. They found the children dirty, full of vermin, sleeping on filthy mattresses, fed on miserable food, punished by being locked in dark rooms for the night, forced to go without their suppers, and even beaten. The number of officials and employees in the schools was nothing less than criminal. In one school, for instance, there were 138 of them to 125 children. In another, 40 to 25 children. All these parasites were taking the bread from the very mouths of the unfortunate children.

The Zorins had spoken to me repeatedly of Lillina, the woman in charge of the Petrograd Educational Department. She was a wonderful worker, they said, devoted and able. I had heard her speak on several occasions, but was not impressed: she looked prim and self-satisfied, a typical Puritan schoolma'am. But I would not form an opinion until I had talked with her. At the publication of the school disclosures I decided to see Lillina. We conversed over an hour about the schools in her charge, about education in general, the problem of defective children and their treatment. She made light of the abuses in her schools, claiming that "the young comrades had exaggerated the defects." At any rate, she added, the guilty had already been removed from the schools.

Similarly to many other responsible Communists Lillina was consecrated to her work and gave all her time and energies to it. Naturally, she could not personally oversee everything; the show schools being the most important in her estimation, she devoted most of her time to them. The other schools were left in the care of her numerous assistants, whose fitness for the work was judged largely according to their political usefulness. Our talk strengthened my conviction that I could have no part in the work of the Bolshevik Board of Education.

The Board of Health offered as little opportunity for real service — service that should not discriminate in favour of show hospitals or the political views of the patients. This principle of discrimination prevailed, unfortunately, even in the sick rooms. Like all Communist institutions, the Board of Health was headed by a political Commissar, Doctor Pervukhin. He was anxious to secure my assistance, proposing to put me in charge of factory, dispensary, or district nursing — a very flattering and tempting offer, and one that appealed to me strongly. I had several conferences with Doctor Pervukhin, but they led to no practical result.

Whenever I visited his department I found groups of men and women waiting, endlessly waiting. They were doctors and nurses, members of the intelligentsia — none of them Communists — who were employed in various medical branches, but their time and energies were being wasted in the waiting rooms of Doctor Pervukhin, the political Commissar. They were a sorry lot, dispirited and dejected, those men and women, once the flower of Russia. Was I to join this tragic procession, submit to the political yoke? Not until I should become convinced that the yoke was indispensable to the revolutionary process would I consent to it. I felt that I must first secure work of a non-partisan character, work that would enable me to study conditions in Russia and get into direct touch with the people, the workers and peasants. Only then should I be able to find my way out of the chaos of doubt and mental anguish that I had fallen prey to.

Chapter 13: Joining The Museum Of The Revolution

The Museum of the Revolution is housed in the Winter Palace, in the suite once used as the nursery of the Tsar's children. The entrance to that part of the palace is known as *detsky podyezd*. From the windows of the palace the Tsar must have often looked across the Neva at the Peter-and-Paul Fortress, the living tomb of his political enemies. How different things were now! The thought of it kindled my imagination. I was full of the wonder and the magic of the great change when I paid my first visit to the Museum.

I found groups of men and women at work in the various rooms, huddled up in their wraps and shivering with cold. Their faces were bloated and bluish, their hands frost-bitten, their whole appearance shadow-like. What must be the devotion of these people, I thought, when they an continue to work under such conditions. The secretary of the Museum, M. B. Kaplan, the Communist machine. "The Bolsheviki," he would say, "always complain about lack of able help, yet no one — unless a Communist — has much of a chance." The Museum was among the least interfered with institutions, and work there had been progressing well. Then a group of twenty youths were sent over, young and inexperienced boys unfamiliar with the work. Being Communists they were placed in positions of authority, and friction and confusion resulted. Everyone felt himself watched and spied upon. "The Bolsheviki care not about merit," he said "their chief concern is a membership card." He was not enthusiastic about the future of the Museum, yet believed that the cooperation of the "Americans" would aid its proper development.

Finally I decided on the Museum as offering the most suitable work for me, mainly because that institution was non-partisan. I had hoped for a more vital share in Russia's life than the collecting of historical material; still I considered it valuable and necessary work. When I had definitely consented to become a member of the expedition, I visited the Museum daily to help with the preparations for the long journey. There was much work. It was no easy matter to obtain a car, equip it for the arduous trip, and secure the documents which would give us access to the material we set out to collect.

While I was busy aiding in these preparations Angelica Balabanova arrived in Petrograd to meet the Italian Mission. She seemed transformed. She had longed for her Italian comrades: they would bring her a breath of her beloved Italy, of her former life and work there. Though Russian by birth, training, and revolutionary traditions, Angelica had become rooted in the soil of Italy. Well I understood her and her sense of strangeness in the country, the hard soil of which was to bear a new and radiant life. Angelica would not admit even to herself that the much hoped-for life was stillborn. But knowing her as I did, it was not difficult for me to understand how bitter was her grief over the hapless and formless thing that had come to Russia. But now her beloved Italians were coming! They would bring with them the warmth and colour of Italy.

The Italians came and with them new festivities, demonstrations, meetings, and speeches. How different it all appeared to me from my memorable first days on Belo-Ostrov. No doubt the Italians now felt as awed as I did then, as inspired by the seeming wonder of Russia. Six months and the close proximity with the reality of things quite changed the picture for me. The spontaneity, the enthusiasm, the vitality had all gone out of it. Only a pale shadow remained, a grinning phantom that clutched at my heart.

On the Uritski Square the masses were growing weary with long waiting. They had been kept there for hours before the Italian Mission arrived from the Tauride Palace. The ceremonies were just beginning when a woman leaning against the platform, wan and pale, began to weep. I stood close by. " It is easy for them to talk," she moaned, "but we've had no food all day. We received orders to march directly from our work on pain of losing our bread rations. Since five this morning I am on my feet. We were not permitted to go home after work to our bit of dinner. We had to come here. Seventeen hours on a piece of bread and some *kipyatok* [boiled water]. Do the visitors know anything about us?" The speeches went on, the "Internationale" was being repeated for the tenth time, the sailors performed their fancy exercises and the claqueurs on the reviewing stand were shouting hurrahs. I rushed away. I, too, was weeping, though my eyes remained dry.

The Italian, like the English, Mission was quartered in the Narishkin Palace. One day, on visiting Angelica there, I found her in a perturbed state of mind. Through one of the servants she had learned that the ex-princess Narishkin, former owner of the palace, had come to beg for the silver ikon which had been in the family for generations. "Just that ikon," she had implored. But the ikon was now state property, and Balabanova could do nothing about it. "Just think," Angelica said, "Narishkin, old and desolate, now stands on the street corner begging, and I live in this palace. How dreadful is life! I am no good for it; I must get away."

But Angelica was bound by party discipline; she stayed on in the palace until she returned to Moscow. I know she did not feel much happier than the ragged and starving ex-princess begging on the street corner.

Balabanova, anxious that I should find suitable work, informed me one day that Petrovsky, known in America as Doctor Goldfarb, had arrived in Petrograd. He was Chief of the Central Military Education Department, which included Nurses' Training Schools. I had never met the man in the States, but I had heard of him as the labour editor of the New York *Forward*, the Jewish Socialist daily. He offered me the position of head instructress in the military Nurses' Training School, with a view to introducing American methods of nursing, or to send me with a medical train to the Polish front. I had proffered my services at the first news of the Polish attack on Russia: I felt the Revolution in danger, and I hastened to Zorin to ask to be assigned as a nurse. He promised to bring the matter before the proper authorities, but I heard nothing further about it. I was, therefore, somewhat surprised at the proposition of Petrovsky.

However, it came too late. What I had since learned about the situation in the Ukraina, the Bolshevik methods toward Makhno and the *povstantsi* movement, the persecution of Anarchists, and the Tcheka activities, had completely shaken my faith in the Bolsheviki as revolutionists. The offer came too late. But Moscow perhaps thought it unwise to let me see behind the scenes at the front; Petrovsky failed to inform me of the Moscow decision. I felt relieved.

At last we received the glad tidings that the greatest difficulty had been overcome: a car for the Museum Expedition had been secured. It consisted of six compartments and was newly painted and cleaned. Now began the work of equipment. Ordinarily it would have taken another two months, but we had the cooperation of the man at the head of the Museum, Chairman Yatmanov, a Communist. He was also in charge of all the properties of the Winter Palace where the Museum is housed. The largest part of the linen, silver, and glassware from the Tsar's storerooms had been removed, but there was still much left. Supplied with an order of the chairman I was shown over what was once guarded as sacred precincts by Romanov flunkeys. I found rooms stacked to the ceiling with rare and beautiful china and compartments filled with the finest linen. The basement, running the whole length of the Winter Palace, was stocked with kitchen utensils of every size and variety. Tin plates and pots would have been more appropriate for the Expedition, but owing to the ruling that no institution may draw upon another for anything it has in its own possession, there was nothing to do but to choose the simplest obtainable at the Winter Palace. I went home reflecting upon the strangeness of life: revolutionists eating out of the crested service of the Romanovs. But I felt no elation over it.

Chapter 14: Petropavlovsk And Schlüsselburg

As some time was to pass before we could depart, I took advantage of the opportunity which presented itself to visit the historic prisons, the Peter-and-Paul Fortress and Schlüsselburg. I recollected the dread and awe the very names of these places filled me with when I first came to Petrograd as a child of thirteen. In fact, my dread of the Petropavlovsk Fortress dated back to a much earlier time. I think I must have been six years old when a great shock had come to our family: we learned that my mother's oldest brother, Yegor, a student at the University of Petersburg, had been arrested and was held in the Fortress. My mother at once set out for the capital. We children remained at home in fear and trepidation lest Mother should not find our uncle among the living. We spent anxious weeks and months till finally Mother returned. Great was our rejoicing to hear that she had rescued her brother from the living dead. But the memory of the shock remained with me for a long time.

Seven years later, my family then living in Petersburg, I happened to be sent on an errand which took me past the Peter-and-Paul Fortress. The shock I had received many years before revived within me with paralyzing force. There stood the heavy mass of stone, dark and sinister. I was terrified. The great prison was still to me a haunted house, causing my heart to palpitate with fear whenever I had to pass it. Years later, when I had begun to draw sustenance from the lives and heroism of the great Russian revolutionists, the Peter-and-Paul Fortress became still more hateful. And now I was about to enter its mysterious walls and see with my own eyes the place which had been the living grave of so many of the best sons and daughters of Russia.

The guide assigned to take us through the different *ravelins* had been in the prison for ten years. He knew every stone in the place. But the silence told me more than all the information of the guide. The martyrs who had beaten their wings against the cold stone, striving upward toward the light and air, came to life for me. The Dekabristi Tchernishevsky, Dostoyevsky, Bakunin, Kropotkin, and scores of others spoke in a thousand-throated voice of their social idealism and their personal suffering—of their high hopes and fervent faith in the ultimate liberation of Russia. Now the fluttering spirits of the heroic dead may rest in peace: their dream has come true. But what is this strange writing on the wall? "To-night I am to be shot because I had once acquired an education." I had almost lost consciousness of the reality. The inscription roused me to it. "What is this?" I asked the guard. "Those are the last words of an intelligent," he replied. "After the October Revolution the intelligentsia filled this prison. From here they were taken out and shot, or were loaded on barges never to return. Those were dreadful days and still more dreadful nights." So the dream of those who had given their lives for the liberation of Russia had not come true, after all. Is there any change in the world ? Or is it all an eternal recurrence of man's inhumanity to man?

We reached the strip of enclosure where the prisoners used to be permitted a half-hour's recreation. One by one they had to walk up and down the narrow lane in dead silence, with the sentries on the wall ready to shoot for the slightest infraction of the rules. And while the caged and fettered ones treaded the treeless walk, the all-powerful Romanovs looked out of the Winter Palace toward the golden spire topping the Fortress to reassure themselves that their hated enemies would never again threaten their safety. But not even Petropavlovsk could save the Tsars from the slaying hand of Time and Revolution. Indeed, there is change; slow and painful, but come it does.

In the enclosure we met Angelica Balabanova and the Italians. We walked about the huge prison, each absorbed in his own thoughts set in motion by what he saw. Would Angelica notice the writing on the wall, I wondered. "To-night I am to be shot because I had once acquired an education."

Some time later several of our group made a trip to Schlüsselburg, the even more dreadful tomb of the political enemies of Tsarism. It is a journey of several hours by boat up the beautiful River Neva. The day was chilly and gray, as was our mood; just the right state of mind to visit Schlüsselburg. The fortress was strongly guarded, but our Museum permit secured for us immediate admission. Schlüsselburg is a compact mass of stone perched upon a high rock in the open sea. For many decades only the victims of court intrigues and royal disfavour were immured within its impenetrable walls, but later it became the Golgotha of the political enemies of the Tsarist regime.

I had heard of Schlüsselburg when my parents first came to Petersburg; but unlike my feeling toward the Peter-and-Paul Fortress, I had no personal reaction to the place. It was Russian revolutionary literature which brought the meaning of Schlüsselburg home to me. Especially the story of Volkenstein, one of the two women who had spent long years in the dreaded place, left an indelible impression on my mind. Yet nothing I had read made the place quite so real and terrifying as when I climbed up the stone steps and stood before the forbidding gates. As far as any effect upon the physical condition of the Peter-and-Paul Fortress was concerned, the Revolution might never have taken place. The prison remained intact, ready for immediate use by the new regime. Not so Schlüsselburg. The wrath of the proletariat struck that house of the dead almost to the ground.

How cruel and perverse the human mind which could create a Schlüsselburg! Verily, no savage could be guilty of the fiendish spirit that conceived this appalling tomb. Cells built like a bag, without doors or windows and with only a small opening through which the victims were lowered into their living grave. Other cells were stone cages to drive the mind to madness and lacerate the heart of the unfortunates. Yet men and women endured twenty years in this terrible place. What fortitude, what power of endurance, what sublime faith one must have had to hold out, to emerge from it alive! Here Netchaev, Lopatin, Morosov, Volkenstein, Figner, and others of the splendid band spent their tortured lives. Here is the common grave of Ulianov, Mishkin, Kalayev, Balmashev, and many more. The black tablet inscribed with their names speaks louder than the voices silenced for ever. Not even the roaring waves dashing against the rock of Schlüsselburg can drown that accusing voice.

Petropavlovsk and Schlüsselburg stand as the living proof of how futile is the hope of the mighty to escape the Frankensteins of their own making.

Chapter 15: The Trade Unions

It was the month of June and the time of our departure was approaching. Petrograd seemed more beautiful than ever; the white nights had come — almost broad daylight without its glare, the mysterious soothing white nights of Petrograd. There were rumours of counter-revolutionary danger and the city was guarded against attack. Martial law prevailing, it was forbidden to be out on the streets after 1 A. M., even though it was almost daylight. Occasionally special permits were obtained by friends and then we would walk through the deserted streets or along the banks of the dark Neva, discussing in whispers the perplexing situation. I sought for some outstanding feature in the blurred picture — the Russian Revolution, a huge flame shooting across the world illuminating the black horizon of the disinherited and oppressed — the Revolution, the new hope, the great spiritual awakening. And here I was in the midst of it, yet nowhere could I see the promise and fulfilment of the great event. Had I misunderstood the meaning and nature of revolution? Perhaps the wrong and the evil I have seen during those five months were inseparable from a revolution. Or was it the political machine which the Bolsheviki have created — is that the force which is crushing the Revolution ? If I had witnessed the birth of the latter I should now be better able to judge. But apparently I arrived at the end — the agonizing end of a people. It is all so complex, so impenetrable, a *tupik,* a blind alley, as the Russians call it. Only time and earnest study, aided by sympathetic understanding, will show me the way out. Meanwhile, I must keep up my courage and—away from Petrograd, out among the people.

Presently the long-awaited moment arrived. On June 30, 1920, our car was coupled to a slow train called "Maxim Gorki," and we pulled out of the Nikolayevski station, bound for Moscow.

In Moscow there were many formalities to go through with. We thought a few days would suffice, but we remained two weeks. However, our stay was interesting. The city was alive with delegates to the Second Congress of the Third International; from all parts of the world the workers had sent their comrades to the promised land, revolutionary Russia, the first republic of the workers. Among the delegates there were also Anarchists and syndicalists who believed as firmly as I did six months previously that the Bolsheviki were the symbol of the Revolution. They had responded to the Moscow call with enthusiasm. Some of them I had met in Petrograd and now they were eager to hear of my experiences and learn my opinions. But what was I to tell them, and would they believe me if I did ? Would I have believed any adverse criticism before I came to Russia? Besides, I felt that my views regarding the Bolsheviki were still too unformed, too vague, a conglomeration of mere impressions. My old values had been shattered and so far I have been unable to replace them. I could therefore not speak on the fundamental questions, but I did inform my friends that the Moscow and Petrograd prisons were crowded with Anarchists and other revolutionists, and I advised them not to content themselves with the official explanations but to investigate for themselves. I warned them that they would be surrounded by guides and interpreters, most of them men of the Tcheka, and that they would not be able to learn the facts unless they made a determined, independent effort.

There was considerable excitement in Moscow at the time. The Printers' Union had been suppressed and its entire managing board sent to prison. The Union had called a public meeting to which members of the British Labour Mission were invited. There the famous Socialist Revolutionist Tchernov had unexpectedly made his appearance. He severely criticised the Bolshevik regime, received an ovation from the huge audience of workers, and then vanished as mysteriously as he had come. The Menshevik Dan was less successful.

He also addressed the meeting, but he failed to make his escape: he landed in the Tcheka. The next morning the Moscow *Pravda* and the *Izvestia* denounced the action of the Printers' Union as counter-revolutionary, and raged about Tchernov having been permitted to speak. The papers called for exemplary punishment of the printers who dared defy the Soviet Government.

The Bakers' Union, a very militant organization, had also been suppressed, and its management replaced by Communists. Several months before, in March, I had attended a convention of the bakers. The delegates impressed me as a courageous group who did not fear to criticise the Bolshevik regime and present the demands of the workers. I wondered then that they were permitted to continue the conference, for they were outspoken in their opposition to the Communists. "The bakers are '*shkurniki*' [skinners]," I was told; "they always instigate strikes, and only counter-revolutionists can wish to strike in the workers' Republic." But it seemed to me that the workers could not follow such reasoning. They did strike. They even committed a more heinous crime: they refused to vote for the Communist candidate, electing instead a man of their own choice. This action of the bakers was followed by the arrest of several of their more active members. Naturally the workers resented the arbitrary methods of the Government

Later I met some of the bakers and found them much embittered against the Communist Party and the Government. I inquired about the condition of their union, telling them that I had been informed that the Russian unions were very powerful and had practical control of the industrial life of the country. The bakers laughed. "The trade unions are the lackeys of the Government," they said; "they have no independent function, and the workers have no say in them. The trade unions are doing mere police duty for the Government." That sounded quite different from the story told by Melnichansky, the chairman of the Moscow Trade Union Soviet, whom I had met on my first visit to Moscow.

On that occasion he had shown me about the trade union headquarters known as the Dom Soyusov, and explained how the organization worked. Seven million workers were in the trade unions, he said; all trades and professions belonged to it. The workers themselves managed the industries and owned them. "The building you are in now is also owned by the unions," he remarked with pride;

"formerly it was the House of the Nobility." The room we were in had been used for festive assemblies and the great nobles sat in crested chairs around the table in the centre. Melnichansky showed me the secret underground passage hidden by a little turntable, through which the nobles could escape in case of danger. They never dreamed that the workers would some day gather around the same table and sit in the beautiful hall of marble columns. The educational and cultural work done by the trade unions, the chairman further explained, was of the greatest scope. "We have our workers' colleges and other cultural institutions giving courses and lectures on various subjects. They are all managed by the workers. The unions own their own means of recreation, and we have access to all the theatres." It was apparent from his explanation that the trade unions of Russia had reached a point far beyond anything known by labour organizations in Europe and America.

A similar account I had heard from Tsiperovitch, the chairman of the Petrograd trade unions, with whom I had made my first trip to Moscow. He had also shown me about the Petrograd Labour Temple, a beautiful and spacious building where the Petrograd unions had their offices. His recital also made it clear that the workers of Russia had at last come into their own.

But gradually I began to see the other side of the medal. I found that like most things in Russia the trade union picture had a double facet: one paraded before foreign visitors and "investigators," the other known by the masses. The bakers and the printers had recently been shown the other side. It was a lesson of the benefits that accrued to the trade unions in the Socialist Republic.

In March I had attended an election meeting arranged by the workers of one of the large Moscow factories. It was the most exciting gathering I had witnessed in Russia — the dimly lit hall in the factory club rooms, the faces of the men and women worn with privation and suffering, the intense feeling over the wrong done them, all impressed me very strongly. Their chosen representative, an Anarchist, had been refused his mandate by the Soviet authorities. It was the third time the workers gathered to re-elect their delegate to the Moscow Soviet, and every time they elected the same man. The Communist candidate opposing him was Semashko, the Commissar of the Department of Health. I had expected to find an educated and cultured man. But the behaviour and language of the Commissar at that election meeting would have put a hod-carrier to shame. He raved against the workers for choosing a non-Communist, called anathema upon their heads, and threatened them with the Tcheka and the curtailment of their rations. But he had no effect upon the audience except to emphasize their opposition to him, and to arouse antagonism against the party he represented. The final victory, however, was with Semashko. The workers' choice was repudiated by the authorities and later even arrested and imprisoned. That was in March. In May, during the visit of the British Labour Mission, the factory candidate together with other political prisoners declared a hunger strike, which resulted in their liberation.

The story told me by the bakers of their election experiences had the quality of our own Wild West during its pioneer days. Tchekists with loaded guns were in the habit of attending gatherings of the unions and they made it clear what would happen if the workers should fail to elect a Communist. But the bakers, a strong and militant organization, would not be intimidated. They declared that no bread would be baked in Moscow unless they were permitted to elect their own candidate. That had the desired effect. After the meeting the Tchekists tried to arrest the candidate-elect, but the bakers surrounded him and saw him safely home. The next day they sent their ultimatum to the authorities, demanding recognition of their choice and threatening to strike in case of refusal. Thus the bakers triumphed and gained an advantage over their less courageous brothers in the other labour organizations of minor importance. In starving Russia the work of the bakers was as vital as life itself.

Chapter 16: Maria Spiridonova

The Commissariat of Education also included the Department of Museums. The Petrograd Museum of the Revolution had two chairmen; Lunacharsky being one of them, it was necessary to secure his signature to our credentials which had already been signed by Zinonev, the second chairman of the Museum. I was commissioned to see Lunacharsky.

I felt rather guilty before him. I left Moscow in March promising to return within a week to join him in his work. Now, four months later, I came to ask his cooperation in an entirely different field. I went to the Kremlin determined to tell Lunacharsky how I felt about the situation in Russia. But I was relieved of the necessity by the presence of a number of people in his office; there was no time to take the matter up. I could merely inform Lunacharsky of the purpose of the expedition and request his aid in the work. It met with his approval. He signed our credentials and also supplied me with letters of introduction and recommendation to facilitate our efforts in behalf of the Museum.

While our Commission was making the necessary preparations for the trip to the Ukraine, I found time to visit various institutions in Moscow and to meet some interesting people. Among them were certain well-known Left Social Revolutionists whom I had met on my previous visit. I had told them then that I was eager to visit Maria Spiridonova, of whose condition I had heard many conflicting stories. But at that time no meeting could be arranged: it might have exposed Spiridonova to danger, for she was living illegally, as a peasant woman. History indeed repeats itself. Under the Tsar Spiridonova, also disguised as a country girl, had shadowed Lukhanovsky, the Governor of Tamboy, of peasant-flogging fame. Having shot him, she was arrested, tortured, and later sentenced to death. The western world became aroused, and it was due to its protests that the sentence of Spiridonova was changed to Siberian exile for life. She spent eleven years there; the February Revolution brought her freedom and back to Russia. Maria Spiridonova immediately threw herself into revolutionary activity. Now, in the Socialist Republic, Maria was again living in disguise after having escaped from the prison in the Kremlin.

Arrangements were finally made to enable me to visit Spiridonova, and I was cautioned to make sure that I was not followed by Tcheka men. We agreed with Maria's friends upon a meeting place and from there we zigzagged a number of streets till we at last reached the top floor of a house in the back of a yard. I was led into a small room containing a bed, small desk, bookcase, and several chairs. Before the desk, piled high with letters and papers, sat a frail little woman, Maria Spiridonova. This, then, was one of Russia's great martyrs, this woman who had so unflinchingly suffered the tortures inflicted upon her by the Tsar's henchmen. I had been told by Zorin and Jack Reed that Spiridonova had suffered a breakdown, and was kept in a sanatorium. Her malady, they said, was acute neurasthenia and hysteria. When I came face to face with Maria, I immediately realized that both men had deceived me. I was no longer surprised at Zorin: much of what he had told me I gradually discovered to be utterly false. As to Reed, unfamiliar with the language and completely under the sway of the new faith, he took too much for granted. Thus, on his return from Moscow he came to inform me that the story of the shooting of prisoners en masse on the eve of the abolition of capital punishment was really true; but, he assured me, it was all the fault of a certain official of the Tcheka who had already paid with his life for it. I had opportunity to investigate the matter. I found that Jack had again been misled. It was not that a certain man was responsible for the wholesale killing on that occasion. The act was conditioned in the whole system and character of the Tcheka.

I spent two days with Maria Spiridonova, listening to her recital of events since October, 1917. She spoke at length about the enthusiasm and zeal of the masses and the hopes held out by the Bolsheviki; of their ascendancy to power and gradual turn to the right. She explained the Brest-Litovsk peace which she considered as the first link in the chain that has since fettered the Revolution. She dwelt on the *razverstka*, the system of forcible requisition, which was devastating Russia and discrediting everything the Revolution had been fought for; she referred to the terrorism practiced by the Bolsheviki against every revolutionary criticism, to the new Communist bureaucracy and inefficiency, and the hopelessness of the whole situation. It was a crushing indictment against the Bolsheviki, their theories and methods.

If Spiridonova had really suffered a breakdown, as I had been assured, and was hysterical and mentally unbalanced, she must have had extraordinary control of herself. She was calm, self-contained, and clear on every point. She had the fullest command of her material and information. On several occasions during her narrative, when she detected doubt in my face, she remarked: "I fear you don't quite believe me. Well, here is what some of the peasants write me," and she would reach over to a pile of letters on her desk and read to me passages heartrending with misery and bitter against the Bolsheviki. In stilted handwriting, sometimes almost illegible, the peasants of the Ukraine and Siberia wrote of the horrors of the *razverstka* and what it had done to them and their land. "They have taken away everything, even the last seeds for the next sowing." "The Commissars have robbed us of everything." Thus ran the letters. Frequently peasants wanted to know whether Spiridonova had gone over to the Bolsheviki. "If you also forsake us, *matushka*, we have no one to turn to," one peasant wrote.

The enormity of her accusations challenged credence. After all, the Bolsheviki were revolutionists. How could they be guilty of the terrible things charged against them? Perhaps they were not responsible for the situation as it had developed; they had the whole world against them. There was the Brest peace, for instance. When the news of it first reached America I happened to be in prison. I reflected long and carefully whether Soviet Russia was justified in negotiating with German imperialism. But I could see no way out of the situation. I was in favour of the Brest peace. Since I came to Russia I heard conflicting versions of it. Nearly everyone, excepting the Communists, considered the Brest agreement as much a betrayal of the Revolution as the role of the German Socialists in the warÛa betrayal of the spirit of internationalism. The Communists, on the other hand, were unanimous in defending the peace and denouncing as counter-revolutionist everybody who questioned the wisdom and the revolutionary justification of that agreement. "We could do nothing else," argued the Communists. "Germany had a mighty army, while we had none. Had we refused to sign the Brest treaty we should have sealed the fate of the Revolution. We realized that Brest meant a compromise, but we knew that the workers of Russia and the rest of the world would understand that we had been forced to it. Our compromise was similar to that of workers when they are forced to accept the conditions of their masters after an unsuccessful strike."

But Spiridonova was not convinced. "There is not one word of truth in the argument advanced by the Bolsheviki," she said. It is true that Russia had no disciplined army to meet the German advance, but it had something infinitely more effective: it had a conscious revolutionary people who would have fought back the invaders to the last drop of blood. As a matter of fact, it was the people who had checked all the counter-revolutionary military attempts against Russia. Who else but the people, the peasants and the workers, made it impossible for the German and Austrian army to remain in the Ukraine ? Who defeated Denikin and the other counter-revolutionary generals? Who triumphed over Koltchak and Yudenitch? Lenin and Trotsky claim that it was the Red Army. But the historic truth was that the voluntary military units of the workers and peasants — the *povstantsi,* in Siberia as well as in the south of Russia — had borne the brunt of the fighting on every front, the Red Army usually only completing the victories of the former. Trotsky would have it now that the Brest treaty had to be accepted, but he himself had at one time refused to sign the treaty and Radek, Joffe, and other leading Communists had also been opposed to it. It is claimed now that they submitted to the shameful terms because they realized the hopelessness of their expectation that the German workers would prevent the Junkers from marching against revolutionary Russia. But that was not the true reason. It was the whip of the party discipline which lashed Trotsky and others into submission.

"The trouble with the Bolsheviki," continued Spiridonova, "is that they have no faith in the masses. They proclaimed themselves a proletarian party, but they refused to trust the workers." It was this lack of faith, Maria emphasized, which made the Communists bow to German imperialism. And as concerns the Revolution itself, it was precisely the Brest peace which struck it a fatal blow. Aside from the betrayal of Finland, White Russia, Latvia and the Ukraine—which were turned over to the mercy of the German Junkers by the Brest peace—the peasants saw thousands of their brothers slain, and had to submit to being robbed and plundered. The simple peasant mind could not understand the complete reversal of the former Bolshevik slogans of "no indemnity and no annexations." But even the simplest peasant could understand that his toil and his blood were to pay the indemnities imposed by the Brest conditions. The peasants grew bitter and antagonistic to the Soviet regime. Disheartened and discouraged they turned from the Revolution. As to the effect of the Brest peace upon the German workers, how could they continue in their faith in the Russian Revolution in view of the fact that the Bolsheviki negotiated and accepted the peace terms with the German masters over the heads of the German proletariat? The historic fact remains that the Brest peace was the beginning of the end of the Russian Revolution. No doubt other factors contributed to the debacle, but Brest was the most fatal of them.

Spiridonova asserted that the Left Socialist Revolutionary elements had warned the Bolsheviki against that peace and fought it desperately. They refused to accept it even after it had been signed. The presence of Mirbach in Revolutionary Russia they considered an outrage against the Revolution, a crying injustice to the heroic Russian people who had sacrificed and suffered so much in their struggle against imperialism and capitalism. Spiridonova's party decided that Mirbach could not be tolerated in Russia: Mirbach had to go. Wholesale arrests and persecutions followed upon the execution of Mirbach, the Bolsheviki rendering service to the German Kaiser. They filled the prisons with the Russian revolutionists.

In the course of our conversation I suggested that the method of *razverstka* was probably forced upon the Bolsheviki by the refusal of the peasants to feed the city. In the beginning of the revolutionary period, Spiridonova explained, so long as the peasant Soviets existed, the peasants gave willingly and generously. But when the Bolshevik Government began to dissolve these Soviets and arrested 500 peasant delegates, the peasantry became antagonistic. Moreover, they daily witnessed the inefficiency of the Communist regime: they saw their products lying at side stations and rotting away, or in possession of speculators on the market. Naturally under such conditions they would not continue to give. The fact that the peasants had never refused to contribute supplies to the Red Army proved that other methods than those used by the Bolsheviki could have been employed. The *razverstka* served only to widen the breach between the village and the city. The Bolsheviki resorted to punitive expeditions which became the terror of the country. They left death and ruin wherever they came. The peasants, at last driven to desperation, began to rebel against the Communist regime. In various parts of Russia, in the south, on the Ural, and in Siberia, peasants' insurrections have taken place, and everywhere they were being put down by force of arms and with an iron hand.

Spiridonova did not speak of her own sufferings since she had parted ways with the Bolsheviki. But I learned from others that she had been arrested twice and imprisoned for a considerable length of time. Even when free she was kept under surveillance, as she had been in the time of the Tsar. On several occasions she was tortured by being taken out at night and informed that she was to be shot—a favoured Tcheka method. I mentioned the subject to Spiridonova. She did not deny the facts, though she was loath to speak of herself. She was entirely absorbed in the fate of the Revolution and of her beloved peasantry. She gave no thought to herself, but she was eager to have the world and the international proletariat learn the true condition of affairs in Bolshevik Russia.

Of all the opponents of the Bolsheviki I had met Maria Spiridonova impressed me as one of the most sincere, well-poised, and convincing. Her heroic past and her refusal to compromise her revolutionary ideas under Tsarism as well as under Bolshevism were sufficient guarantee of her revolutionary integrity.

Chapter 17: Another Visit To Peter Kropotkin

A few days before our Expedition started for the Ukraine the opportunity presented itself to pay another visit to Peter Kropotkin. I was delighted at the chance to see the dear old man under more favourable conditions than I had seen in March. I expected at least that we would not be handicapped by the presence of newspaper men as we were on the previous occasion.

On my first visit, in snow-clad March I arrived at the Kropotkin cottage late in the evening. The place looked deserted and desolate. But now it was summer time. The country was fresh and fragrant; the garden at the back of the house, clad in green, smiled cheerfully, the golden rays of the sun spreading warmth and light. Peter, who was having his afternoon nap, could not be seen, but Sofya Grigorievna, his wife, was there to greet us. We had brought some provisions given to Sasha Kropotkin for her father, and several baskets of things sent by an Anarchist group. While we were unpacking those treasures Peter Alekseyevitch surprised us. He seemed a changed man: the summer had wrought a miracle in him. He appeared healthier, stronger, more alive than when I had last seen him. He immediately took us to the vegetable garden which was almost entirely Sofya's own work and served as the main support of the family. Peter was very proud of it. "What do you say to this!" he exclaimed; "all Sofya's labour. And see this new species of lettuce" — pointing at a huge head. He looked young; he was almost gay, his conversation sparkling. His power of observation, his keen sense of humour and generous humanity were so refreshing, he made one forget the misery of Russia, one's own conflicts and doubts, and the cruel reality of life.

After dinner we gathered in Peter's study — a small room containing an ordinary table for a desk, a narrow cot, a wash-stand, and shelves of books. I could not help making a mental comparison between this simple, cramped study of Kropotkin and the gorgeous quarters of Radek and Zinoviev. Peter was interested to know my impressions since he saw me last. I related to him how confused and harassed I was, how everything seemed to crumble beneath my feet. I told him that I had come to doubt almost everything, even the Revolution itself. I could not reconcile the ghastly reality with what the Revolution had meant to me when I came to Russia. Were the conditions I found inevitable — the callous indifference to human life, the terrorism, the waste and agony of it all? Of course, I knew revolutions could not be made with kid gloves. It is a stern necessity involving violence and destruction, a difficult and terrible process. But what I had found in Russia was utterly unlike revolutionary conditions, so fundamentally unlike as to be a caricature.

Peter listened attentively; then he said: "There is no reason whatever to lose faith. I consider the Russian Revolution even greater than the French, for it has struck deeper into the soul of Russia, into the hearts and minds of the Russian people. Time alone can demonstrate its full scope and depth. What you see to-day is only the surface, conditions artificially created by a governing class. You see a small political party which by its false theories, blunders, and inefficiency has demonstrated how revolutions must not be made." It was unfortunate, Kropotkin continued, that so many of the Anarchists in Russia and the masses outside of Russia had been carried away by the ultra-revolutionary pretenses of the Bolsheviki. In the great upheaval it was forgotten that the Communists are a political party firmly adhering to the idea of a centralized State, and that as such they were bound to misdirect the course of the Revolution. The Bolsheviki were the Jesuits of the Socialist Church: they believed in the Jesuitic motto that the end justifies the means. Their end being political power, they hesitate at nothing. The means, however, have paralysed the energies of the masses and have terrorized the people.

Yet without the people, without the direct participation of the masses in the reconstruction of the country, nothing essential could be accomplished. The Bolsheviki had been carried to the top by the high tide of the Revolution. Once in power they began to stem the tide. They have been trying to eliminate and suppress the cultural forces of the country not entirely in agreement with their ideas and methods. They destroyed the cooperatives which were of utmost importance to the life of Russia, the great link between the country and the city. They created a bureaucracy and officialdom which surpasses even that of the old regime. In the village where he lived, in little Dmitrov, there were more Bolshevik officials than ever existed there during the reign of the Romanovs. All those people were living off the masses. They were parasites on the social body, and Dmitrov was only a small example of what was going on throughout Russia. It was not the fault of any particular individuals: rather was it the State they had created, which discredits every revolutionary ideal, stifles all initiative, and sets a premium on incompetence and waste. It should also not be forgotten Kropotkin emphasized, that the blockade and the continuous attacks on the Revolution by the interventionists had helped to strengthen the power of the Communist regime. Intervention and blockade were bleeding Russia to death, and were preventing the people from understanding the real nature of the Bolshevik regime.

Discussing the activities and role of the Anarchists in the Revolution, Kropotkin said: "We Anarchists have talked much of revolutions, but few of us have been prepared for the actual work to be done during the process. I have indicated some things in this relation in my *Conquest of Bread*. Pouget and Pataud have also sketched a line of action in their work on *How to Accomplish the Social Revolution.*" Kropotkin thought that the Anarchists had not given sufficient consideration to the fundamental elements of the social revolution. The real facts in a revolutionary process do not consist so much in the actual fighting — that is, merely the destructive phase necessary to clear the way for constructive effort. The basic factor in a revolution is the organization of the economic life of the country. The Russian Revolution had proved conclusively that we must prepare thoroughly for that. Everything else is of minor importance. He had come to think that syndicalism was likely to furnish what Russia most lacked: the channel through which the industrial and economic reconstruction of the country may flow. He referred to Anarcho-syndicalism. That and the cooperatives would save other countries some of the blunders and suffering Russia was going through.

I left Dmitrov much comforted by the warmth and light which the beautiful personality of Peter Kropotkin radiated; and I was much encouraged by what I had heard from him. I returned to Moscow to help with the completion of the preparations for our journey. At last, on July 15, 1920, our car was coupled to a train bound for the Ukraine.

Chapter 18: En Route

Our train was about to leave Moscow when we were surprised by an interesting visitor—Krasnoschekov, the president of the Far Eastern Republic, who had recently arrived in the capital from Siberia. He had heard of our presence in the city, but for some reason he could not locate us. Finally he met Alexander Berkman who invited him to the Museum car.

In appearance Krasnoschekov had changed tremendously since his Chicago days, when, known as Tobinson, he was superintendent of the Workers' Institute in that city. Then he was one of the many Russian emigrants on the West Side, active as organizer and lecturer in the Socialist movement. Now he looked a different man; his expression stern, the stamp of authority on him, he seemed even to have grown taller. But at heart he remained the same—simple and kind, the Tobinson we had known in Chicago. We had only a short time at our disposal and our visitor employed it to give us an insight into the conditions in the Far East and the local form of government. It consisted of representatives of various political factions and "even Anarchists are with us," said Krasnoschekov; "thus, for instance, Shatov is Minister of Railways. We are independent in the East and there is free speech. Come over and try us, you will find a field for your work." He invited Alexander Berkman and myself to visit him in Chita and we assured him that we hoped to avail ourselves of the invitation at some future time. He seemed to have brought a different atmosphere.

On the way from Petrograd to Moscow the Expedition had been busy putting its house in order. As already mentioned, the car consisted of six compartments, two of which were converted into a dining room and kitchen. They were of diminutive size, but we managed to make a presentable dining room of one, and the kitchen might have made many a housekeeper envy us. A large Russian samovar and all necessary copper and zinc pots and kettles were there, making a very effective appearance. We were especially proud of the decorative curtains on our car windows. The other compartments were used for office and sleeping quarters. I shared mine with our secretary, Miss A.T. Shakol.

Besides Alexander Berkman, appointed by the Museum as chairman and general manager, Shakol as secretary, and myself as treasurer and housekeeper, the Expedition consisted of three other members, including a young Communist, a student of the Petrograd University. En route we mapped out our plan of work, each member of the Expedition being assigned some particular branch of it. I was to gather data in the Departments of Education and Health, the Bureaus of Social Welfare and Labour Distribution, as well as in the organization known as Workers' and Peasants' Inspection. After the day's work all the members were to meet in the car to consider and classify the material collected during the day.

Our first stop was Kursk. Nothing of importance was collected there except a pair of *kandai* [iron handcuffs] which had been worn by a revolutionist in Schlusselburg. It was donated to us by a chance passer-by who, noticing the inscription on our car, "Extraordinary Commission of the Museum of the Revolution," became interested and called to pay us a visit. He proved to be an intellectual, a Tolstoian, the manager of a children's colony. He succeeded in maintaining the latter by giving the Soviet Government a certain amount of labour required of him: three days a week he taught in the Soviet schools of Kursk. The rest of his time he devoted to his little colony, or the "Children's Commune," as he affectionately called it. With the help of the children and some adults they raised the vegetables necessary for the support of the colony and made all the repairs of the place. He stated that he had not been directly interfered with by the Government, but that his work was considerably handicapped by discrimination against him as a pacifist and Tolstoian. He feared that because of it his place could not be continued much longer. There was no trading of any sort in Kursk at the time, and one had to depend for supplies on the local authorities. But discrimination and antagonism manifested themselves against independent initiative and effort. The Tolstoian, however, was determined to make a fight, spiritually speaking, for the life of his colony. He was planning to go to the centre, to Moscow, where he hoped to get support in favour of his commune.

The personality of the man, his eagerness to make himself useful, did not correspond with the information I had received from Communists about the intelligentsia, their indifference and unwillingness to help revolutionary Russia. I broached the subject to our visitor. He could only speak of the professional men and women of Kursk, his native city, but he assured us that he found most of them, and especially the teachers, eager to cooperate and even self-sacrificing. But they were the most neglected class, living in semi-starvation all the time. Like himself, they were exposed to general antagonism, even on the part of the children whose minds had been poisoned by agitation against the intelligentsia.

Kursk is a large industrial centre and I was interested in the fate of the workers there. We learned from our visitor that there had been repeated skirmishes between the workers and the Soviet authorities. A short time before our arrival a strike had broken out and soldiers were sent to quell it. The usual arrests followed and many workers were still in the Tcheka. This state of affairs, the Tolstoian thought, was due to general Communist incompetence rather than to any other cause. People were placed in responsible positions not because of their fitness but owing to their party membership. Political usefulness was the first consideration and it naturally resulted in general abuse of power and confusion. The Communist dogma that the end justifies all means was also doing much harm. It had thrown the door wide open to the worst human passions, and discredited the ideals of the Revolution. The Tolstoian spoke sadly, as one speaks of a hope cherished and loved, and lost.

The next morning our visitor donated to our collection the *kandali* he had worn for many years in prison. He hoped that we might return by way of Kursk so that we could pay a visit to some Tolstoian communes in the environs of the city. Not far from Yasnaya Polyana there lived an old peasant friend of Tolstoi, he told us. He had much valuable material that he might contribute to the Museum. Our visitor remained to the moment of our departure; he was starved for intellectual companionship and was loath to see us go.

Chapter 19: In Kharkov

Arriving in Kharkov, I visited the Anarchist book store, the address of which I had secured in Moscow. There I met many friends whom I had known in America. Among them were Joseph and Leah Goodman, formerly from Detroit; Fanny Baron, from Chicago, and Sam Fleshin who had worked in the Mother Earth office in New York, in 1917, before he left for Russia. With thousands of other exiles they had all hastened to their native country at the first news of the Revolution, and they had been in the thick of it ever since. They would have much to tell me, I thought; they might help me to solve some of the problems that were perplexing me.

Kharkov lay several miles away from the railroad station, and it would have therefore been impractical to continue living in the car during our stay in the city. The Museum credentials would secure quarters for us, but several members of the Expedition preferred to stay with their American friends. Through the help of one of our comrades, who was commandant of an apartment house, I secured a room.

It had been quite warm in Moscow, but Kharkov proved a veritable furnace, reminding me of New York in July. Sanitary and plumbing arrangements had been neglected or destroyed, and water had to be carried from a place several blocks distant up three flights of stairs. Still it was a comfort to have a private room.

The city was alive. The streets were full of people and they looked better fed and dressed than the population of Petrograd and Moscow. The women were handsomer than in northern Russia; the men of a finer type. It was rather odd to see beautiful women, wearing evening gowns in the daytime, walk about barefoot or clad in wooden sandals without stockings. The coloured kerchiefs most of them had on lent life and colour to the streets, giving them a cheerful appearance which contrasted favourably with the gray tones of Petrograd.

My first official visit was paid to the Department of Education. I found a long line of people waiting admission, but the Museum credentials immediately opened the doors, the chairman receiving me most cordially. He listened attentively to my explanation of the purposes of the Expedition and promised to give me an opportunity to collect all the available material in his department, including the newly prepared charts of its work. On the chairman's desk I noticed a copy of such a chart, looking like a futurist picture, all lined and dotted with red, blue, and purple. Noticing my puzzled expression the chairman explained that the red indicated the various phases of the educational system, the other colours representing literature, drama, music, and the plastic arts. Each department was subdivided into bureaus embracing every branch of the educational and cultural work of the Socialist Republic.

Concerning the system of education the chairman stated that from three to eight years of age the child attended the kindergarten or children's home. War orphans from the south, children of Red Army soldiers and of proletarians in general received preference. If vacancies remained, children of the bourgeoisie were also accepted. From eight to thirteen the children attended the intermediary schools where they received elementary education which inculcates the general idea of the political and economic structure of R.S.F.S.R. Modern methods of instruction by means of technical apparatus, so far as the latter could be secured, had been introduced. The children were taught processes of production as well as natural sciences. The period from twelve to seventeen embraced vocational training. There were also higher institutions of learning for young people who showed special ability and inclination. Besides this, summer schools and colonies had been established where instruction was given in the open. All children belonging to the Soviet Republic were fed, clothed, and housed at the expense of the Government. The scheme of education also embraced workers' colleges and evening courses for adults of both sexes. Here also everything was supplied to the pupils free, even special rations. For further particulars the chairman referred me to the literature of his department and advised me to study the plan in operation. The educational work was much handicapped by the blockade and counterrevolutionary attempts; else Russia would demonstrate to the world what the Socialist Republic could do in the way of popular enlightenment. They lacked even the most elemental necessaries, such as paper, pencils, and books. In the winter most of the schools had to be closed for lack of fuel. The cruelty and infamy of the blockade was nowhere more apparent and crying than in its effect upon the sick and the children. "It is the blackest crime of the century," the chairman concluded. It was agreed that I return within a week to receive the material for our collection. In the Social Welfare Department I also found a very competent man in charge. He became much interested in the work of the Expedition and promised to collect the necessary material for us, though he could not offer very much because his department had but recently been organized. Its work was to look after the disabled and sick proletarians and those of old age exempt from labour. They were given certain rations in food and clothing; in case they were employed they received also a certain amount of money, about half of their earnings. Besides that the Department was supporting living quarters and dining rooms for its charges.

In the corridor leading to the various offices of the Department there were lines of emaciated and crippled figures, men and women, waiting for their turn to receive aid. They looked like war veterans awaiting their pittance in the form of rations; they reminded me of the decrepit unemployed standing in line in the Salvation Army quarters in America. One woman in particular attracted my attention. She was angry and excited and she complained loudly. Her husband had been dead two days and she was trying to obtain a permit for a coffin. She had been in line ever since but could procure no order. "What am I to do?" she wailed; "I cannot carry him on my own back or bury him without a coffin, and I cannot keep him in my room much longer in this heat." The woman's lament remained unanswered for everyone was absorbed in his own troubles. Sick and disabled workers are thrown everywhere on the scrap pile—I thought—but in Russia an effort is being made to prevent such cruelty. Yet judging from what I saw in Kharkov I felt that not much was being accomplished. It was a most depressing picture, that long waiting line. I felt as if it was adding insult to injury.

I visited a house where the social derelicts lived. It was fairly well kept, but breathing the spirit of cold institutionalism. It was, of course, better than sleeping in the streets or lying all night in the doorways, as the sick and poor are often compelled to do in capitalist countries, in America, for instance. Still it seemed incongruous that something more cheerful and inviting could not be devised in Soviet Russia for those who had sacrificed their health and had given their labour to the common good. But apparently it was the best that the Social Welfare Department could do in the present condition of Russia.

In the evening our American friends visited us. Each of them had a rich experience of struggle, suffering, and persecution and I was surprised to learn that most of them had also been imprisoned by the Bolsheviki. They had endured much for the sake of their ideas and had been hounded by every government of Ukraina, there having been fourteen political changes in some parts of the south during the last two years. The Communists were no different: they also persecuted the Anarchists as well as other revolutionists of the Left. Still the Anarchists continued their work. Their faith in the Revolution, in spite of all they endured, and even in the face of the worst reaction, was truly sublime. They agreed that the possibilities of the masses during the first months after the October Revolution were very great, but expressed the opinion that revolutionary development had been checked, and gradually entirely paralysed, by the deadening effect of the Communist State.

In the Ukraina, they explained, the situation differed from that of Russia, because the peasants lived in comparatively better material conditions. They had also retained greater independence and more of a rebellious spirit. For these reasons the Bolsheviki had failed to subdue the south.

Our visitors spoke of Makhno as a heroic popular figure, and related his daring exploits and the legends the peasants had woven about his personality. There was considerable difference of opinion, however, among the Anarchists concerning the significance of the Makhno movement. Some regarded it as expressive of Anarchism and believed that the Anarchists should devote all their energies to it. Others held that the *povstantsi* represented the native rebellious spirit of the southern peasants, but that their movement was not Anarchism, though anarchistically tinged. They were not in favour of limiting themselves to that movement; they believed their work should be of a more embracing and universal character. Several of our friends took an entirely different position, denying to the Makhno movement any anarchist meaning whatever.

Most enthusiastic about Makhno and emphatic about the Anarchist value of that movement was Joseph, known as the "Emigrant" — the very last man one would have expected to wax warm over a military organization. Joseph was as mild and gentle as a girl. In America he had participated in the Anarchist and Labour movements in a quiet and unassuming manner, and very few knew the true worth of the man. Since his return to Russia he had been in the thick of the struggle. He had spent much time with Makhno and had learned to love and admire him for his revolutionary devotion and courage. Joseph related an interesting experience of his first visit to the peasant leader. When he arrived the *povstantsi* for some reason conceived the notion that he had come to harm their chief. One of Makhno's closest friends claimed that Joseph, being a Jew, must also be an emissary of the Bolsheviki sent to kill Makhno. When he saw how attached Makhno became to Joseph, he decided to kill "the Jew." Fortunately he first warned his leader, whereupon Makhno called his men together and addressed them somewhat in this manner: "Joseph is a Jew and an idealist; he is an Anarchist. I consider him my comrade and friend and I shall hold everyone responsible for his safety." Idolized by his army, Makhno's word was enough: Joseph became the trusted friend of the *povstantsi*. They believed in him because their *batka* [father] had faith in him, and Joseph in return became deeply devoted to them. Now he insisted that he must return to the rebel camp: they were heroic people, simple, brave, and devoted to the cause of liberty. He was planning to join Makhno again. Yet I could not free myself of the feeling that if Joseph went back I should never see him alive any more. He seemed to me like one of those characters in Zola's "Germinal" who loves every living thing and yet is able to resort to dynamite for the sake of the striking miners.

I expressed the view to my friends that, important as the Makhno movement might be, it was of a purely military nature and could not, therefore, be expressive of the Anarchist spirit. I was sorry to see Joseph return to the Makhno camp, for his work for the Anarchist movement in Russia could be of much greater value. But he was determined, and I felt that it was Joseph's despair at the reactionary tendencies of the Bolsheviki which drove him, as it did so many others of his comrades, away from the Communists and into the ranks of Makhno.

During our stay in Kharkov I also visited the Department of Labour Distribution, which had come into existence since the militarization of labour. According to the Bolsheviki it became necessary then to return the workers from the villages to which they had streamed from the starving cities. They had to be registered and classified according to trades and distributed to points where their services were most needed. In the carrying out of this plan many people were daily rounded up on the streets and in the market place. Together with the large numbers arrested as speculators or for possession of Tsarist money, they were put on the list of the Labour Distribution Department. Some were sent to the Donetz Basin, while the weaker ones went on to concentration camps. The Communists justified this system and method as necessary during a revolutionary period in order to build up the industries. Everybody must work in Russia, they said, or be forced to work. They claimed that the industrial output had increased since the introduction of the compulsory labour law.

I had occasion to discuss these matters with many Communists and I doubted the efficacy of the new policy.

One evening a woman called at my room and introduced herself as the former owner of the apartment. Since all the houses had been nationalized she was allowed to keep three rooms, the rest of her apartment having been put in charge of the House Bureau. Her family consisted of eight members, including her parents and a married daughter with her family. It was almost impossible to crowd all into three rooms, especially considering the terrific heat of the Kharkov summer; yet somehow they had managed. But two weeks prior to our arrival in Kharkov Zinoviev visited the city. At a public meeting he declared that the bourgeoisie of the city looked too well fed and dressed. "It proves," he said, "that the comrades and especially the Tcheka are neglecting their duty." No sooner had Zinoviev departed than wholesale arrests and night raids began. Confiscation became the order of the day. Her apartment, the woman related, had also been visited and most of her effects taken away. But worst of all was that the Tcheka ordered her to vacate one of the rooms, and now the whole family was crowded into two small rooms. She was much worried lest a member of the Tcheka or a Red Army man be assigned to the vacant room. "We felt much relieved," she said, "when we were informed that someone from America was to occupy this room. We wish you would remain here for a long time."

Till then I had not come in personal contact with the members of the expropriated bourgeoisie who had actually been made to suffer by the Revolution. The few middle-class families I had met lived well, which was a source of surprise to me. Thus in Petrograd a certain chemist I had become acquainted with in Shatov's house lived in a very expensive way. The Soviet authorities permitted him to operate his factory, and he supplied the Government with chemicals at a cost much less than the Government could manufacture them at. He paid his workers comparatively high wages and provided them with rations. On a certain occasion I was invited to dinner by the chemist's family. I found them living in a luxurious apartment, containing many valuable objects and art treasures. My hostess, the chemist's wife, was expensively gowned and wore a costly necklace. Dinner consisted of several courses and was served in an extravagant manner with exquisite damask linen in abundance. It must have cost several hundred thousand rubles, which in 1920 was a small fortune in Russia. The astonishing thing to me was that almost everybody in Petrograd knew the chemist and was familiar with his mode of life. But I was informed that he was needed by the Soviet Government and that he was therefore permitted to live as he pleased. Once I expressed my surprise to him that the Bolsheviki had not confiscated his wealth. He assured me that he was not the only one of the bourgeoisie who had retained his former condition. "The bourgeoisie is by no means dead," he said; "it has only been chloroformed for a while, so to speak, for the painful operation. But it is already recovering from the effect of the anesthetic and soon it will have recuperated entirely. It only needs a little more time." The woman who visited me in the Kharkov room had not managed so well as the Petrograd chemist. She was a part of the wreckage left by the revolutionary storm that had swept over Russia.

During my stay in the Ukrainian capital I met some interesting people of the professional classes, among them an engineer who had just returned from the Donetz Basin and a woman employed in a Soviet Bureau. Both were cultured persons and keenly alive to the fate of Russia. We discussed the Zinoviev visit. They corroborated the story told me before. Zinoviev had upbraided his comrades for their laxity toward the bourgeoisie and criticized them for not suppressing trade. Immediately upon Zinoviev's departure the Tcheka began indiscriminate raids, the members of the bourgeoisie losing on that occasion almost the last things they possessed. The most tragic part of it, according to the engineer, was that the workers did not benefit by such raids. No one knew what became of the things confiscated — they just disappeared. Both the engineer and the woman Soviet employee spoke with much concern about the general disintegration of ideas. The Russians once believed, the woman said, that hovels and palaces were equally wrong and should be abolished. It never occurred to them that the purpose of a revolution is merely to cause a transfer of possessions to put the rich into the hovels and the poor into the palaces. It was not true that the workers have gotten into the palaces. They were only made to believe that that is the function of a revolution. In reality, the masses remained where they had been before. But now they were not alone there: they were in the company of the classes they meant to destroy.

The civil engineer had been sent by the Soviet Government to the Donetz Basin to build homes for the workers, and I was glad of the opportunity to learn from him about the conditions there. The Communist press was publishing glowing accounts about the intensive coal production of the Basin, and official calculations claimed that the country would be provided with sufficient coal for the approaching winter. In reality, the Donetz mines were in a most deplorable state, the engineer informed me. The miners were herded like cattle. They received abominable rations, were almost barefoot, and were forced to work standing in water up to their ankles. As a result of such conditions very little coal was being produced. "I was one of a committee ordered to investigate the situation and report our findings," said the engineer. "Our report is far from favourable. We know that it is dangerous to relate the facts as we found them: it may land us in the Tcheka. But we decided that Moscow must face the facts. The system of political Commissars, general Bolshevik inefficiency, and the paralysing effect of the State machinery have made our constructive work in the Basin almost impossible. It was a dismal failure."

Could such a condition of affairs be avoided in a revolutionary period and in a country so little developed industrially as Russia? I questioned. The Revolution was being attacked by the bourgeoisie within and without; there was compelling need of defence and no energies remained for constructive work. The engineer scorned my viewpoint. The Russian bourgeoisie was weak and could offer practically no resistance, he claimed. It was numerically insignificant and it suffered from a sick conscience. There was neither need nor justification for Bolshevik terrorism and it was mainly the latter that paralysed the constructive efforts. Middle-class intellectuals had been active for many years in the liberal and revolutionary movements of Russia, and thus the members of the bourgeoisie had become closer to the masses. When the great day arrived the bourgeoisie, caught unawares, preferred to give up rather than to put up a fight. It was stunned by the Revolution more than any other class in Russia. It was quite unprepared and has not gotten its bearings even to this day. It was not true, as the Bolsheviki claimed, that the Russian bourgeoisie was an active menace to the Revolution.

I had been advised to see the Chief of the Department of Workers' and Peasants' Inspection, the position being held by a woman, formerly an officer of the Tcheka, reputed to be very severe, even cruel, but efficient. She could supply me with much valuable material, I was told, and give me entrance to the prisons and concentration camps. On my visiting the Workers' and Peasants' Inspection offices I found the lady in charge not at all cordial at first. She ignored my credentials, apparently not impressed by Zinoviev's signature. Presently a man stepped out from an inner office. He proved to be Dibenko, a high Red Army officer, and he informed me that he had heard of me from Alexandra Kollontay, whom he referred to as his wife. He promised that I should get all available material and asked me to return later in the day. When I called again I found the lady much more amiable and willing to give me information about the activities of her department. It appeared that the latter had been organized to fight growing sabotage and graft. It was part of the duties of the Tcheka, but it was found necessary to create the new department for the inspection and correction of abuses. "It is the tribunal to which cases may be appealed," said the woman; "just now, for instance, we are investigating complaints of prisoners who had been wrongly convicted or received excessive sentences." She promised to secure for us permission to inspect the penal institutions and several days later several members of the Expedition were given the opportunity.

First we visited the main concentration camp of Kharkov. We found a number of prisoners working in the yard, digging a new sewer. It was certainly needed, for the whole place was filled with nauseating smells. The prison building was divided into a number of rooms, all of them overcrowded. One of the compartments was called the "speculator's apartment," though almost all its inmates protested against being thus classed. They looked poor and starved, everyone of them anxious to tell us his tale of woe, apparently under the impression that we were official investigators. In one of the corridors we found several Communists charged with sabotage. Evidently the Soviet Government did not discriminate in favour of its own people.

There were in the camp White officers taken prisoners at the Polish front and scores of peasant men and women held on various charges. They presented a pitiful sight, sitting there on the floor for lack of benches, a pathetic lot, bewildered and unable to grasp the combination of events which had caught them in the net.

More than one thousand able-bodied men were locked up in the concentration camp, of no service to the community and requiring numerous officials to guard and attend them. And yet Russia was badly in need of labour energy. It seemed to me an impractical waste.

Later we visited the prison. At the gates an angry mob was gesticulating and shouting. I learned that the weekly parcels brought by relatives of the inmates had that morning been refused acceptance by the prison authorities. Some of the people had come for miles and had spent their last ruble for food for their arrested husbands and brothers. They were frantic. Our escort, the woman in charge of the Bureau, promised to investigate the matter. We made the rounds of the big prison—a depressing sight of human misery and despair. In the solitary were those condemned to death. For days their look haunted me—their eyes full of terror at the torturing uncertainty, fearing to be called at any moment to face death. We had been asked by our Kharkov friends to find a certain young woman in the prison. Trying to avoid arousing attention we sought her with our eyes in various parts of the institution, till we saw someone answering her description. She was an Anarchist, held as a political. The prison conditions were bad, she told us. It had required a protracted hunger strike to compel the authorities to treat the politicals more decently and to keep the doors of those condemned to death open during the day, so that they could receive a little cheer and comfort from the other prisoners. She told of many unjustly arrested and pointed out an old stupid-looking peasant woman locked up in solitary as a Makhno spy, a charge obviously due to a misunderstanding.

The prison régime was very rigid. Among other things, it was forbidden the prisoners to climb up on the windows or to look out into the yard. The story was related to us of a prisoner being shot for once disobeying that rule. He had heard some noise in the street below and, curious to know what was going on, he climbed up on the window sill of his cell. The sentry in the yard gave no warning. He fired, severely wounding the man. Many similar stories of severity and abuse we heard from the prisoners. On our way to town I expressed surprise at the conditions that were being tolerated in the prisons. I remarked to our guide that it would cause a serious scandal if the western world were to learn under what conditions prisoners live and how they are treated in Socialist Russia. Nothing could justify such brutality, I thought. But the chairman of the Workers' and Peasants' Inspection remained unmoved. "We are living in a revolutionary period," she replied; "these matters cannot be helped." But she promised to investigate some cases of extreme injustice which we had pointed out to her. I was not convinced that the Revolution was responsible for the existing evils. If the Revolution really had to support so much brutality and crime, what was the purpose of the Revolution, after all?

At the end of our first week in Kharkov I returned to the Department of Education where I had been promised material. To my surprise I found that nothing had been prepared. I was informed that the chairman was absent, and again assured that the promised data would be collected and ready before our departure. I was then referred to the man in charge of a certain school experimental department. The chairman had told me that some interesting educational methods were being developed, but I found the manager unintelligent and dull. He could tell me nothing of the new methods, but he was willing to send for one of the instructors to explain things to me. A messenger was dispatched, but he soon returned with the information that the teacher was busy demonstrating to his class and could not come. The manager flew into a rage. "He must come," he shouted; "the bourgeoisie are sabotaging like the other damnable intelligentsia. They ought all to be shot. We can do very well without them." He was one of the type of narrow-minded fanatical and persecuting Communists who did more harm to the Revolution than any counter-revolutionary.

During our stay in Kharkov we also had time to visit some factories. In a plough manufacturing plant we found a large loft stacked with the finished product. I was surprised that the ploughs were kept in the factory instead of being put to practical use on the farms. "We are awaiting orders from Moscow.' the manager explained; "it was a rush order and we were threatened with arrest for sabotage in case it should not be ready for shipment within six weeks. That was six months ago, and as you see the ploughs are still here. The peasants need them badly, and we need their bread. But we cannot exchange. We must await orders from Moscow.

I recalled a remark of Zinoviev when on our first meeting he stated that Petrograd lacked fuel, notwithstanding the fact that less than a hundred *versts* from the city there was enough to supply almost half the country. I suggested on that occasion that the workers of Petrograd be called upon to get the fuel to the city. Zinoviev thought it very naive. "Should we grant such a thing in Petrograd," he said, "the same demand would be made in other cities. It would create communal competition which is a bourgeois institution. It would interfere with our plan of nationalized and centralized control." That was the dominating principle, and as a result of it the Kharkov workers lacked bread until Moscow should give orders to have the ploughs sent to the peasants. The supremacy of the state was the cornerstone of Marxism.

Several days before leaving Kharkov I once more visited the Board of Education and again I failed to find its chairman. To my consternation I was informed that I would receive no material because it had been decided that Ukraina was to have its own museum and the chairman had gone to Kiev to organize it. I felt indignant at the miserable deception practised upon us by a man in high Communist position. Surely Ukraina had the right to have its own museum, but why this petty fraud which caused the Expedition to lose so much valuable time.

The sequel to this incident came a few days later when we were surprised by the hasty arrival of our secretary who informed us that we must leave Kharkov immediately and as quietly as possible, because the local executive committee of the party had decided to prevent our carrying out statistical material from Ukraina. Accordingly, we made haste to leave in order to save what we had already collected. We knew the material would be lost if it remained in Kharkov and that the plan of an independent Ukrainian museum would for many years remain only on paper.

Before departing we made arrangements for a last conference with our local friends. We felt that we might never see them again. On that occasion the work of the *Nabat* Federation was discussed in detail. That general Anarchist organization of the south had been founded as a result of the experiences of the Russian Anarchists and the conviction that a unified body was necessary to make their work more effective. They wanted not merely to die but to live for the Revolution. It appeared that the Anarchists of Russia had been divided into several factions, most of them numerically small and of little practical influence upon the progress of events in Russia. They had been unable to establish a permanent hold in the ranks of the workers. It was therefore decided to gather all the Anarchist elements of the Ukraina into one federation and thus be in condition to present a solid front in the struggle not only against invasion and counter-revolution, but also against Communist persecution.

By means of unified effort the *Nabat* was able to cover most of the south and get in close touch with the life of the workers and the peasantry. The frequent changes of government in the Ukraina finally drove the Anarchists to cover, the relentless persecution of the Bolsheviki having depleted their ranks of the most active workers. Still the Federation had taken root among the people. The little band was in constant danger, but it was energetically continuing its educational and propaganda work.

The Kharkov Anarchists had evidently expected much from our presence in Russia. They hoped that Alexander Berkman and myself would join them in their work. We were already seven months in Russia but had as yet taken no direct part in the Anarchist movement. I could sense the disappointment and impatience of our comrades. They were eager we should at least inform the European and American Anarchists of what was going on in Russia, particularly about the ruthless persecution of the Left revolutionary elements. Well could I understand the attitude of my Ukrainian friends. They had suffered much during the last years: they had seen the high hopes of the Revolution crushed and Russia breaking down beneath the heel of the Bolshevik State. Yet I could not comply with their wishes. I still had faith in the Bolsheviki, in their revolutionary sincerity and integrity. Moreover, I felt that as long as Russia was being attacked from the outside I could not speak in criticism. I would not add fuel to the fires of counter-revolution. I therefore had to keep silent, and stand by the Bolsheviki as the organized defenders of the Revolution. But my Russian friends scorned this view. I was confounding the Communist Party with the Revolution, they said; they were not the same; on the contrary, they were opposed, even antagonistic. The Communist State, according to the *Nabat* Anarchists, had proven fatal to the Revolution.

Within a few hours before our departure we received the confidential information that Makhno had sent a call for Alexander Berkman and myself to visit him. He wished to place his situation before us, and, through us, before the Anarchist movement of the world. He desired to have it widely understood that he was not the bandit, Jew-baiter, and counter-revolutionist the Bolsheviki had proclaimed him. He was devoted to the Revolution and was serving the interests of the people as he conceived them.

It was a great temptation to meet the modern Stenka Rasin, but we were pledged to the Museum and could not break faith with the other members of the Expedition.

Chapter 20: Poltava

In the general dislocation of life in Russia and the breaking down of her economic machinery the railroad system had suffered most. The subject was discussed in almost every meeting and every Soviet paper often wrote about it. Between Petrograd and Moscow, however, the real state of affairs was not so noticeable, though the main stations were always overcrowded and the people waited for days trying to secure places. Still, trains between Petrograd and Moscow ran fairly regularly. If one was fortunate enough to procure the necessary permission to travel, and a ticket, one could manage to make the journey without particular danger to life or limb. But the farther south one went the more apparent became the disorganization. Broken cars dotted the landscape, disabled engines lay along the route, and frequently the tracks were torn up. Everywhere in the Ukraina the stations were filled to suffocation, the people making a wild rush whenever a train was sighted. Most of them remained for weeks on the platforms before succeeding in getting into a train. The steps and even the roofs of the cars were crowded by men and women loaded with bundles and bags. At every station there was a savage scramble for a bit of space. Soldiers drove the passengers off the steps and the roofs, and often they had to resort to arms. Yet so desperate were the people and so determined to get to some place where there was hope of securing a little food, that they seemed indifferent to arrest and risked their lives continuously in this mode of travel. As a result of this situation there were numberless accidents, scores of travellers being often swept to their death by low bridges. These sights had become so common that practically no attention was paid to them. Travelling southward and on our return we frequently witnessed these scenes. Constantly the *meshotchniki* [people with bags] mobbed the cars in search of food, or when returning laden with their precious burden of flour and potatoes.

Day and night the terrible scenes kept repeating themselves at every station. It was becoming a torture to travel in our well-equipped car. It contained only six persons, leaving considerable room for more; yet we were forbidden to share it with others. It was not only because of the danger of infection or of insects but because the Museum effects and the material collected would have surely vanished had we allowed strangers on board. We sought to salve our conscience by permitting women and children or cripples to travel on the rear platform of our car, though even that was contrary to orders.

Another feature which caused us considerable annoyance was the inscription on our car, which read: Extraordinary Commission of the Museum of the Revolution. Our friends at the Museum had assured us that the "title" would help us to secure attention at the stations and would also be effective in getting our car attached to such trains as we needed. But already the first few days proved that the inscription roused popular feeling against us. The name "Extraordinary Commission" signified to the people the Tcheka. They paid no attention to the other words, being terrorized by the first. Early in the journey we noticed the sinister looks that met us at the stations and the unwillingness of the people to enter into friendly conversation. Presently it dawned on us what was wrong; but it required considerable effort to explain the misunderstanding. Once put at his ease, the simple Russian opened up his heart to us. A kind word, a solicitous inquiry, a cigarette, changed his attitude. Especially when assured that we were not Communists and that we had come from America, the people along the route would soften and become more talkative, sometimes even confidential. They were unsophisticated and primitive, often crude. But illiterate and undeveloped as they were, these plain folk were clear about their needs. They were unspoiled and possessed of a deep faith in elementary justice and equality. I was often moved almost to tears by these Russian peasant men and women clinging to the steps of the moving train, every moment in danger of their lives, yet remaining good-humoured and indifferent to their miserable condition. They would exchange stories of their lives or sometimes break out in the melodious, sad songs of the south. At the stations, while the train waited for an engine, the peasants would gather into groups, form a large circle, and then someone would begin to play the accordion, the bystanders accompanying with song. It was strange to see these hungry and ragged peasants, huge loads on their backs, standing about entirely forgetful of their environment, pouring their hearts out in folk songs. A peculiar people, these Russians, saint and devil in one, manifesting the highest as well as the most brutal impulses, capable of almost anything except sustained effort. I have often wondered whether this lack did not to some extent explain the disorganization of the country and the tragic condition of the Revolution.

We reached Poltava in the morning. The city looked cheerful in the bright sunlight, the streets lined with trees, with little garden patches between them. Vegetables in great variety were growing on them, and it was refreshing to note that no fences were about and still the vegetables were safe, which would surely not have been the case in Petrograd or Moscow. Apparently there was not so much hunger in this city as in the north.

Together with the Expedition Secretary I visited the government headquarters. Instead of the usual *Ispolkom* [Executive Committee of the Soviet] Poltava was ruled by a revolutionary committee known as the *Revkom*. This indicated that the Bolsheviki had not yet had time to organize a Soviet in the city. We succeeded in getting the chairman of the *Revkom* interested in the purpose of our journey and he promised to cooperate and to issue an order to the various departments that material be collected and prepared for us. Our gracious reception augured good returns.

In the Bureau for the Care of Mothers and Infants I met two very interesting women — one the daughter of the great Russian writer, Korolenko, the other the former chairman of the Save-the-Children Society. Learning of the purpose of my presence in Poltava the women offered their aid and invited me to visit their school and the near-by home of Korolenko.

The school was located in a small house set deep in a beautiful garden, the place hardly visible from the street. The reception room contained a rich collection of dolls of every variety. There were handsome Ukranian lassies, competing in colourful dress and headgear with their beautiful sisters from the Caucasus; dashing Cossacks from the Don looked proudly at their less graceful brothers from the Volga. There were dolls of every description, representing local costumes of almost every part of Russia. The collection also contained various toys, the handwork of the villages, and beautiful designs of the *kustarny* manufacture, representing groups of children in Russian and Siberian peasant attire

The ladies of the holly related the story of the Save-the-Children Society. The organization, in existence for a number of years, was of very limited scope until the February Revolution. Then new elements mainly of revolutionary type, joined the society. They strove to extend its work and to provide not only for the physical well-being of the children but also to educate them, teach them to love work, and develop their appreciation of beauty. Toys and dolls, made chiefly of waste material, were exhibited and the proceeds applied to the needs of the children. After the October Revolution, when the Bolsheviki possessed themselves of Poltava, the society was repeatedly raided and some of the instructors arrested on suspicion that the institution was a counter-revolutionary nest. The small band which remained went on, however, with their efforts on behalf of the children. They succeeded in sending a delegation to Lunacharsky to appeal for permission to carry on their work. Lunacharsky proved sympathetic, issued the requested document, and even provided them with a letter to the local authorities pointing out the importance of their labours.

But the society continued to be subjected to annoyance and discrimination. To avoid being charged with sabotage the women offered their services to the Poltava Department of Education. There they worked from nine in the morning till three in the afternoon, devoting their leisure time to their school. But the antagonism of the Communist authorities was not appeased: the society remained in disfavour.

The women pointed out that the Soviet Government pretended to stand for self-determination and yet every independent effort was being discredited and all initiative discouraged, if not entirely suppressed. Not even the Ukrainian Communists were permitted self-determination. The majority of the chiefs of the departments were Moscow appointees, and Ukraina was practically deprived of opportunity for independent action. A bitter struggle was going on between the Communist Party of Ukraina and the Central authorities in Moscow. The policy of the latter was to control everything.

The women were devoted to the cause of the children and willing to suffer misunderstanding and even persecution for the sake of their interest in the welfare of their charted. Both had understanding and sympathy with the Revolution, though they could not approve of the terroristic methods of the Bolsheviki. They were intelligent and cultured people and I felt their home an oasis in the desert of Communist thought and feeling. Before I left the ladies supplied me with a collection of the children's work and some exquisite colour drawings by Miss Korolenko, begging me to send the things to America as specimens of their labours. They were very eager to have the American people learn about their society and its efforts.

Subsequently I had the opportunity of meeting Korolenko who was still very feeble from his recent illness. He looked the patriarch, venerable and benign; he quickly warmed one's heart by his melodious voice and the fine face that lit up when he spoke of the people. He referred affectionately to America and his friends there. But the light faded out of his eyes and his voice quivered with grief as he spoke of the great tragedy of Russia and the sufferings of the people.

"You want to know my views on the present situation and my attitude toward the Bolsheviki?" he asked. "It would take too long to tell you about it. I am writing to Lunacharsky a series of letters for which he had asked and which he promised to publish. The letters deal with this subject. Frankly speaking, I do not believe they will ever appear in print, but I shall send you a copy of the letters for the Museum as soon as they are complete. There will be six of them. I can give you two right now. Briefly, my opinion is summarized in a certain passage in one of these letters. I said there that if the gendarmes of the Tsar would have had the power not only to arrest but also to shoot us, the situation would have been like the present one. That is what is happening before my eyes every day. The Bolsheviki claim that such methods are inseparable from the Revolution. But I cannot agree with them that persecution and constant shooting will serve the interests of the people or of the Revolution. It was always my conception that revolution meant the highest expression of humanity and of justice. In Russia to-day both are absent. At a time when the fullest expression and coöperation of all intellectual and spiritual forces are necessary to reconstruct the country, a gag has been placed upon the whole people. To dare question the wisdom and efficacy of the so-called dictatorship of the proletariat or the Communist Party leaders is considered a crime. We lack the simplest requisites of the real essence of a social revolution, and yet we pretend to have placed ourselves at the head of a world revolution. Poor Russia will have to pay dearly for this experiment. It may even delay for a long time fundamental changes in other countries. The bourgeoisie will be able to defend its reactionary methods by pointing to what has happened in Russia."

With heavy heart I took leave of the famous writer, one of the last of the great literary men who had been the conscience and the spiritual voice of intellectual Russia. Again I felt him uttering the cry of that part of the Russian intelligentsia whose sympathies were entirely with the people and whose life and work were inspired only by the love of their country and the interest for its welfare.

In the evening I visited a relative of Korolenko, a very sympathetic old lady who was the chairman of the Poltava Political Red Cross. She told me much about things that Korolenko himself was too modest to mention. Old and feeble as he was, he was spending most of his time in the Tcheka, trying to save the lives of those innocently condemned to death. He frequently wrote letters of appeal to Lenin, Gorki, and Lunacharsky, begging them to intervene to prevent senseless executions. The present chairman of the Poltava Tcheka was a man relentless and cruel. His sole solution of difficult problems was shooting. The lady smiled sadly when I told her that the man had been very gracious to the members of our Expedition. "That was for show," she said, "we know him better. We have daily occasion to see his graciousness from this balcony. Here pass the victims taken to slaughter. "

Poltava is famous as a manufacturing centre of peasant handicrafts. Beautiful linen, embroidery, laces, and basket work were among the products of the province's industry. I visited the Department of Social Economy, the *Sovnarkhoz*, where I learned that those industries were practically suspended. Only a small collection remained in the Department. "We used to supply the whole world, even America, with our *kustarny* work," said the woman in charge who had formerly been the head of the *Zemstvo* which took special pride in fostering those peasant efforts. "Our needlework was known all over the country as among the finest specimens of art, but now it has all been destroyed. The peasants have lost their art impulse, they have become brutalized and corrupted." She was bemoaning the loss of peasant art as a mother does that of her child.

During our stay in Poltava we got in touch with representatives of various other social elements. The reaction of the Zionists toward the Bolshevik régime was particularly interesting. At first they refused to speak with us, evidently made very cautious by previous experience. It was also the presence of our secretary, a Gentile, that aroused their distrust. I arranged to meet some of the Zionists alone, and gradually they became more confidential. I had learned in Moscow, in connection with the arrest of the Zionists there, that the Bolsheviki were inclined to consider them counter-revolutionary. But I found the Poltava Zionists very simple orthodox Jews who certainly could not impress any one as conspirators or active enemies. They were passive, though bitter against the Bolshevik régime. It was claimed that the Bolsheviki made no pogroms and that they do not persecute the Jews, they said; but that was true only in a certain sense. There were two kinds of pogroms: the loud, violent ones, and the silent ones. Of the two the Zionists considered the former preferable. The violent pogrom might last a day or a week; the Jews are attacked and robbed, sometimes even murdered; and then it is over. But the silent pogroms continued all the time. They consisted of constant discrimination, persecution, and hounding. The Bolsheviki had closed the Jewish hospitals and now sick Jews were forced to eat *treife* in the Gentile hospitals. The same applied to the Jewish children in the Bolshevik feeding houses. If a Jew and a Gentile happened to be arrested on the same charge, it was certain that the Gentile would go free while the Jew would be sent to prison and sometimes even shot. They were all the time exposed to insult and indignities, not to mention the fact that they were doomed to slow starvation, since all trade had been suppressed. The Jews in the Ukraina were suffering a continuous silent pogrom.

I felt that the Zionist criticism of the Bolshevik régime was inspired by a narrow religious and nationalistic attitude. They were Orthodox Jews, mostly tradesmen whom the Revolution had deprived of their sphere of activity. Nevertheless, their problem was real—the problem of the Jew suffocating in the atmosphere of active anti-Semitism. In Poltava the leading Communist and Bolshevik officials were Gentiles. Their dislike of the Jews was frank and open.

Anti-Semitism throughout the Ukraine was more virulent than even in pre-revolutionary days.

After leaving Poltava we continued on our journey south, but we did not get farther than Fastov owing to the lack of engines. That town, once prosperous, was now impoverished and reduced to less than one third of its former population. Almost all activity was at a stand-still. We found the market place, in the centre of the town, a most insignificant affair, consisting of a few stalls having small supplies of white flour, sugar, and butter. There were more woman about than men and I was especially struck by the strange expression in their eyes. They did not look you full in the face; they stared past you with a dumb, hunted animal expression. We told the women that we had heard many terrible pogroms had taken place in Fastov and we wished to get data on the subject to be sent to America to enlighten the people there on the condition of the Ukrainian Jews. As the news of our presence spread many women and children surrounded us, all much excited and each trying to tell her story of the horrors of Fastov. Fearful pogroms, they related, had taken place in that city, the most terrible of them by Denikin, in September, 1919. It lasted eight days, during which 4,000 persons were killed while several thousand died as the result of wounds and shock. Seven thousand perished from hunger and exposure on the road to Kiev, while trying to escape the Denikin savages. The greater part of the city had been destroyed or burned; many of the older Jews were trapped in the synagogue and there murdered, while others had been driven to the public square where they were slaughtered. Not a woman, young or old, that had not been outraged, most of them in the very sight of their fathers, husbands, and brothers. The young girls, some of them mere children, had suffered repeated violation at the hands of the Denikin soldiers. I understood the dreadful look in the eyes of the women of Fastov.

Men and women besieged us with appeals to inform their relatives in America about their miserable condition. Almost everyone, it seemed, had some kin in that country. They crowded into our car in the evenings, bringing scores of letters to be forwarded to the States. Some of the messages bore no addresses, the simple folk thinking the name sufficient. Others had not heard from their American kindred during the years of war and revolution but still hoped that they were to be found somewhere across the ocean. It was touching to see the people's deep faith that their relatives in America would save them.

Every evening our car was filled with the unfortunates of Fastov. Among them was a particularly interesting visitor, a former attorney, who had repeatedly braved the pogrom makers and saved many Jewish lives. He had kept a diary of the pogroms and we spent a whole evening listening to the reading of his manuscript. It was a simple recital of facts and dates, terrible in its unadorned objectivity. It was the soul cry of a people continuously violated and tortured and living in daily fear of new indignities and outrages. Only one bright spot there was in the horrible picture: no pogroms had taken place under the Bolsheviki. The gratitude of the Fastov Jews was pathetic. They clung to the Communists as to a saving straw. It was encouraging to think that the Bolshevik régime was at least free from that worst of all Russian curses, pogroms against Jews.

Chapter 21: Kiev

Owing to the many difficulties and delays the journey from Fastov to Kiev lasted six days and was a continuous nightmare. The railway situation was appalling. At every station scores of freight cars clogged the lines. Nor were they loaded with provisions to feed the starving cities; they were densely packed with human cargo among whom the sick were a large percentage. All along the route the waiting rooms and platforms were filled with crowds, bedraggled and dirty. Even more ghastly were the scenes at night. Everywhere masses of desperate people, shouting and struggling to gain a foothold on the train. They resembled the damned of Dante's Inferno, their faces ashen gray in the dim light, all frantically fighting for a place. Now and then an agonized cry would ring through the night and the already moving train would come to a halt: somebody had been thrown to his death under the wheels.

It was a relief to reach Kiev. We had expected to find the city almost in ruins, but we were pleasantly disappointed. When we left Petrograd the Soviet Press contained numerous stories of vandalism committed by Poles before evacuating Kiev. They had almost demolished the famous ancient cathedral in the city, the papers wrote, destroyed the water works and electric stations, and set fire to several parts of the city. Tchicherin and Lunacharsky issued passionate appeals to the cultured people of the world in protest against such barbarism. The crime of the Poles against Art was compared with that committed by the Germans in Rheims, whose celebrated cathedral had been injured by Prussian artillery. We were, therefore, much surprised to find Kiev in even better condition than Petrograd. In fact, the city had suffered very little, considering the numerous changes of government and the accompanying military operations. It is true that some bridges and railroad tracks had been blown up on the outskirts of the city, but Kiev itself was almost unharmed. People looked at us in amazement when we made inquiries about the condition of the cathederal: they had not heard the Moscow report.

Unlike our welcome in Kharkov and Poltava, Kiev proved a disappointment. The secretary of the Ispolkom was not very amiable and appeared not at all impressed by Zinoviev's signature on our credentials. Our secretary succeeded in seeing the chairman of the Executive Committee, but returned very discouraged: that high official was too impatient to listen to her representations. He was busy, he said, and could not be troubled. It was decided that I try my luck as an American, with the result that the chairman finally agreed to give us access to the available material. It was a sad reflection on the irony of life. America was in league with world imperialism to starve and crush Russia. Yet it was sufficient to mention that one came from America to find the key to everything Russian. It was pathetic, and rather distasteful to make use of that key.

In Kiev antagonism to Communism was intense, even the local Bolsheviki being bitter against Moscow. It was out of the question for any one coming from " the centre" to secure their cooperation unless armed with State powers. The Government employees in Soviet institutions took no interest in anything save their rations. Bureaucratic indifference and incompetence in Ukraina were even worse than in Moscow and were augmented by nationalistic resentment against the "Russians." It was true also of Kharkov and Poltava, though in a lesser degree. Here the very atmosphere was charged with distrust and hatred of everything Muscovite. The deception practiced on us by the chairman of the Educational Department of Kharkov was characteristic of the resentment almost every Ukrainian official felt toward Moscow. The chairman was a Ukrainian to the core, but he could not openly ignore our credentials signed by Zinoviev and Lunacharsky. He promised to aid our efforts but he disliked the idea of Petrograd "absorbing" the historic material of the Ukraina. In Kiev there was no attempt to mask the opposition to Moscow. One was made to feel it everywhere. But the moment the magic word "America" was spoken and the people made to understand that one was not a Communist, they became interested and courteous, even confidential. The Ukrainian Communists were also no exception.

The information and documents collected in Kiev were of the same character as the data gathered in former cities. The system of education, care of the sick, distribution of labour and so forth were similar to the general Bolshevik scheme. "We follow the Moscow plan," said a Ukrainian teacher, "with the only difference that in our schools the Ukrainian language is taught together with Russian." The people, and especially the children, looked better fed and clad than those of Russia proper: food was comparatively more plentiful and cheaper. There were show schools as in Petrograd and Moscow, and no one apparently realized the corrupting effect of such discrimination upon the teachers as well as the children. The latter looked with envy upon the pupils of the favoured schools and believed that they were only for Communist children, which in reality was not the case. The teachers, on the other hand knowing how little attention was paid to ordinary schools, were negligent in their work. All tried to get a position in the show schools which were enjoying special and varied rations.

The chairman of the Board of Health was an alert and competent man, one of the few officials in Kiev who showed interest in the Expedition and its work. He devoted much time to explaining to us the methods of his organization and pointing out interesting places to visit and the material which could be collected for the Museum. He especially called our attention to the Jewish hospital for crippled children.

I found the latter in charge of a cultivated and charming man, Dr. N--. For twenty years he had been head of the hospital and he took interest as well as pride in showing us about his institution and relating its history.

The hospital had formerly been one of the most famous in Russia, the pride of the local Jews who had built and maintained it. But within recent years its usefulness had become curtailed owing to the frequent changes of government. It had been exposed to persecution and repeated pogroms. Jewish patients critically ill were often forced out of their beds to make room for the favourites of this or that régime. The officers of the Denikin army were most brutal. They drove the Jewish patients out into the street, subjected them to indignities and abuse, and would have killed them had it not been for the intercession of the hospital staff who at the risk of their own lives protected the sick. It was only the fact that the majority of the staff were Gentiles that saved the hospital and its inmates. But the shock resulted in numerous deaths and many patients were left with shattered nerves.

The doctor also related to me the story of some of the patients, most of them victims of the Fastov pogroms. Among them were children between the ages of six and eight, gaunt and sickly looking, terror stamped on their faces. They had lost all their kin, in some cases the whole family having been killed before their eyes. These children often waked at night, the physician said, in fright at their horrible dreams. Everything possible was being done for them, but so far the unfortunate children had not been freed from the memory of their terrible experiences at Fastov. The doctor pointed out a group of young girls between the ages of fourteen and eighteen, the worst victims of the Denikin pogrom. All of them had been repeatedly outraged and were in a mutilated state when they came to the hospital; it would take years to restore them to health. The doctor emphasized the fact that no pogroms had taken place during the Bolshevik régime. It was a great relief to him and his staff to know that his patients were no longer in such danger. But the hospital had other difficulties. There was the constant interference by political Commissars and the daily struggle for supplies. "I spend most of my time in the various bureaus," he said, "instead of devoting myself to my patients. Ignorant officials are given power over the medical profession, continuously harassing the doctors in their work." The doctor himself had been repeatedly arrested for sabotage because of his inability to comply with the numerous decrees and orders, frequently mutually contradictory. It was the result of a system in which political usefulness rather than professional merit played the main rôle. It often happened that a first-class physician of well-known repute and long experience would be suddenly ordered to some distant part to place a Communist doctor in his position. Under such conditions the best efforts were paralysed. Moreover, there was the general suspicion of the intelligentsia, which was a demoralizing factor. It was true that many of that class had sabotaged, but there were also those who did heroic and self-sacrificing work. The

Bolsheviki, by their indiscriminate antagonism toward the intelligentsia as a class, roused prejudices and passions which poisoned the mainsprings of the cultural life of the country. The Russian intelligentsia had with its very blood fertilized the soil of the Revolution, yet it was not given it to reap the fruits of its long struggle. "A tragic fate," the doctor remarked; "unless one forget it in his work, existence would be impossible."

The institution for crippled children proved a very model and modern hospital, located in the heart of a large park. It was devoted to the marred creatures with twisted limbs and deformed bodies, victims of the great war, disease, and famine. The children looked aged and withered; like Father Time, they had been born old. They lay in rows on clean white beds, baking in the warm sun of the Ukrainian summer. The head physician, who guided us through the institution, seemed much beloved by his little charges. They were eager and pleased to see him as he approached each helpless child and bent over affectionately to make some inquiries about its health. The hospital had been in existence for many years and was considered the first of its kind in Russia. Its equipment for the care of deformed and crippled children was among the most modern. " Since the war and the Revolution we feel rather behind the times," the doctor said; "we have been cut off from the civilized world for so many years. But in spite of the various government changes we have striven to keep up our standards and to help the unfortunate victims of strife and disease." The supplies for the institution were provided by the Government and the hospital force was exposed to no interference, though I understood from the doctor that because of his political neutrality he was looked upon by the Bolsheviki as inclined to counter-revolution.

The hospital contained a large number of children; some of those who could walk about studied music and art, and we had the opportunity of attending an informal concert arranged by the children and their teachers in our honour. Some of them played the balalaika in a most artistic manner, and it was consoling to see those marred children finding forgetfulness in the rhythm of the folk melodies of the Ukraina.

Early during our stay in Kiev we learned that the most valuable material for the Museum was not to be found in the Soviet institutions, but that it was in the possession of other political groups and private persons. The best statistical information on pogroms, for instance, was in the hands of a former Minister of the Rada régime in the Ukraina. I succeeded in locating the man and great was my surprise when, upon learning my identity, he presented me with several copies of the Mother Earth magazine I had published in America. The ex-Minister arranged a small gathering to which were invited some writers and poets and men active in the Jewish *Kulturliga* to meet several members of our Expedition. The gathering consisted of the best elements of the local Jewish intelligentsia. We discussed the Revolution, the Bolshevik methods, and the Jewish problem. Most of those present, though opposed to the Communist theories, were in favour of the Soviet Government. They felt that the Bolsheviki, in spite of their many blunders, were striving to further the interests of Russia and the Revolution. At any rate, under the Communist régime the Jews were not exposed to the pogroms practised upon them by all the other régimes of Ukraina. Those Jewish intellectuals argued that the Bolsheviki at least permitted the Jews to live, and that they were therefore to be preferred to any other governments and should be supported by the Jews. They were fearful of the growth of anti-Semitism in Russia and were horrified at the possibility of the Bolsheviki being overthrown. Wholesale slaughter of the Jews would undoubtedly follow, they believed.

Some of the younger set held a different view. The Bolshevik régime had resulted in increased hatred toward the Jews, they said, for the masses were under the impression that most of the Communists were Jews. Communism stood for forcible tax-collection, punitive expeditions, and the Tcheka. Popular opposition to the Communists therefore expressed itself in the hatred of the whole Jewish race. Thus Bolshevik tyranny had added fuel to the latent anti-Semitism of the Ukraina. Moreover, to prove that they were not discriminating in favour of the Jews, the Bolsheviki had gone to the other extreme and frequently arrested and punished Jews for things that the Gentiles could do with impunity. The Bolsheviki also fostered and endowed cultural work in the south in the Ukrainian language, while at the same time they discouraged such efforts in the Jewish language. It was true that the *Kulturliga* was still permitted to exist, but its work was hampered at every step. In short, the Bolsheviki permitted the Jews to live, but only in a physical sense. Culturally, they were condemned to death. The *Yevkom* (Jewish Communist Section) was receiving, of course, every advantage and support from the Government, but then its mission was to carry the gospel of the proletarian dictatorship to the Jews of the Ukraina. It was significant that the *Yevkom* was more anti-Semitic than the Ukrainians themselves. If it had the power it would pogrom every non-Communist Jewish organization and destroy all Jewish educational efforts. This young element emphasized that they did not favour the overthrow of the Bolshevik Government; but they could not support it, either.

I felt that both Jewish factions took a purely nationalistic view of the Russian situation. I could well understand their personal attitude, the result of their own suffering and the persecution of the Jewish race. Still, my chief concern was the Revolution and its effects upon Russia as a whole. Whether the Bolsheviki should be supported or not could not depend merely on their attitude to the Jews and the Jewish question. The latter was surely a very vital and pressing issue, especially in the Ukraina; yet the general problem involved was much greater. It embraced the complete economic and social emancipation of the whole people of Russia, the Jews included. If the Bolshevik methods and practices were not imposed upon them by the force of circumstances, if they were conditioned in their own theories and principles, and if their sole object was to secure their own power, I could not support them. They might be innocent of pogroms against the Jews, but if they were pogroming the whole of Russia then they had failed in their mission as a revolutionary party. I was not prepared to say that I had reached a clear understanding of all the problems involved, but my experience so far led me to think that it was the basic Bolshevik conception of the Revolution which was false, its practical application necessarily resulting in the great Russian catastrophe of which the Jewish tragedy was but a minor part.

My host and his friends could not agree with my viewpoint: we represented opposite camps. But the gathering was nevertheless intensely interesting and it was arranged that we meet again before our departure from the city.

Returning to our car one day I saw a detachment of Red Army soldiers at the railway station. On inquiry I found that foreign delegates were expected from Moscow and that the soldiers had been ordered out to participate in a demonstration in their honour. Groups of the uniformed men stood about discussing the arrival of the mission. There were many expressions of dissatisfaction because the soldiers had been kept waiting so long. "These people come to Russia just to look us over," one of the Red Army men said; "do they know anything about us or are they interested in how we live? Not they. It's a holiday for them. They are dressed up and fed by the Government, but they never talk to us and all they see is how we march past. Here we have been lying around in the burning sun for hours while the delegates are probably being feasted at some other station. That's comradeship and equality for you!"

I had heard such sentiments voiced before, but it was surprising to hear them from soldiers. I thought of Angelica Balabanova, who was accompanying the Italian Mission, and I wondered what she would think if she knew how the men felt. It had probably never occurred to her that those "ignorant Russian peasants" in military uniform had looked through the sham of official demonstrations.

The following day we received an invitation from Balabanova to attend a banquet given in honour of the Italian delegates. Anxious to meet the foreign guests, several members of our Expedition accepted the invitation.

The affair took place in the former Chamber of Commerce building, profusely decorated for the occasion. In the main banquet hall long tables were heavily laden with fresh-cut flowers, several varieties of southern fruit, and wine. The sight reminded one of the feasts of the old bourgeoisie, and I could see that Angelica felt rather uncomfortable at the lavish display of silverware and wealth. The banquet opened with the usual toasts, the guests drinking to Lenin, Trotsky, the Red Army, and the Third International, the whole company rising as the revolutionary anthem was intoned after each toast, with the soldiers and officers standing at attention in good old military style.

Among the delegates were two young French Anarcho-syndicalists. They had heard of our presence in Kiev and had been looking for us all day without being able to locate us. After the banquet they were immediately to leave for Petrograd, so that we had only a short time at our disposal. On our way to the station the delegates related that they had collected much material on the Revolution which they intended to publish in France. They had become convinced that all was not well with the Bolshevik régime: they had come to realize that the dictatorship of the proletariat was in the exclusive hands of the Communist Party, while the common worker was enslaved as much as ever. It was their intention, they said, to speak frankly about these matters to their comrades at home and to substantiate their attitude by the material in their possession. "Do you expect to get the documents out?" I asked La Petit, one of the delegates. "You don't mean that I might be prevented from taking out my own notes," he replied. "The Bolsheviki would not dare to go so far—not with foreign delegates, at any rate." He seemed so confident that I did not care to pursue the subject further. That night the delegates left Kiev and a short time afterward they departed from Russia. They were never seen alive again. Without making any comment upon their disappearance I merely want to mention that when I returned to Moscow several months later it was generally related that the two Anarcho-syndicalists, with several other men who had accompanied them, were overtaken by a storm somewhere off the coast of Finland, and were all drowned. There were rumours of foul play, though I am not inclined to credit the story, especially in view of the fact that together with the Anarcho-syndicalists also perished a Communist in good standing in Moscow. But their disappearance with all the documents they had collected has never been satisfactorily explained.

The rooms assigned to the members of our Expedition were located in a house within a passage leading off the Kreschatik, the main street of Kiev. It had formerly been the wealthy residential section of the city and its fine houses, though lately neglected, still looked imposing. The passage also contained a number of shops, ruins of former glory, which catered to the well-to-do of the neighbourhood. Those stores still had good supplies of vegetables, fruit, milk, and butter. They were owned mostly by old Jews whose energies could not be applied to any other usefulness—Orthodox Jews to whom the Revolution and the Bolsheviki were a *bête noire*, because that had "ruined all business." The little shops barely enabled their owners to exist; moreover, they were in constant danger of Tcheka raids, on which occasions the provisions would be expropriated. The appearance of those stores did not justify the belief that the Government would find it worth while raiding them. "Would not the Tcheka prefer to confiscate the goods of the big delicatessen and fruit stores on the Kreschatik?" I asked an old Jew storekeeper. "Not at all," he replied; "those stores are immune because they pay heavy taxes."

The morning following the banquet I went down to the little grocery store I used to do my shopping in. The place was closed, and I was surprised to find that not one of the small shops near by was open. Two days later I learned that the places had all been raided on the eve of the banquet in order to feast the foreign delegates. I promised myself never to attend another Bolshevik banquet.

Among the members of the *Kulturliga* I met a man who had lived in America, but for several years now was with his family in Kiev. His home proved one of the most hospitable during my stay in the south, and as he had many callers belonging to various social classes I was able to gather much information about the recent history of Ukraina. My host was not a Communist: though critical of the Bolshevik régime, he was by no means antagonistic. He used to say that the main fault of the Bolsheviki was their lack of psychological perception. He asserted that no government had ever such a great opportunity in the Ukraina as the Communists. The people had suffered so much from the various occupations and were so oppressed by every new régime that they rejoiced when the Bolsheviki entered Kiev. Everybody hoped that they would bring relief. But the Communists quickly destroyed all illusions. Within a few months they proved themselves entirely incapable of administering the affairs of the city; their methods antagonized the people, and the terrorism of the Tcheka turned even the friends of the Communists to bitter enmity. Nobody objected to the nationalization of industry and it was of course expected that the Bolsheviki would expropriate. But when the Bourgeoisie had been relieved of its possessions it was found that only the raiders benefited. Neither the people at large nor even the proletarian class gained anything. Precious jewelry, silverware, furs, practically the whole wealth of Kiev seemed to disappear and was no more heard of. Later members of the Tcheka strutted about the streets with their women gowned in the finery of the bourgeoisie. When private business places were closed, the doors were locked and sealed and guards placed there. But within a few weeks the stores were found empty. This kind of "management" and the numerous slew laws and edicts, often mutually conflicting, served the Tcheka as a pretext to terrorize the citizens and aroused general hatred against the Bolsheviki. The people had turned against Petlura, Denikin, and the Poles. They welcomed the Bolsheviki with open arms. But the last disappointed them as the first.

"Now we have gotten used to the situation," my host said, "we just drift and manage as best we can." But he thought it a pity that the Bolsheviki lost such a great chance. They were unable to hold the confidence of the people and to direct that confidence into constructive channels. Not only had the Bolsheviki failed to operate the big industries: they also destroyed the small *kustarnaya* work. There had been thousands of artisans in the province of Kiev for instance; most of them had worked by themselves, without exploiting any one. They were independent producers who supplied a certain need of the community. The Bolsheviki in their reckless scheme of nationalization suspended those efforts without being able to replace them by aught else. They had nothing to give either to the workers or to the peasants. The city proletariat faced the alternative of starving in the city or going back to the country. They preferred the latter, of course. Those who could not get to the country engaged in trade, buying and selling jewelry, for instance. Practically everybody in Russia had become a tradesman, the Bolshevik Government no less than private speculators. "You have no idea of the cement of illicit business carried on by officials in Soviet institutions," my host informed me; "nor is the army free from it. My nephew, a Red Army officer, a Communist, has just returned from the Polish front. He can tell you about these practices in the army."

I was particularly eager to talk to the young officer. In my travels I had met many soldiers, and I found that most of them had retained the old slave psychology and bowed absolutely to military discipline. Some, however, were very wide awake and could see clearly what was happening about them. A certain small element in the Red Army was entirely transformed by the Revolution. It was proof of the gestation of new life and new forms which set Russia apart from the rest of the world, notwithstanding Bolshevik tyranny and oppression. For that element the Revolution had a deep significance. They saw in it something vital which even the daily decrees could not compress within the narrow Communist mould. It was their attitude and general sentiment that the Bolsheviki had not kept faith with the people. They saw the Communist State growing at the cost of the Revolution, and some of them even went so far as to voice the opinion that the Bolsheviki had become the enemies of the Revolution. But they all felt that for the time being they could do nothing. They were determined to dispose of the foreign enemies first. "Then," they would say, "we will face the enemy at home."

Red Army officer proved a fine-looking fellow very deeply in earnest. At first he was disinclined to talk, but in the course of the evening he grew less embarrassed and expressed his feelings freely. He had found much corruption at the front, he said. But it was even worse at the base of supplies where he had done duty for some time. The men at the front were practically without clothes or shoes. The food was insufficient and the Army was ravaged by typhoid and cholera. Yet the spirit of the men was wonderful. They fought bravely, enthusiastically, because they believed in their ideal of a free Russia. But while they were fighting and dying for the great cause, the higher officers, the so-called *tovaristchi*, sat in safe retreat and there drank and gambled and got rich by speculation. The supplies so desperately needed at the front were being sold at fabulous prices to speculators.

The young officer had become so disheartened by the situation, he had thought of committing suicide. But now he was determined to return to the front. "I shall go back and tell my comrades what I have seen," he said; "our real work will begin when we have defeated foreign invasion. Then we shall go after those who are trading away the Revolution."

I felt there was no cause to despair so long as Russia possessed such spirits.

I returned to my room to find our secretary waiting to report the valuable find she had made. It consisted of rich Denikin material stacked in the city library and apparently forgotten by everybody. The librarian, a zealous Ukrainian nationalist, refused to permit the "Russian" Museum to take the material, though it was of no use to Kiev, literally buried in an obscure corner and exposed to danger and ruin. We decided to appeal to the Department of Education and to apply the "American amulet." It grew to be a standing joke among the members of the Expedition to resort to the "amulet" in difficult situations. Such matters were always referred to Alexander Berkman and myself as the "Americans."

It required considerable persuasion to interest the chairman in the matter. He persisted in refusing till I finally asked him: "Are you willing that it become known in America that you prefer to have valuable historical material rot away in Kiev rather than give it to the Petrograd Museum, which is sure to become a world centre for the study of the Russian Revolution and where Ukraina is to have such an important part?" At last the chairman issued the required order and our Expedition took possession of the material, to the great elation of our secretary, to whom the Museum represented the most important interest in life.

In the afternoon of the same day I was visited by a woman Anarchist who was accompanied by a young peasant girl, confidentially introduced as the wife of Makhno. My heart stood still for a moment: the presence of that girl in Kiev meant certain death were she discovered by the Bolsheviki. It also involved grave danger to my landlord and his family, for in Communist Russia harbouring even if unwittingly—a member of the Makhno *povstantsi* often incurred the worst consequences. I expressed surprise at the young woman's recklessness in thus walking into the very jaws of the enemy. But she explained that Makhno was determined to reach us; he would trust no one else with the message, and therefore she had volunteered to come. It was evident that danger had lost all terror for her. "We have been living in constant peril for years," she said simply.

Divested of her disguise, she revealed much beauty. She was a woman of twenty-five, with a wealth of jet-black hair of striking lustre. "Nestor had hoped that you and Alexander Berkman would manage to come, but he waited in vain," she began. "Now he sent me to tell you about the struggle he is waging and he hopes that you will make his purpose known to the world outside." Late into the night she related the story of Makhno which tallied in all important features with that told us by the two Ukrainian visitors in Petrograd. She dwelt on the methods employed by the Bolsheviki to eliminate Makhno and the agreements they had repeatedly made with him, every one of which had been broken by the Communists the moment immediate danger from invaders was over. She spoke of the savage persecution of the members of the Makhno army and of the numerous attempts of the Bolsheviki to trap and kill Nestor. That failing, the Bolsheviki had murdered his brother and had exterminated her own family, including her father and brother. She praised the revolutionary devotion, the heroism and endurance of the *povstantsi* in the face of the greatest difficulties, and she entertained us with the legends the peasants had woven about the personality of Makhno. Thus, for instance, there grew up among the country folk the belief that Makhno was invulnerable because he had never been wounded during all the years of warfare, in spite of his practice of always personally leading every charge.

She was a good conversationalist, and her tragic story was relieved by bright touches of humour. She told many anecdotes about the exploits of Makhno. Once he had caused a wedding to be celebrated in a village occupied by the enemy. It was a gala affair, everybody attending. While the people were making merry on the market place and the soldiers were succumbing to the temptation of drink, Makhno's men surrounded the village and easily routed the superior forces stationed there. Having taken a town it was always Makhno's practice to compel the rich peasants, the *kulaki*, to give up their surplus wealth, which was then divided among the poor, Makhno keeping a share for his army. Then he would call a meeting of the villagers, address them on the purposes of the *povstantsi* movement, and distribute his literature.

Late into the night the young woman related the story of Makhno and *makhnovstchina*. Her voice, held low because of the danger of the situation, was rich and mellow, her eyes shore with the intensity of emotion. "Nestor wants you to tell the comrades of America and Europe," she concluded, "that he is one of them — an Anarchist whose aim is to defend the Revolution against all enemies. He is trying to direct the innate rebellious spirit of the Ukrainian peasant into organized Anarchist channels. He feels that he cannot accomplish it himself without the aid of the Anarchists of Russia. He himself is entirely occupied with military matters, and he has therefore invited his comrades throughout the country to take charge of the educational work. His ultimate plan is to take possession of a small territory in Ukraina and there establish a free commune. Meanwhile, he is determined to fight every reactionary force."

Makhno was very anxious to confer personally with Alexander Berkman and myself, and he proposed the following plan. He would arrange to take any small town or village between Kiev and Kharkov where our car might happen to be. It would be carried out without any use of violence, the place being captured by surprise. The stratagem would have the appearance of our having been taken prisoners, and protection would be guaranteed to the other members of the Expedition. After our conference we would be given safe conduct to our car. It would at the same time insure us against the Bolsheviki, for the whole scheme would be carried out in military manner, similar to a regular Makhno raid. The plan promised a very interesting adventure and we were anxious for an opportunity to meet Makhno personally. Yet we could not expose the other members of the Expedition to the risk involved in such an undertaking. We decided not to avail ourselves of the offer, hoping that another occasion might present itself to meet the *povstantsi* leader.

Makhno's wife had been a country school teacher; she possessed considerable information and was intensely interested in all cultural problems. She plied me with questions about American women, whether they had really become emancipated and enjoyed equal rights. The young woman had been with Makhno and his army for several years, but she could not reconcile herself to the primitive attitude of her people in regard to woman. The Ukrainian woman she said, was considered an object of sex and motherhood only. Nestor himself was no exception in this matter. Was it different in America? Did the American woman believe in free motherhood and was she familiar with the subject of birth control?

It was astonishing to hear such questions from a peasant girl. I thought it most remarkable that a woman born and reared so far from the scene of woman's struggle for emancipation should yet be so alive to its problems. I spoke to the girl of the activities of the advanced women of America, of their achievements and of the work yet to be done for woman's emancipation. I mentioned some of the literature dealing with these subjects. She listened eagerly. "I must get hold of something to help our peasant women. They are just beasts of burden," she said.

Early the next morning we saw her safely out of the house. The same day, while visiting the Anarchist club, I witnessed a peculiar sight. The club had recently been reopened after having been raided by the Tcheka. The local Anarchists met in the club rooms for study and lectures; Anarchist literature was also to be had there. While conversing with some friends I noticed a group of prisoners passing on the street below. Just as they neared the Anarchist headquarters several of them looked up, having evidently noticed the large sign over the club rooms. Suddenly they straightened up, took off their caps, bowed, and then passed on. I turned to my friends. "Those peasants are probably *makhnovstsi*," they said; "the Anarchist headquarters are sacred precincts to them." How exceptional the Russian soul, I thought, wondering whether a group of American workers or farmers could be so imbued with an ideal as to express it in the simple and significant way the *makhnovstsi* did. To the Russian his belief is indeed an inspiration.

Our stay in Kiev was rich in varied experiences and impressions. It was a strenuous time during which we met people of different social strata and gathered much valuable information and material. We closed our visit with a short trip on the river Dniepr to view some of the old monasteries and cathedrals, among them the celebrated Sophievski and Vladimir. Imposing edifices, which remained intact during all the revolutionary changes, even their inner life continuing as before. In one of the monasteries we enjoyed the hospitality of the sisters who treated us to real Russian tea, black bread, and honey. They lived as if nothing had happened in Russia since 1914; it was as if they had passed the last years outside of the world. The monks still continued to show to the curious the sacred caves of the Vladimir Cathedral and the places where the saints had been walled in, their ossified bodies now on exhibition. Visitors were daily taken through the vaults, the accompanying priests pointing out the cells of the celebrated martyrs and reciting the biographies of the most important of the holy family. Some of the stories related were wonderful beyond all human credence, breathing holy superstition with every pore. The Red Army soldiers in our group looked rather dubious at the fantastic tales of the priests. Evidently the Revolution had influenced their religious spirit and developed a skeptical attitude toward miracle workers.

Chapter 22: Odessa

At the numerous stations between Kiev and Odessa we frequently had to wait for days before we managed to make connections with trains going south. We employed our leisure in visiting the small towns and villages, and formed many acquaintances. The markets were especially of interest to us.

In the Kiev province by far the greater part of the population is Jewish. They had suffered many pogroms and were now living in constant terror of their repetition. But the will to live is indestructible, particularly in the Jew; otherwise centuries of persecution and slaughter would long since have destroyed the race. Its peculiar perseverance was manifest everywhere: the Jews continued to trade as if nothing had happened. The news that Americans were in town would quickly gather about us crowds of people anxious to hear of the New World. To them it was still a "new" world, of which they were as ignorant as they had been fifty years before. But not only America—Russia itself was a sealed book to them. They knew that it was a country of pogroms, that some incomprehensible thing called revolution had happened, and that the Bolsheviki would not let them ply their trade. Even the younger element in the more distant villages was not much better informed.

The difference between a famished population and one having access to food supplies was very noticeable. Between Kiev and Odessa products were extremely cheap as compared with northern Russia. Butter, for instance, was 250 rubles a pound as against 3,000 in Petrograd; sugar 350 rubles, while in Moscow it was 5,000. White flour, almost impossible to obtain in the capitals, was here sold at 80 rubles a pound. Yet all along the journey we were besieged at the stations by hungry people, begging for food. The country possessed plenty of supplies, but evidently the average person had no means of purchase. Especially terrible was the sight of the emaciated and ragged children, pleading for a crust of bread at the car windows.

While in the neighbourhood of Zhmerenka we received the appalling news of the retreat of the Twelfth Army and the quick advance of the Polish forces. It was a veritable rout in which the Bolsheviki lost great stores of food and medical supplies, of which Russia stood so much in need. The Polish operations and the Wrangel attacks from the Crimea threatened to cut our journey short. It had been our original purpose to visit the Caucasus but the new developments made travel farther than Odessa impracticable. We still hoped, however, to continue our trip provided we could secure and extension of time for our car permit, which was to expire on October 1st.

We reached Odessa just after a fire had completely destroyed the main telegraph and electric stations, putting the city in total darkness. As it would require considerable time to make repairs, the situation increased the nervousness of the city, for darkness favoured counter-revolutionary plots. Rumours were afloat of Kiev having been taken by the Poles and of the approach of Wrangel.

It was our custom to pay our first official visit to the *Ispolkom* (Executive Committee) in order to familiarize ourselves with the situation and the general work scheme of the local institutions. In Odessa there was a Revkom instead, indicating that the affairs of the city had not yet been sufficiently organized to establish a Soviet and its Executive Committee. The Chairman of the *Revkom* was a young man, not over thirty, with a hard face. After scrutinizing our documents carefully and learning the objects of our mission he stated that he could not be of any assistance to us. The situation in Odessa was precarious, and as he was busy with many pressing matters, the Expedition would have to look out for itself. He gave us permission, however, to visit the Soviet institutions and to collect whatever we might be able to procure. He did not consider the Petrograd Museum and its work of much importance. He was an ordinary worker appointed to a high government position, not over-intelligent and apparently antagonistic to everything "intellectual."

The prospects did not look promising, but, of course, we could not leave Odessa without making a serious effort to collect the rich historical material which we knew to be in the city. Returning from the *Revkom* we happened to meet a group of young people who recognized us, they having lived in America before. They assured us that we could expect no aid from the Chairman who was known as a narrow fanatic embittered against the intelligentsia. Several of the group offered to introduce us to other officials who would be able and willing to assist us in our efforts. We learned that the Chairman of Public Economy in Odessa was an Anarchist, and that the head of the Metal Trade Unions was also an Anarchist. The information held out hope that we might accomplish something in Odessa, after all.

We lost no time in visiting the two men, but the result was not encouraging. Both were willing to do everything in their power, but warned us to expect no returns because Odessa, as they phrased it, was The City of Sabotage.

It must unfortunately be admitted that our experience justified that characterization. I had seen a great deal of sabotage in various Soviet institutions in every city I had visited. Everywhere the numerous employees deliberately wasted their time while thousands of applicants spent days and weeks in the corridors and offices without receiving the least attention. The greater part of Russia did nothing else but stand in line, waiting for the bureaucrats, big and little, to admit them to their sanctums. But bad as conditions were in other cities, nowhere did I find such systematic sabotage as in Odessa. From the highest to the lowest Soviet worker everyone was busy with something other than the work entrusted to him. Office hours were supposed to begin at ten, but as a rule no official could be found in any of the departments till noon or even later. At three in the afternoon the institutions closed, and therefore very little work was accomplished.

We remained in Odessa two weeks, but so far as material collected through official channels was concerned, we got practically nothing. Whatever we accomplished was due to the aid of private persons and members of outlawed political parties. From them we received valuable material concerning the persecution of the Mensheviki and the labour organizations where the influence of the former was strongest. The management of several unions had been entirely suspended at the time we arrived in Odessa, and there began a complete reorganization of them by the Communists, for the purpose of eliminating all opposing elements.

Among the interesting people we met in Odessa were the Zionists, including some well known literary and professional men. It was at Doctor N---'s house that we met them. The Doctor himself was the owner of a sanatorium located on a beautiful spot overlooking the Black Sea and considered the best in the South. The institution had been nationalized by the Bolsheviki, but Doctor N--- was left in charge and was even permitted to take in private patients. In return for that privilege he had to board and give medical attention to Soviet patients for one third of the established price.

Late into the night we discussed the Russian situation with the guests at the Doctor's house. Most of them were antagonistic to the Bolshevik régime. "Lenin let loose the motto 'Rob the robbers,' and at least here in the Ukraina his followers have carried out the order to the letter," said the Doctor. It was the general opinion of the gathering that the confusion and ruin which resulted were due to that policy. It robbed the old bourgeoisie but did not benefit the workers. The Doctor cited his sanatorium as an illustration. When the Bolsheviki took it over they declared that the proletariat was to own and enjoy the place, but not a single worker had since been received as patient, not even a proletarian Communist. The people the Soviet sent to the sanatorium were members of the new bureaucracy, usually the high officials. The Chairman of the Tcheka, for instance, who suffered from nervous breakdown, had been in the institution several times. "He works sixteen hours a day sending people to their death," the doctor commented. "You can easily imagine how it feels to take care of such a man."

One of the Bundist writers present held that the Bolsheviki were trying to imitate the French Revolution. Corruption was rampant; it put in the shade the worst crimes of the Jacobins. Not a day passed but that people were arrested for trading in Tsarist or Kerensky money; yet it was an open secret that the Chairman of the Tcheka himself speculated in *valuta*. The depravity of the Tcheka was a matter of common knowledge. People were shot for slight offences, while those who could afford to give bribes were freed even after they had been sentenced to death. It repeatedly happened that the rich relatives of an arrested man would be notified by the Tcheka of his execution. A few weeks later, after they had somewhat recovered from their shock and grief, they would be informed that the report of the man's death was erroneous, that he was alive and could be liberated by paying a fine, usually a very high one. Of course, the relatives would strain every effort to raise the money. Then they would suddenly be arrested for attempted bribery, their money confiscated and the prisoner shot.

One of the Doctor's guests, who lived in the "Tcheka Street" told of the refinements of terrorism practised to awe the population. Almost daily he witnessed the same sights: early in the morning mounted Tchekists would dash by, shooting into the air — a warning that all windows must be closed. Then came motor trucks loaded with the doomed. They lay in rows, faces downward, their hands tied, soldiers standing over them with rifles. They were being carried to execution outside the city. A few hours later the trucks would return empty save for a few soldiers. Blood dripped from the wagons, leaving a crimson streak on the pavement all the way to the Tcheka headquarters.

It was not possible that Moscow did not know about these things, the Zionists asserted. The fear of the central power was too great to permit of the local Tcheka doing anything not approved by Moscow. But it was no wonder that the Bolsheviki had to resort to such methods. A small political party trying to control a population of 150,000,000 which bitterly hated the Communists, could not hope to maintain itself without such an institution as the Tcheka. The latter was characteristic of the basic principles of Bolshevik conception: the country must be forced to be saved by the Communist Party. The pretext that the Bolsheviki were defending the Revolution was a hollow mockery. As a matter of fact, they had entirely destroyed it.

It had grown so late that the members of our expedition could not return to the car, fearing difficulty in locating it, because of the dark night. We therefore remained at the home of our host, to meet next day a group of men of national reputation, including Bialeck, the greatest living Jewish poet, known to Jews the world over. There was also present a literary investigator, who had made a special study of the question of pogroms. He had visited seventy-two cities, collecting the richest material to be had on the subject. It was his opinion that, contrary to accepted notion, the pogrom wave during the civil war period, between the years 1918 and 1921, under the various Ukrainian governments, was even worse than the most terrible Jewish massacres under the Tsars. There had taken place no pogroms during the Bolshevik régime, but he believed that the atmosphere created by them intensified the anti-Jewish spirit and would some day break out in the wholesale slaughter of the Jews. He did not think that the Bolsheviki were particularly concerned in defending his race. In certain localities of the South the Jews, constantly exposed to assault and pillage by robber bands and occasionally by individual Red soldiers, had appealed to the Soviet Government for permission to organize themselves for self-defence, requesting that arms be given them. But in all such cases the Government refused.

It was the general sentiment of the Zionists that the continuation of the Bolsheviki in power meant the destruction of the Jews. The Russian Jews, as a rule, were not workers. From time immemorial they had engaged in trade; but business had been destroyed by the Communists, and before the Jew could be turned into a worker he would deteriorate, as a race, and become extinct. Specific Jewish culture, the most priceless thing to the Zionists, was frowned upon by the Bolsheviki. That phase of the situation seemed to affect them even more deeply than pogroms.

These intellectual Jews were not of the proletarian class. They were bourgeois without any revolutionary spirit. Their criticism of the Bolsheviki did not appeal to me for it was a criticism from the Right. If I had still believed in the Communists as the true champions of the Revolution I could have defended them against the Zionist complaints. But I myself had lost faith in the revolutionary integrity of the Bolsheviki.

Chapter 23: Returning To Moscow

In a country where speech and press are so completely suppressed as in Russia it is not surprising that the human mind should feed on fancy and out of it weave the most incredible stories. Already, during my first months in Petrograd, I was amazed at the wild rumours that circulated in the city and were believed even by intelligent people. The Soviet press was inaccessible to the population at large and there was no other news medium. Every morning Bolshevik bulletins and papers were pasted on the street corners, but in the bitter cold few people cared to pause to read them. Besides, there was little faith in the Communist press. Petrograd was therefore completely cut off, not only from the Western world but even from the rest of Russia. An old revolutionist once said to me: "We not only don't know what is going on in the world or in Moscow; we are not even aware of what is happening in the next street." However, the human mind will not be bottled up all the time. It must have and generally finds an outlet. Rumours of attempted raids on Petrograd, stories that Zinoviev had been ducked in "Sovietsky soup" by some factory workers and that Moscow was captured by the Whites were afloat.

Of Odessa it was related that enemy ships had been sighted off the coast, and there was much talk of an impending attack. Yet when we arrived we found the city quiet and leading its ordinary life. Except for the large markets, Odessa impressed me as a complete picture of Soviet rule. But we had not been gone a day from the city when, on our return to Moscow, we again met the same rumours. The success of the Polish forces and the hasty retreat of the Red Army furnished fuel to the over-excited imagination of the people. Everywhere the roads were blocked with military trains and the stations filled with soldiers spreading the panic of the rout.

At several points the Soviet authorities were getting ready to evacuate at the first approach of danger. The population, however, could not do that. At the railroad stations along the route groups of people stood about discussing the impending attack. Fighting in Rostov, other cities already in the hands of Wrangel, bandits holding up trains and blowing up bridges, and similar stories kept everybody in a panic. It was of course impossible to verify the rumours. But we were informed that we could not continue to Rostov-on-the-Don, that city being already within the military zone. We were advised to start for Kiev and thence return to Moscow. It was hard to give up our plan of reaching Baku, but we had no choice. We could not venture too far, especially as our car permit was to expire within a short time. We decided to return to Moscow via Kiev.

When we left Petrograd, we had promised to bring back from the South some sugar, white flour, and cereals for our starved friends who had lacked these necessities for three years. On the way to Kiev and Odessa we found provisions comparatively cheap; but now the prices had risen several hundred per cent. From an Odessa friend we learned of a place twenty *versts* [about thirteen miles] from Rakhno, a small village near Zhmerenka, where sugar, honey, and apple jelly could be had at small cost. We were not supposed to transport provisions to Petrograd, though our car was immune from the usual inspection by the Tcheka. But as we had no intention of selling anything, we felt justified in bringing some food for people who had been starving for years. We had our car detached at Zhmerenka, and two men of the expedition and myself went to Rakhno.

It was no easy matter to induce the Zhmerenka peasants to take us to the next village. Would we give them salt, nails, or some other merchandise? Otherwise they would not go. We lost the best part of a day in a vain search, but at last we found a man who consented to drive us to the place in return for Kerensky rubles. The journey reminded me of the rocky road of good intentions: we were heaved up and down, jerked back and forth, like so many dice. After a seemingly endless trip, aching in every limb, we reached the village. It was poor and squalid, Jews constituting the main population. The peasants lived along the Rakhno road and visited the place only on market days. The Soviet officials were Gentiles.

We carried a letter of introduction to a woman physician, the sister of our Odessa Bundist friend. She was to direct us how to go about procuring the provisions., Arriving at the Doctor's house we found her living in two small rooms, ill kept and unclean, with a dirty baby crawling about. The woman was busy making apple jelly. She was of the type of disillusioned intellectual now so frequently met in Russia. From her conversation I learned that she and her husband, also a physician, had been detailed to that desolate spot. They were completely isolated from all intellectual life, having neither papers, books, nor associates. Her husband would begin his rounds early in the morning and return late at night, while she had to attend to her baby and household, besides taking care of her own patients. She had only recently recovered from typhus and it was hard for her to chop wood, carry water, wash and cook and look after her sick. But what made their life unbearable was the general antagonism to the intelligentsia. They had it constantly thrown up to them that they were bourgeois and counter-revolutionists, and they were charged with sabotage. It was only for the sake of her child that she continued the sordid life, the woman said; "otherwise it were better to be dead."

A young woman, poorly clad, but clean and neat, came to the house and was introduced as a school teacher. She at once got into conversation with me. She was a Communist, she announced, who was "doing her own thinking." "Moscow may be autocratic," she said, "but the authorities in the towns and villages here beat Moscow. They do as they please." The provincial officials were flotsam washed ashore by the great storm. They had no revolutionary past—they had known no suffering for their ideals. They were just slaves in positions of power. If she had not been a Communist herself, she would have been eliminated long ago, but she was determined to make a fight against the abuses in her district. As to the schools, they were doing as best they could under the circumstances, but that was very little. They lacked everything. It was not so bad in the summer, but in the winter the children had to stay home because the classrooms were not heated. Was it true that Moscow was publishing glowing accounts of the great reduction in illiteracy? Well, it was certainly exaggerated. In her village the progress was very slow. She had often wondered whether there was really much to so-called education. Supposing the peasants should learn to read and write. Would that make them better and kinder men? If so, why is there so much cruelty, injustice, and strife in countries where people are not illiterate? The Russian peasant cannot read or write, but he has an innate sense of right and beauty. He can do wonderful things with his hands and he is no more brutal than the rest of the world.

I was interested to find such an unusual viewpoint in one so young and in such an out-of-the-way place. The little teacher could not have been more than twenty-five. I encouraged her to speak of her reactions to the general policies and methods of her party. Did she approve of them, did she think them dictated by the revolutionary process? She was not a politician, she said; she did not know. She could judge only by the results and they were far from satisfactory. But she had faith in the Revolution. It had uprooted the very soil, it had given life a new meaning. Even the peasants were not the same — no one was the same. Something great must come of all the confusion.

The arrival of the Doctor turned the conversation into other channels. When informed of our errand he went in search of some tradesmen, but presently he returned to say that nothing could be done: it was the eve of Yom Kippur, and every Jew was in the synagogue. Heathen that I am, I did not know that I had come on the eve of that most solemn fast day. As we could not remain another day, we decided to return without having accomplished our purpose.

Here a new difficulty arose. Our driver would not budge unless we got an armed guard to accompany us. He was afraid of bandits: two nights previously, he said, they had attacked travellers in the forest. It became necessary to apply to the Chairman of the Militia. The latter was willing to help us, but all his men were in the synagogue, praying. Would we wait until the services were over?

At last the people filed out from the synagogue and we were given two armed militiamen. It was rather hard on those Jewish boys, for it was a sin to ride on Yom Kippur. But no inducement could persuade the peasant to venture through the woods without military protection. Life is indeed a crazy quilt made of patches. The peasant, a true Ukrainian, would not have hesitated a moment to beat and rob Jews in a pogrom; yet he felt secure in the protection of Jews against the possible attack of his own coreligionists.

We rode into the bright fall night, the sky dotted with stars. It was soothingly still, with all nature asleep. The driver and our escort discussed the bandits, competing in bloodcurdling stories of the outrages committed by them. As we reached the dark forest I reflected that their loud voices would be the signal of our approach for any highwaymen who might be lying in wait. The soldiers stood up in the wagon, their rifles ready for action; the peasant crossed himself and lashed the horses into a mad gallop, keeping up the pace till we reached the open road again. It was all very exciting but we met no bandits. They must have been sabotaging that night.

We reached the station too late to make connections and had to wait until the morning. I spent the night in the company of a girl in soldier uniform, a Communist. She had been at every front, she declared, and had fought many bandits. She was a sort of Playboy of the Eastern World, romancing by the hour. Her favourite stories were of shooting. "A bunch of counter-revolutionists, White Guards and speculators," she would say; "they should all be shot." I thought of the little school teacher, the lovely spirit in the village, giving of herself in hard and painful service to the children, to beauty in life; and here, her comrade, also a young woman, but hardened and cruel, lacking all sense of revolutionary values — both children of the same school, yet so unlike each other.

In the morning we rejoined the Expedition in Zhmerenka and proceeded to Kiev, where we arrived by the end of September, to find the city completely changed. The panic of the Twelfth Army was in the air; the enemy was supposed to be only 150 *versts* [about ninety-nine miles] away and many Soviet Departments were being evacuated, adding to the general uneasiness and fright. I visited Wetoshkin, the Chairman of the *Revkom*, and his secretary. The latter inquired about Odessa, anxious to know how they were doing there, whether they had suppressed trade, and how the Soviet Departments were working. I told him of the general sabotage, of the speculation and the horrors of the Tcheka. As to trade, the stores were closed and all signs were down, but the markets were doing big business. "Indeed? Well, you must tell this to Comrade Wetoshkin," the Secretary cried gleefully. "What do you suppose — Rakovsky was here and told us perfect wonders about the accomplishments of Odessa. He put us on the rack because we had not done as much. You must tell Wetoshkin all about Odessa; he will enjoy the joke on Rakovsky."

I met Wetoshkin on the stairs as I was leaving the office. He looked thinner than when I had last seen him, and very worried. When asked about the impending danger, he made light of it. "We are not going to evacuate," he said, "we remain right here. It is the only way to reassure the public."' He, too, inquired about Odessa. I promised to call again later, as, I had no time just then, but I did not have the chance to see Wetoshkin again to furnish that joke on Rakovsky. We left Kiev within two days.

At Bryansk, an industrial centre not far away from Moscow, we came upon large posters announcing that Makhno was again with the Bolsheviki, and that he was distinguishing himself by daring exploits against Wrangel. It was startling news, in view of the fact that the Soviet papers had constantly painted Makhno as a bandit, counter-revolutionary, and traitor. What had happened to bring about this change of attitude and tone? The thrilling adventure of having our car held up and ourselves carried off as prisoners, by the Makhnovtsi did not come off. By the time we reached the district where Makhno h ad been operating in September, he was cut off from us. It would have been very interesting to meet the peasant leader face to face and hear at first hand what he was about. He was undoubtedly the most picturesque and vital figure brought to the fore by the Revolution in the South—and now he was again with the Bolsheviki. What had happened? There was no way of knowing until we should reach Moscow.

From a copy of the *Izvestia* that fell into our hands en route, we learned the sad news of the death of John Reed. It was a great blow to those of us who had known Jack. The last time I saw him was at the guest house, the Hotel International, in Petrograd. He had just returned from Finland, after his imprisonment there, and was ill in bed. I was informed that Jack was alone and without proper care, and I went up to nurse him. He was in a bad state, all swollen and with a nasty rash on his arms, the result of malnutrition. In Finland he had been fed almost exclusively on dried fish and had been otherwise wretchedly treated. He was a very sick man, but his spirit remained the same. No matter how radically one disagreed with Jack, one could not help loving his big, generous spirit, and now he was dead, his life laid down in the service of the Revolution, as he believed.

Arriving in Moscow I immediately went to the guest house, the Delovoi Dvor, where stayed Louise Bryant, Jack's wife. I found her terribly distraught and glad to see one who had known Jack so well. We talked of him, of his illness, his suffering and his untimely death. She was much embittered because, she claimed, Jack had been ordered to Baku to attend the Congress of the Eastern peoples when he was already very ill. He returned a dying man. But even then he could have been saved had he been given competent medical attention. He lay in his room for a week without the doctors making up their mind as to the nature of his illness. Then it was too late. I could well understand Louise's feelings, though I was convinced that everything humanly possible had been done for Reed. I knew that whatever else might be said against the Bolsheviki, it could not be charged that they neglect those who serve them. On the contrary, they are generous masters. But Louise had lost what was most precious to her.

During the conversation she asked me about my experiences and I told her of the conflict within me, of the desperate effort I had been making to find my way out of the chaos, and that now the fog was lifting, and I was beginning to differentiate between the Bolsheviki and the Revolution. Ever since I had come to Russia I had begun to sense that all was not well with the Bolshevik régime, and I felt as if caught in a trap. "How uncanny!" Louise suddenly gripped my arm and stared at me with wild eyes. "'Caught in a trap' were the very words Jack repeated in his delirium." I realized that poor Jack had also begun to see beneath the surface. His was the free, unfettered spirit striving for the real values of life. It would be chafed when bound by a dogma which proclaimed itself immutable. Had Jack lived he would no doubt have clung valiantly to the thing which had caught him in the trap. But in the face of death the mind of man sometimes becomes luminous: it sees in a flash what in man's normal condition is obscure and hidden from him. It was not at all strange to me that Jack should have felt as I did, as everyone who is not a zealot must feel in Russia—caught in a trap.

Chapter 24: Back In Petrograd

The Expedition was to proceed to Petrograd the next day, but Louise begged me to remain for the funeral. Sunday, October 23rd, several friends rode with her to the Trade Union House where Reed's body lay in state. I accompanied Louise when the procession started for the Red Square. There were speeches—much cold stereotyped declamation about the value of Jack Reed to the Revolution and to the Communist Party. It all sounded mechanical, far removed from the spirit of the dead man in the fresh grave. One speaker only dwelt on the real Jack Reed—Alexandra Kollontay. She had caught the artist's soul, infinitely greater in its depth and beauty than any dogma. She used the occasion to admonish her comrades. "We call ourselves Communists," she said, "but are we really that? Do we not rather draw the life essence from those who come to us, and when they are no longer of use, we let them fall by the wayside, neglected and forgotten? Our Communism and our comradeship are dead letters if we do not give out of ourselves to those who need us. Let us beware of such Communism. It slays the best in our ranks. Jack Reed was among the best."

The sincere words of Kollontay displeased the high Party members. Bukharin knitted his brows, Reinstein fidgeted about, others grumbled. But I was glad of what Kollontay had said. Not only because what she said expressed Jack Reed better than anything else said that day, but also because it brought her nearer to me. In America we had repeatedly tried to meet but never succeeded. When I reached Moscow, in March, 1920, Kollontay was ill. I saw her only for a little while before I returned to Petrograd. We spoke of the things that were troubling me. During the conversation Kollontay remarked: "Yes, we have many dull sides in Russia." "Dull," I queried; "nothing more?" I was unpleasantly affected by what seemed to me a rather superficial view. But I reassured myself that Kollontay's inadequate English caused her to characterize as "dull" what to me was a complete collapse of all idealism.

Among other things Kollontay had then said was that I could find a great field for work among the women as very little had been attempted up to that time to enlighten and broaden them. We parted in a friendly manner, but I did not sense in her the same feeling of warmth and depth that I had found in Angelica Balabanova. Now at the open grave of Reed her words brought her closer to me. She, too, felt deeply, I thought.

Louise Bryant had fallen in a dead faint and was lying face downward on the damp earth. After considerable effort we got her to her feet. Hysterical, she was taken in the waiting auto to her hotel and put to bed. Outside, the sky was clothed in gray and was weeping upon the fresh grave of Jack Reed. And all of Russia seemed a fresh grave.

While in Moscow we found the explanation of the sudden change of tone of the Communist press toward Makhno. The Bolsheviki, hard pressed by Wrangel, sought the aid of the Ukrainian *povstantsi* army. A politico-military agreement was about to be entered into between the Soviet Government and Nestor Makhno. The latter was to coöperate fully with the Red Army in the campaign against the counterrevolutionary enemy. On their side, the Bolsheviki accepted the following conditions of Makhno:

(1) The immediate liberation and termination of persecution of all Makhnovtsi and Anarchists, excepting cases of armed rebellion against the Soviet Government. (2) Fullest liberty of speech, press and propaganda for Makhnovtsi and Anarchists, without, however, the right of calling for armed uprisings against the Soviet Government, and subject to military censorship. (3) Free participation in Soviet elections; the right of Makhnovtsi and Anarchists to be candidates, and to hold the fifth All-Ukrainian Congress of Soviets.

The agreement also included the right of the Anarchists to call a congress in Kharkov, and preparations were being made to hold it in the month of October. Many Anarchists were getting ready to attend it and were elated over the outlook. But my faith in the Bolsheviki had received too many shocks. Not only did I believe that the Congress would not take place,. but I saw in it a Bolshevik ruse to gather all the Anarchists in one place in order to destroy them. Yet the fact was that several Anarchists, among them the well-known writer and lecturer Volin, had already been released and were now free in Moscow.

We left for Petrograd to deliver to the Museum the carload of precious material we had gathered in the South. More valuable still was the experience the members of the Expedition had been enriched with through personal contact with people of various shades of opinion, or of no opinion, and the impressions of the social panorama as it was being unrolled day by day. That was a treasure of far greater worth than any paper documents. But better insight into the situation intensified my inner struggle. I longed to close my eyes and ears — not to see the accusing hand which pointed to the blind errors and conscious crimes that were stifling the Revolution. I wanted not to hear the compelling voice of facts, which no personal attachments could silence any longer. I knew that the Revolution and the Bolsheviki, proclaimed as one and the same, were opposites, antagonistic in aim and purpose. The Revolution had its roots deep down in the life of the people. The Communist State was based on a scheme forcibly applied by a political party. In the contest the Revolution was being slain, but the slayer also was gasping for breath. I had known in America that the Interventionists, the blockade and the conspiracy of the Imperialists were wrecking the Revolution. But what I had not known then was the part the Bolsheviki were playing in the process. Now I realized that they were the grave-diggers.

I was oppressively conscious of the great debt I owed to the workers of Europe and America: I should tell them the truth about Russia. But how could I speak out when the country was still besieged on several fronts? It would mean working into the hands of Poland and Wrangel. For the first time in my life I refrained from exposing grave social evils. I felt as if I were betraying the trust of the masses, particularly of the American workers, whose faith I dearly cherished.

Arrived in Petrograd, I went to live temporarily in the Hôtel International. I intended to find a room somewhere else, determined to accept no privileges at the hands of the Government. The International was filled with foreign visitors. Many had no idea of why or wherefore they had come. They had simply flocked to the land they believed to be the paradise of the workers. I remember my experience with a certain I.W.W. chap. He had brought to Russia a small supply of provisions, needles, thread, and other similar necessities. He insisted that I let him share with me. "But you will need every bit of it yourself," I told him. Of course, he knew there was great scarcity in Russia. But the proletariat was in control and as a worker he would receive everything he needed. Or he would "get a piece of land and build a homestead". He had been fifteen years in the Wobbly movement and he "didn't mind settling down." What was there to say to such an innocent? I had not the courage to disillusion him. I knew he would learn soon enough. It was pathetic, though, to see such people flood starving Russia. Yet they could not do her the harm the other kind was doing—creatures from the four corners of the earth to whom the Revolution represented a gold mine. There were many of them in the International. They all came with legends of the wonderful growth of Communism in America, Ireland, China, Palestine. Such stories were balm to the hungry souls of the men in power. They welcomed them as an old maid welcomes the flattery of her first suitor. They sent these impostors back home well provided financially and equipped to sing the praises of the Workers' and Peasants' Republic. It was both tragic and comic to observe the breed all inflated with "important conspiratory missions."

I received many visitors in my room, among them my little neighbour from the Astoria with her two children, a Communist from the French Section, and several of the foreigners. My neighbour looked sick and worn since I had seen her last in June,1920. "Are you ill?" I inquired on one occasion. "Not exactly," she said; "I am hungry most of the time and exhausted. The summer has been hard: as inspectress of children's homes I have to do much walking. I return home completely exhausted. My nine-year-old girl goes to a children's colony, but I would not risk sending my baby boy there because of his experience last year, when he was so neglected that he nearly died. I had to keep him in the city all summer, which made it doubly hard for me. Still, it would not have been so bad had it not been for the *subotniki* and *voskresniki* (Communist Saturday and

Sunday voluntary work-days). They drain my energies completely. You know how they began—like a picnic, with trumpets and singing, marching and festivities. We all felt inspired, especially when we saw our leading comrades take pick and shovel and pitch in. But that is all a matter of the past. The *subotniki* have become gray and spiritless, beneath an obligation imposed without regard to inclination, physical fitness, or the amount of other work one has to do. Nothing ever succeeds in our poor Russia. If I could only get out to Sweden, Germany, anywhere, far away from it all." Poor little woman, she was not the only one who wanted to forsake the country. It was their love for Russia and their bitter disappointment which made most people anxious to run away.

Several other Communists I knew in Petrograd were even more embittered. Whenever they called on me they would repeat their determination to get out of the Party. They were suffocating—they said—in the atmosphere of intrigue, blind hatred, and senseless persecution. But it requires considerable will power to leave the Party which absolutely controls the destiny of more than a hundred million people, and my Communist visitors lacked the strength. But that did not lessen their misery, which affected even their physical condition, although they received the best rations and they had their meals at the exclusive Smolny dining room. I remember my surprise on first finding that there were two separate restaurants in Smolny, one where wholesome and sufficient food was served to the important members of the Petrograd Soviet and of the Third International, while the other was for the ordinary employees of the Party. At one time there had even been three restaurants. Somehow the Kronstadt sailors learned of it. They came down in a body and closed two of the eating places. "We made the Revolution that all should share alike," they said. Only one restaurant functioned for a time but later the second was opened. But even in the latter the meals were far superior to the Sovietsky dining rooms for the "common people."

Some of the Communists objected to the discrimination. They saw the blunders, the intrigues, the destruction of life practised in the name of Communism, but they had not the strength and courage to protest or to disassociate themselves from the Party responsible for the injustice and brutality. They would often unburden themselves to me of the matters they dared not discuss in their own circles. Thus I came to know many things about the inner workings of the Party and the Third International that were carefully hidden from the outside world. Among them was the story of the alleged Finnish White conspiracy, which resulted in the killing in Petrograd of seven leading Finnish Communists. I had read about it in the Soviet papers while I was in the Ukraina. I remember my feeling of renewed impatience with myself that I should be critical of the Bolshevik regime at a time when counter-revolutionary conspiracies were still so active. But from my Communist visitors I learned that the published report was false from beginning to end. It was no White conspiracy but a fight between two groups of Bolsheviki: the moderate Finnish Communists in control of the propaganda carried on from Petrograd, and the Left Wing working in Finland. The Moderates were Zinoviev adherents and had been put in charge of the work by him. The Lefts had repeatedly complained to the Third International about the conservatism and compromises of their comrades in Petrograd and the harm they were doing to the movement in Finland. They asked that these men be removed. They were ignored. On the 3Ist of August, 1920, the Lefts came to Petrograd and proceeded to the headquarters of the Moderates. At the session of the latter they demanded that the Executive Committee resign and turn over all books and accounts to them. Their demand refused, the young Finnish Communists opened fire, killing seven of their comrades. The affair was heralded to the world as a counter-revolutionary conspiracy of White Finns.

The third anniversary of the October Revolution was celebrated November 7th (October 25th old style), on the Uritsky Square. I had seen so many official demonstrations that they had lost interest for me. Still I went to the Square hoping that a new note might be sounded. It proved a rehash of the thing I had heard over and over again. The pageant especially was a demonstration of Communist poverty in ideas. Kerensky and his cabinet, Tchernov and the Constituent Assembly, and the storming of the Winter Palace again served as puppets to bring out in strong relief the rôle of the Bolsheviki as "saviours of the Revolution." It was badly played and poorly staged, and fell flat. To me the celebration was more like the funeral than the birth of the Revolution.

There was much excitement in Petrograd all through the month of November. Numerous rumours were afloat about strikes, arrests, and dashes between workers and soldiery. It was difficult to get at the facts. But the extraordinary session called by the Party in the First House of the Soviet indicated a serious situation. In the early part of the afternoon the whole square in front of the Astoria was lined with autos of the influential Communists who had been summoned to attend the special conference. The following morning we learned that in obedience to the Moscow decree the Petrograd session had decided to mobilize a number of important Bolshevik workers for the factories and shops. Three hundred Party members, some of them high government officials and others holding responsible positions in the Petro-Soviet, were immediately ordered to work, to prove to the proletariat that Russia was indeed a Workers' Government. The plan was expected to allay the growing discontent of the proletarians and to counteract the influence of the other political parties among them. Zorin was one of the three hundred.

However, the toilers would not be deceived by this move. They knew that most of the mobilized men continued to live in the Astoria and came to work in their autos. They saw them warmly dressed and well shod, while they themselves were almost naked and living in squalid quarters without light or heat. The workers resented the pretense. The matter became a subject of discussion in the shops, and many unpleasant scenes followed. One woman, a prominent Communist, was so tormented in the factory that she went into hysterics and had to be taken away. Some of the mobilized Bolsheviki, among them Zorin and others, were sincere enough, but they had grown away from the toilers and could not stand the hardships of factory life. After a few weeks Zorin collapsed and had to be removed to a place of rest. Though he was generally liked, his collapse was interpreted by the workers as a ruse to get away from the misery of the proletarian's existence. The breach between the masses and the new Bolshevik bureaucracy had grown too wide. It could not be bridged.

Chapter 25: Archangel And Return

On November 28th the Expedition again got under way, this time with three members only: Alexander Berkman, the Secretary, and myself. We travelled by way of Moscow to Archangel, with stops in Vologda and Yaroslavl. Vologdahad been the seat of various foreign embassies, unofficially engaged in aiding the enemies of the Revolution; We expected to find historic material there, but we were informed that most of it had been destroyed or otherwise wasted. The Soviet institutions were uninteresting: it was a plodding, sleepy provincial town. In Yaroslavl, where the so-called Savinkov uprising had taken place two years previously, no significant data were found.

We continued to Archangel. The stories we had heard of the frozen North made us rather apprehensive. But, much to our relief, we found that city no colder than Petrograd, and much drier.

The Chairman of the Archangel Ispolkom was pleasant type of Communist, not at all officious or stern. As soon as we had stated our mission he set the telephone going. Every time he reached some official on the wire he would address him as "dear *tovarishtch*," and inform him that "dear *tovarishtchi* from the Centre" had arrived and must be given every assistance. He thought that our stay would be profitable because many important documents had remained after the Allies had withdrawn. There were files of old newspapers published by the Tchaikovsky Government and photographs of the brutalities perpetrated upon the Communists by the Whites. The Chairman himself had lost his whole family, including his twelve-year-old sister. As he had to leave the next day to attend the Conference of Soviets in Moscow, he promised to issue an order giving us access to the archives.

Leaving the *Ispolkom* to begin our rounds, we were surprised by three sleighs waiting for us, thanks to the thoughtfulness of the Chairman. Tucked up under fur covers and with bells tinkling, each member of the Expedition started in a different direction to cover the departments assigned to him. The Archangel Soviet officials appeared to have great respect for the "Centre"; the word acted like magic, opening every door.

The head of the Department of Education was a hospitable and kindly man. After explaining to me in detail the work done in his institution he called to his office a number of employees, informed them of the purpose of the Expedition and asked them to prepare the material they could gather for the Museum. Among those Soviet workers was a nun, a pleasant-faced young woman. What a strange thing, I thought, to find a nun in a Soviet office! The Chairman noticed my surprise. He had quite a number of nuns in his department, he said. When the monasteries had been nationalized the poor women had no place to go. He conceived the idea of giving them a chance to do useful work in the new world. He had found no cause to regret his action: he did not convert the nuns to Communism, but they became very faithful and industrious workers, and the younger ones had even expanded a little. He invited me to visit the little art studio where several nuns were employed.

The studio was a rather unusual place — not so much because of its artistic value as on account of the people who worked there; two old nuns who had spent forty and twenty-five years, respectively, in monasteries; a young White officer, and an elderly workingman. The last two had been arrested as counter-revolutionists and were condemned to death, but the Chairman rescued them in order to put them to useful work. He wanted to give an opportunity to those who through ignorance or accident were the enemies of the Revolution. A revolutionary period, he remarked, necessitated stern measures, even violence; but other methods should be tried first. He had many in his department who had been considered counter-revolutionary, but now they were all doing good work. It was the most extraordinary thing I had heard from a Communist. "Aren't you considered a sentimental bourgeois?" I asked. "Yes, indeed," he replied smilingly, "but that is nothing. The main thing is that I have been able to prove that my sentimentalism works, as you can see for yourself."

The carpenter was the artist of the studio. He had never been taught, but he did beautiful carving and was a master in every kind of wood work. The nuns made colour drawings of flowers and vegetables, which were used for demonstration by lecturers in the villages. They also painted posters, mainly for the children's festivals.

I visited the studio several times alone so that I might speak freely to the carpenter and the nuns. They had little understanding of the elemental facts that had pulled them out of their moorings. The carpenter lamented that times were hard because he was not permitted to sell his handiwork. "I used to earn a good bit of money, but now I hardly get enough to eat," he would say. The sisters did not complain; they accepted their fate as the will of God. Yet there was a change even in them. Instead of being shut away in a nunnery they were brought in touch with real life, and they had become more human. Their expression was less forbidding, their work showed signs of kinship with the world around them. I noticed it particularly in their drawings of children and children's games. There was a tenderness about them that spoke of the long-suppressed mother instinct struggling for expression. The former White officer was the most intelligent of the four — he had gone through Life's crucible. He had learned the folly and crime of intervention, he said, and would never lend his aid to it again. What had convinced him? The interventionists themselves. They had been in Archangel and they carried on as if they owned the city. The Allies had promised much, but they had done nothing except enrich a few persons who speculated in the supplies intended to benefit the population. Everyone gradually turned against the interventionists. I wondered how many of the countless ones shot as counter-revolutionists would have been won over to the new régime and would now be doing useful work if somebody had saved their lives.

I had seen so many show schools that I decided to say nothing about visiting educational institutions until some unexpected moment when one could take them by surprise. For our first Saturday in Archangel a special performance of Leonid Andreyev's play, "Savva," had been arranged. For a provincial theatre, considering also the lack of preparation, the drama was fairly well done.

After the performance I told the Chairman of the Department, X, that I would like to visit his schools early next morning. Without hesitation he consented and even offered to call for the other members of the Expedition. We visited several schools and in point of cleanliness, comfort, and general cheerfulness, I found them a revelation. It was also beautiful to see the fond relationship that existed between the children and X. Their joy was spontaneous and frank at the sight of him. The moment he appeared they would throw themselves upon him, shouting with delight; they climbed on him and clung to his neck. And he? Never once did I see such a picture in any school in Petrograd or Moscow. He threw himself on the floor, the children about him, and played and frolicked with them as if they were his own. He was one of them; they knew it, and they felt at home with him.

Similar beautiful relationships I found in every school and children's home we visited. The children were radiant when X--- appeared. They were the first happy children I had seen in Russia. It strengthened my conviction of the significance of personality and the importance of mutual confidence and love between teacher and pupil. We visited a number of schools that day. Nowhere did I find any discrimination; everywhere the children had spacious dormitories, spotlessly clean rooms and beds, good food and clothes. The atmosphere of the schools was warm and intimate.

We found in Archangel many historic documents, including the correspondence between Tchaikovsky, of the Provisional Government, and General Miller, the representative of the Allies. It was pathetic to read the pleading, almost cringing words of the old pioneer of the revolutionary movement in Russia, the founder of the Tchaikovsky circles, the man I had known for years, by whom I had been inspired. The letters exposed the weakness of the Tchaikovsky régime and the arbitrary rule of the Allied troops. Particularly significant was the farewell message of a sailor about to be executed by the Whites. He described his arrest and cross-examination and the fiendish third degree applied by an English army officer at the point of a gun. Among the material collected by us were also copies of various revolutionary and Anarchist publications issued sub rosa. From the Department of Education we received many interesting posters and drawings, as well as pamphlets and books, and a collection of specimens of the children's work. Among them was a velvet table cover painted by the nuns and portraying Archangel children in gay colours, presented as their greeting to the children of America.

The schools and the splendid man at their head were not the only noteworthy features of Archangel. The other Soviet institutions also proved efficient. There was no sabotage, the various bureaus worked in good order, and the general spirit was sincere and progressive.

The food distribution was especially well organized. Unlike most other places, there was no loss of time or waste of energy connected with procuring one's rations. Yet Archangel was not particularly well supplied with provisions. One could not help thinking of the great contrast in this regard between that city and Moscow. Archangel probably learned a lesson in organization from contact with Americans — the last thing the Allies intended.

The Archangel visit was so interesting and profitable that the Expedition delayed its departure, and we remained much longer than originally planned. Before leaving, I called on X. If anything could be sent him from "the Centre," what would he like most, I asked. "Paints and canvas for our little studio," he replied. "See Lunacharsky and get him to send us some." Splendid, gracious personality!

We left Archangel for Murmansk, but we had not gone far when we were overtaken by a heavy snowstorm. We were informed that we could not reach Murmansk in less than a fortnight, a journey which under normal conditions required three days. There was also danger of not being able to return to Petrograd on time, the snow often blocking the roads for weeks. We therefore decided to turn back to Petrograd. When we came within seventy-five *versts* [about fifty miles] of that city we ran into a blizzard. It would take days before the track would be cleared sufficiently to enable us to proceed. Not cheerful news, but fortunately we were supplied with fuel and enough provisions for some time.

It was the end of December, and we celebrated Christmas Eve in our car. The night was glorious, the sky brilliant with stars, the earth clad in white. A small pine tree, artfully decorated by the Secretary and enthroned in our diner, graced the occasion. The glow of the little wax candles lent a touch of romance to the scene. Gifts for our fellow travellers came all the way from America; they had been given us by friends in December, 1919, when we were on Ellis Island awaiting deportation. A year had passed since then, an excruciating year.

Arriving in Petrograd we found the city agitated by the heated discussion of the role of the trade unions. Conditions in the latter had resulted in so much discontent among the rank and file that the Communist Party was at last forced to take up the issue. Already in October the trade union question had been brought up at the sessions of the Communist Party. The discussions continued all through November and December, reaching their climax at the Eighth All-Russian Congress of the Soviets. All the leading Communists participated in the great verbal contest which was to decide the fate of the labour organizations. The theses discussed disclosed four different views. First, that of the Lenin-Zinoviev faction. which held that the main "function of the trade unions under the proletarian dictatorship is to serve as schools of Communism." Second, the group represented by the old Communist Ryasanov, which insisted that the trade unions must function as the forum of the workers and their economic protector. Trotsky led the third faction. He believed that the trade unions would in the course of time become the managers and controllers of the industries, but for the present the unions must be subject to strict military discipline and be made entirely subservient to the needs of the State. The fourth and most important tendency was that of the Labour Opposition, headed by Madame Kollontay and Schliapnikov, who expressed the sentiment of the workers themselves and had their support. This opposition argued that the governmental attitude toward the trade unions had destroyed the interest of the toilers in economic reconstruction of the country and paralysed their productive capacity. They emphasized that the October Revolution had been fought to put the proletariat in control of the industrial life of the country. They demanded the liberation of the masses from the yoke of the bureaucratic State and its corrupt officialdom and opportunity for the exercise of the creative energies of the workers. The Labour Opposition voiced the discontent and aspirations of the rank and file.

It was a battle royal, with Trotsky and Zinoviev chasing each other over the country in separate special trains, to disprove each other's contentions. In Petrograd, for instance, Zinoviev's influence was so powerful that it required a big struggle before Trotsky received permission to address the Communist Local on his views in the controversy. The latter engendered intense feeling and for a time threatened to disrupt the Party.

At the Congress, Lenin denounced the Labour Opposition as "anarcho-syndicalist, middle-class ideology" and advocated its entire suppression. Schliapnikov, one of the most influential leaders of the Opposition, was referred to by Lenin as a "peeved Commissar" and was subsequently silenced by being made a member of the Central Committee of the Communist Party. Madame Kollontay was told to hold her tongue or get out of the Party; her pamphlet setting forth the views of the Opposition was suppressed. Some of the lesser lights of the Labour Opposition were given a vacation in the Tcheka, and even Ryasanov, an old and tried Communist, was suppressed for six months from all union activities.

Soon after our arrival in Petrograd we were informed by the Secretary of the Museum that a new institution known as the Ispart had been formed in Moscow to collect material about the history of the Communist Party. This organization also proposed to supervise all future expeditions of the Museum of the Revolution and to place them under the direction of a political Commissar. It became necessary to go to Moscow to ascertain the facts in the case. We had seen too many evils resulting from the dictatorship of the political Commissar, the ever-present espionage and curtailment of independent effort. We could not consent to the change which was about to be made in the character of our expedition.

Chapter 26: Death And Funeral Of Peter Kropotkin

When I reached Moscow in January, 1921, I learned that Peter Kropotkin had been stricken with pneumonia. I immediately offered to nurse him, but as one nurse was already in attendance and the Kropotkin cottage was too small to accommodate extra visitors, it was agreed that Sasha Kropotkin, who was then in Moscow, should go to Dmitrov to find out whether I was needed. I had previously arranged to leave for Petrograd the next day. Till the moment of departure I waited for a call from the village; none coming, I concluded that Kropotkin was improving. Two days later, in Petrograd, I was informed by Ravitch that Kropotkin had grown worse and that I was asked to come to Moscow at once. I left immediately, but unfortunately my train was ten hours overdue, so that I reached Moscow too late to connect with Dmitrov. There were at the time no morning trains to the village and it was not till the eve of February 7th that I was at last seated in a train bound for the place. Then the engine went off for fuel and did not return until 1 A. M. of the next day. When I finally arrived at the Kropotkin cottage, on February 8th, I learned the terrible news that Peter had died about an hour before. He had repeatedly called for me, but I was not there to render the last service to my beloved teacher and comrade, one of the world's greatest and noblest spirits. It had not been given to me to be near him in his last hours. I would at least remain until he was carried to his final resting place.

Two things had particularly impressed me on my two previous visits to Kropotkin: his lack of bitterness toward the Bolskeviki, and the fact that he never once alluded to his own hardships and privations. It was only now, while the family was preparing for the funeral, that I learned some details of his life under the Bolshevik regime. In the early part of 1918 Kropotkin had grouped around him some of the ablest specialists in political economy. His purpose was to make a careful study of the resources of Russia, to compile these in monographs and to turn them to practical account in the industrial reconstruction of the country. Kropotkin was the editor-in-chief of the undertaking. One volume was prepared, but never published. The Federalist League, as this scientific group was known, was dissolved by the Government and all the material confiscated.

On two occasions were the Kropotkin apartments in Moscow requisitioned and the family forced to seek other quarters. It was after these experiences that the Kropotkins moved to Dmitrov, where old Peter became an involuntary exile. Kropotkin, in whose home in the past had gathered from every land all that was best in thought and ideas, was now forced to lead the life of a recluse. His only visitors were peasants and workers of the village and some members of the intelligentsia, whose wont it was to come to him with their troubles and misfortunes. He had always kept in touch with the world through numerous publications, but in Dmitrov he had no access to these sources. His only channels of information now were the two government papers, *Pravda* and *Izvestia* He was also greatly handicapped in his work on the new Ethics while he lived in the village. He was mentally starved, which to him was greater torture than physical malnutrition. It is true that he was given a better payck than the average person, but even that was insufficient to sustain his waning strength. Fortunately he occasionally received from various sources assistance in the form of provisions. His comrades from abroad, as well as the Anarchists of the Ukraina, often sent him food packages. Once he received some gifts from Makhno, at that time heralded by the Bolsheviki as the terror of counter-revolution in Southern Russia. Especially did the Kropotkins feel the lack of light. When I visited them in 1920 they were considering themselves fortunate to be able to have even one room lit. Most of the time

Kropotkin worked by the flicker of a tiny oil lamp that nearly drove him blind. During the short hours of the day he would transcribe his notes on a typewriter, slowly and painfully pounding out every letter.

However, it was not his own discomfort which sapped his strength. It was the thought of the Revolution that had failed. the hardships of Russia, the persecutions, the endless *raztrels*, which made the last two years of his life a deep tragedy. On two occasions he attempted to bring the rulers of Russia to their senses: once in protest against the suppression of all non-Communist publications; the other time against the barbaric practice of taking hostages. Ever since the Tcheka had begun its activities, the Bolshevik Government had sanctioned the taking of hostages. Old and young, mothers, fathers, sisters, brothers, even children, were kept as hostages for the alleged offence of one of their kin, of which they often knew nothing. Kropotkin regarded such methods as inexcusable under any circumstances.

In the fall of 1920, members of the Social Revolutionist Party that had succeeded in getting abroad threatened retaliation if Communist persecution of their comrades continued. The Bolshevik Government announced in its official press that for every Communist victim it would execute ten Social Revolutionists. It was then that the famous revolutionist Vera Figner and Peter Kropotkin sent their protest to the powers that be in Russia. They pointed out that such practices were the worst blot on the Russian Revolution and an evil that had already brought terrible results in its wake: history would never forgive such methods.

The other protest was made in reply to the plan of the Government to "liquidate" all private publishing establishments, including even those of the cooperatives. The protest was addressed to the Presidium of the All-Russian Congress of Soviets, then in session. It is interesting to note that Gorki, himself an official of the Commissariat of Education, had sent a similar protest. In this statement, Kropotkin called attention to the danger of such a policy to all progress, in fact, to all thought, and emphasized that such State monopoly would make creative work utterly impossible. But the protests had no effect. Thereafter Kropotkin felt that it was useless to appeal to a government gone mad with power.

During the two days I spent in the Kropotkin household I learned more of his personal life than during all the years that I had known him. Even his closest friends were not aware that Peter Kropotkin was an artist and a musician of much talent. Among his effects I discovered a collection of drawings of great merit. He loved music passionately and was himself a musician of unusual ability. Much of his leisure he spent at the piano.

And now he lay on his couch, in the little workroom, as if peacefully asleep, his face as kindly in death as it had been in life. Thousands of people made pilgrimages to the Kropotkin cottage to pay homage to this great son of Russia. When his remains were carried to the station to be taken to Moscow, the whole population of the village attended the impressive funeral procession to express their last affectionate greeting to the man who had lived among them as their friend and comrade.

The friends and comrades of Kropotkin decided that the Anarchist organizations should have exclusive charge of the funeral, and a Peter Kropotkin Funeral Commission was formed in Moscow, consisting of representatives of the various Anarchist groups. The Committee wired Lenin, asking him to order the release of all Anarchists imprisoned in the capital in order to give them the opportunity to participate in the funeral.

Owing to the nationalization of all public conveyances, printing establishments, etc., the Anarchist Funeral Commission was compelled to ask the Moscow Soviet to enable it to carry out successfully the funeral programme. The Anarchists being deprived of their own press, the Commission had to apply to the authorities for the publication of the matter necessary in connection with the funeral arrangements. After considerable discussion permission was secured to print two leaflets and to issue a four-page bulletin in commemoration of Peter Kropotkin. The Commission requested that the paper be issued without censorship and stated that the reading matter would consist of appreciations of our dead comrade, exclusive of all polemical questions. This request was categorically refused. Having no choice, the Commission was forced to submit and the manuscripts were sent in for censorship. To forestall the possibility of remaining without any memorial issue because of the delaying tactics of the Government, the Funeral Commission resolved to open, on its own responsibility, a certain Anarchist printing office that had been sealed by the Government. The bulletin and the two leaflets were printed in that establishment.

In answer to the wire sent to Lenin the Central Committee of the All-Russian Executive of the Soviets resolved "to propose to the All-Russian Extraordinary Commissin (Veh-Tcheka) to release, according to its judgment, the imprisoned Anarchists for participation in the funeral of Peter A. Kropotkin." The delegates sent to the Tcheka were asked whether the Funeral Commission would guarantee the return of the prisoners. They replied that the question had not been discussed. The Tcheka thereupon refused to release the Anarchists. The Funeral Commission, informed of the new development in the situation, immediately guaranteed the return of the prisoners after the funeral. Thereupon the Tcheka replied that "there are no Anarchists in prison who, in the judgment of the Chairman of the Extraordinary Commission, could be released for the funeral."

The remains of the dead lay in state in the Hall of Columns in the Moscow Labour Temple. On the morning of the funeral the Kropotkin Funeral Commission decided to inform the assembled people of the breach of faith on the part of the authorities and demonstratively to withdraw from the Temple all the wreaths presented by official Communist bodies. Fearing public exposure, the representatives of the Moscow Soviet definitely promised that all the Anarchists imprisoned in Moscow would immediately be released to attend the funeral. But this promise was also broken, only seven of the Anarchists being released from the "inner jail" of the Extraordinary Commission. None of the Anarchists imprisoned in the Butyrki attended the funeral. The official explanation was that the twenty Anarchists incarcerated in that prison refused to accept the offer of the authorities. Later I visited the prisoners to ascertain the facts in the case. They informed me that a representative of the Extraordinary, Commission insisted on individual attendance, making exceptions in some cases. The Anarchists, aware that the promise of temporary release was collective, demanded that the stipulations be kept. The Tcheka representative went to the telephone to consult the higher authorities, so he said. He did not return.

The funeral was a most impressive sight. It was a unique demonstration never witnessed in any other country. Long lines of members of Anarchist organizations, labour unions, scientific and literary societies and student bodies marched for over two hours from the Labour Temple to the burial place, seven *versts* [nearly five miles] distant. The procession was headed by students and children carrying wreaths presented by various organizations. Anarchist banners of black and scarlet Socialist emblems floated above the multitude. The mile-long procession entirely dispensed with the services of the official guardians of the peace. Perfect order was kept by the multitude itself spontaneously forming in several rows, while students and workers organized a live chain on both sides of the marchers. Passing the Tolstoi Museum the cortege paused, and the banners were lowered in honour of the memory of another great son of Russia. A group of Tolstoians on the steps of the Museum rendered Chopin's Funeral March as an expression of their love and reverence for Kropotkin.

The brilliant winter sun was sinking behind the horizon when the remains of Kropotkin were lowered into the grave, after speakers of many political tendencies had paid the last tribute to their great teacher and comrade.

Chapter 27: Kronstadt

In February, 1921, the workers of several Petrograd factories went on strike. The winter was an exceptionally hard one, and the people of the capital suffered intensely from cold, hunger, and exhaustion. They asked an increase of their food rations, some fuel and clothing. The complaints of the strikers, ignored by the authorities, presently assumed a political character. Here and there was also voiced a demand for the Constituent Assembly and free trade. The attempted street demonstration of the strikers was suppressed, the Government having ordered out the military *kursanti*. Lisa Zorin, who of all the Communists I had met remained closest to the people, was present at the breaking up of the demonstration. One woman became so enraged over the brutality of the military that she attacked Lisa. The latter, true to her proletarian instincts, saved the woman from arrest and accompanied her home. There she found the most appalling conditions. In a dark and damp room there lived a worker's family with its six children, half-naked in the bitter cold. Subsequently Lisa said to me: "I felt sick to think that I was in the Astoria." Later she moved out.

When the Kronstadt sailors learned what was happening in Petrograd they expressed their solidarity with the strikers in their economic and revolutionary demands, but refused to support any call for the Constituent Assembly. On March 1st, the sailors organized a mass meeting in Kronstadt, which was attended also by the Chairman of the All-Russian Central Executive Committee, Kalinin (the presiding officer of the Republic of Russia), the Commander of the Kronstadt Fortress, Kuzmin, and the Chairman of the Kronstadt Soviet, Vassiliev. The meeting, held with the knowledge of the Executive Committee of the Kronstadt Soviet, passed a resolution approved by the sailors, the garrison, and the citizens' meeting of 16,000 persons. Kalinin, Kuzmin, and Vassiliev spoke against the resolution, which later became the basis of the conflict between Kronstadt and the Government. It voiced the popular demand for Soviets elected by the free choice of the people. It is worth reproducing that document in full, that the reader may be enabled to judge the true character of the Kronstadt demands. The Resolution read:

Having heard the Report of the Representatives sent by the General Meeting of Ship Crews to Petrograd to investigate the situation there, Resolved:

(1) In view of the fact that the present Soviets do not express the will of the workers and the peasants, immediately to hold new elections by secret ballot, the pre-election campaign to have full freedom of agitation among the workers and peasants; (2) To establish freedom of speech and press for workers and peasants, for Anarchists and left Socialist parties; (3) To secure freedom of assembly for labour unions and peasant organizations; (4) To call a non-partisan Conference of the workers, Red Army soldiers and sailors of Petrograd, Kronstadt, and of Petrograd Province, no later than March 10, 1921; (5) To liberate all political prisoners of Socialist parties, as well as all workers, peasants, soldiers, and sailors imprisoned in connection with the labour and peasant movements; (6) To elect a Commission to review the cases of those held in prisons and concentration camps; (7) To abolish all *politotdeli* [political bureaus] because no party should be given special privileges in the propagation of its ideas or receive the financial support of the Government for such purposes, Instead there should be established educational and cultural commissions, locally elected and financed by the Government. (8) To abolish immediately all *zagryaditelniye otryadi*; [armed units that requisitioned grain from the peasants] (9) To equalize the rations of all who work, with the exception of those

employed in trades detrimental to health; (10) To abolish the Communist fighting detachments in all branches of the Army, as well as the Communist guards kept on duty in mills and factories. Should such guards or military detachments be found necessary, they are to be appointed in the Army from the ranks, and in the factories according to the judgment of the workers; (11) To give the peasants full freedom of action in regard to their land, and also the right to keep cattle, on condition that the peasants manage with their own means; that is, without employing hired labour; (12) To request all branches of the Army, as well as our comrades the military *kursanti*, to concur in our resolutions; (13) To demand that the press give the fullest publicity to our resolutions; (14) To appoint a Travelling Commission of Control; (15) To permit free *kustarnoye* [individual, small-scale] production by one's own efforts.

On March 4th the Petrograd Soviet was to meet and it was generally felt that the fate of Kronstadt would be decided then. Trotsky was to address the gathering, and as 1 had not yet had an opportunity to hear him in Russia, I was anxious to attend. My attitude in the matter of Kronstadt was still undecided. I could not believe that the Bolsheviki would deliberately fabricate the story about General Kozlovsky as the leader of the sailors. The Soviet meeting, I expected, would clarify the matter.

Tauride Palace was crowded and a special body of *kursanti* surrounded the platform. The atmosphere was very tense. All waited for Trotsky. But when at 10 o'clock he had not arrived, Zinoviev opened the meeting. Before he had spoken fifteen minutes I was convinced that he himself did not believe in the story of Kozlovsky. "Of course Kozlovsky is old and can do nothing," he said, "but the White officers are back of him and are misleading the sailors." Yet for days the Soviet papers had heralded General Kozlovsky as the moving spirit in the "uprising." Kalinin, whom the sailors had permitted to leave Kronstadt unmolested, raved like a fishmonger. He denounced the sailors as counter-revolutionists and called for their immediate subjugation. Several other Communists followed suit. When the meeting was opened for discussion, a workingman from the Petrograd Arsenal demanded to be heard. He spoke with deep emotion and, ignoring the constant interruptions, he fearlessly declared that the workers had been driven to strike because of the

Government's indifference to their complaints; the Kronstadt sailors, far from being counter-revolutionists, were devoted to the Revolution. Facing Zinoviev he reminded him that the Bolshevik authorities were now acting toward the workers and sailors just as the Kerensky Government had acted toward the Bolsheviki. "Then you were denounced as counter-revolutionists and German agents," he said; "we, the workers and sailors, protected you and helped you to power. Now you denounce us and are ready to attack us with arms. Remember, you are playing with fire."

Then a sailor spoke. He referred to the glorious revolutionary past of Kronstadt, appealed to the Communists not to engage in fratricide, and read the Kronstadt resolution to prove the peaceful attitude of the sailors. But the voice of these sons of the people fell on deaf ears. The Petro-Soviet, its passions roused by Bolshevik demagoguery, passed the Zinoviev resolution ordering Kronstadt to surrender on pain of extermination.

The Kronstadt sailors were ever the first to serve the Revolution. They had played an important part in the revolution of 1905; they were in the front ranks in 1917. Under Kerensky's regime they proclaimed the Commune of Kronstadt and opposed the Constituent Assembly. They were the advance guard in the October Revolution. In the great struggle against Yudenitch the sailors offered the strongest defense of Petrograd, and Trotsky praised them as the "pride and glory of the Revolution." Now, however, they had dared to raise their voice in protest against the new rulers of Russia. That was high treason from the Bolshevik viewpoint. The Kronstadt sailors were doomed.

Petrograd was aroused over the decision of the Soviet; some of the Communists even, especially those of the French Section, were filled with indignation. But none of them had the courage to protest, even in the Party circles, against the proposed slaughter. As soon as the Petro-Soviet resolution became known, a group of well-known literary men of Petrograd gathered to confer as to whether something could not be done to prevent the planned crime. Someone suggested that Gorki be approached to head a committee of protest to the Soviet authorities. It was hoped that he would emulate the example of his illustrious countryman Tolstoi, who in his famous letter to the Tsar had raised his voice against the terrible slaughter of workers. Now also such a voice was needed, and Gorki was considered the right man to call on the present Tsars to bethink themselves. But most of those present at the gathering scouted the idea. Gorki was of the Bolsheviki, they said; he would not do anything. On several previous occasions he had been appealed to, but refused to intercede. The conference brought no results. Still, there were some persons in Petrograd who could not remain silent. They sent the following letter to the Soviet of Defense:

To The Petrograd Soviet Of Labour And Defense, Chairman Zinoviev:

To remain silent now is impossible, even criminal. Recent events impel us Anarchists to speak out and to declare our attitude in the present situation.

The spirit of ferment and dissatisfaction manifest among the workers and sailors is the result of causes that demand our serious attention. Cold and hunger have produced dissatisfaction, and the absence of any opportunity for discussion and criticism is forcing the workers and sailors to air their grievances in the open.

White-guardist bands wish and may try to exploit this dissatisfaction in their own class interests. Hiding behind the workers and sailors they throw out slogans of the Constituent Assembly, of free trade, and similar demands.

We Anarchists have long since exposed the fiction of these slogans, and we declare to the whole world that we will fight with arms against any counter-revolutionary attempt, in cooperation with all friends of the Social Revolution and hand in hand with the Bolsheviki.

Concerning the conflict between the Soviet Government and the workers and sailors, we hold that it must be settled not by force of arms but by means of comradely, fraternal revolutionary agreement. Resort to bloodshed on the part of the Soviet Government will not-in the given situation-intimidate or quiet the workers. On the contrary, it will serve only to aggravate matters and will strengthen the bands of the Entente and of internal counter-revolution.

More important still, the use of force by the Workers' and Peasants' Government against workers and sailors will have a reactionary effect upon the international revolutionary movement and will everywhere result in incalculable harm to the Social Revolution.

Comrades Bolsheviki, bethink yourselves before it is too late. Do not play with fire: you are about to make a most serious and decisive step.

We hereby submit to you the following proposition: Let a Commission he selected to consist of five persons, inclusive of two Anarchists. The Commission is to go to Kronstadt to settle the dispute by peaceful means. In the given situation this is the most radical method. It will be of international revolutionary significance.

Petrograd, March 5, 1921.

ALEXANDER BERKMAN.
EMMA GOLDMAN
PERKUS.
PETROVSKY.

But this protest was ignored.

On March 7th Trotsky began the bombardment of Kronstadt, and on the 17th the fortress and city were taken, after numerous assaults involving terrific human sacrifice. Thus Kronstadt was "liquidated" and the "counterrevolutionary plot" quenched in blood. The "conquest" of the city was characterized by ruthless savagery, although not a single one of the Communists arrested by the

Kronstadt sailors had been injured or killed by them. Even before the storming of the fortress the Bolsheviki summarily executed numerous soldiers of the Red Army whose revolutionary spirit and solidarity caused them to refuse to participate in the bloodbath.

Several days after the "glorious victory" over Kronstadt Lenin said at the Tenth Congress of the Communist Party of Russia: "The sailors did not want the counter-revolutionists, but they did not want us, either." And—irony of Bolshevism!--at that very Congress Lenin advocated free trade-a more reactionary step than any charged to the Kronstadt sailors.

Between the 1st and the 17th of March several regiments of the Petrograd garrison and all the sailors of the port were disarmed and ordered to the Ukraina and the Caucasus. The Bolsheviki feared to trust them in the Kronstadt situation: at the first psychological moment they might make common cause with Kronstadt. In fact, many Red soldiers of the Krasnaya Gorka and the surrounding garrisons were also in sympathy with Kronstadt and were forced at the point of guns to attack the sailors.

On March 17th the Communist Government completed its "victory" over the Kronstadt proletariat and on the 18th of March it commemorated the martyrs of the Paris Commune. It was apparent to all who were mute witnesses to the outrage committed by the Bolsheviki that the crime against Kronstadt was far more enormous than the slaughter of the Communards in 1871, for it was done in the name of the Social Revolution, in the name of the Socialist Republic. History will not be deceived. In the annals of the Russian Revolution the names of Trotsky, Zinoviev, and Dibenko will be added to those of Thiers and Gallifet.

Seventeen dreadful days, more dreadful than anything I had known in Russia. Agonizing days, because of my utter helplessness in the face of the terrible things enacted before my eyes. It was just at that time that I happened to visit a friend who had been a patient in a hospital for months. I found him much distressed. Many of those wounded in the attack on Kronstadt had been brought to the same hospital, mostly *kursanti*. I had opportunity to speak to one of them. His physical suffering, he said, was nothing as compared with his mental agony. Too late he had realized that he had been duped by the cry of "counter-revolution." There were no Tsarist generals in

Kronstadt, no White Guardists—he found only his own comrades, sailors and soldiers who had heroically fought for the Revolution.

The rations of the ordinary patients in the hospitals were far from satisfactory, but the wounded *kursanti* received the best of everything, and a select committee of Communist members was assigned to look after their comfort. Some of the *kursanti*, among them the man I had spoken to, refused to accept the special privileges. "They want to pay us for murder", they said. Fearing that the whole institution would be influenced by these awakened victims, the management ordered them removed to a separate ward, the "Communist ward," as the patients called it.

Kronstadt broke the last thread that held me to the Bolsheviki. The wanton slaughter they had instigated spoke more eloquently against them than aught else. Whatever their pretences in the past, the Bolsheviki now proved themselves the most pernicious enemies of the Revolution. I could have nothing further to do with them.

Chapter 28: Persecution Of Anarchists

In a country State-owned and controlled as completely as Russia it is almost impossible to live without the "grace" of the Government. However, I was determined to make the attempt. I would accept nothing, not even bread rations, from the hands stained with the blood of the brave Kronstadt sailors. Fortunately, I had some clothing left me by an American friend; it could be exchanged for provisions. I had also received some money from my own people in the United States. That would enable me to live for some time.

In Moscow I procured a small room formerly occupied by the daughter of Peter Kropotkin. From that day on I lived like thousands of other Russians, carrying water, chopping wood, washing and cooking, all in my little room. But I felt freer and better for it.

The new economic policy turned Moscow into a vast market place. Trade became the new religion. Shops and stores sprang up overnight, mysteriously stacked with delicacies Russia had not seen for years. Large quantities of butter, cheese, and meat were displayed for sale; pastry, rare fruit, and sweets of every variety were to be purchased. In the building of the First House of the Soviet one of the biggest pastry shops had been opened. Men, women, and children with pinched faces and hungry eyes stood about gazing into the windows and discussing the great miracle: what was but yesterday considered a heinous offence was now flaunted before them in an open and legal manner. I overheard a Red soldier say: "Is this what we made the Revolution for? For this our comrades had to die ?" The slogan, "Rob the robbers," was now turned into "Respect the robbers," and again was proclaimed the sanctity of private property.

Russia was thus gradually resurrecting the social conditions that the great Revolution had come to destroy. But the return to capitalism in no way changed the Bolshevik attitude toward the Left elements. Bourgeois ideas and practices were to be encouraged to develop the industrial life of Russia, but revolutionary tendencies were to be suppressed as before.

In connection with Kronstadt a general raid on Anarchists took place in Petrograd and Moscow. The prisons were filled with these victims. Almost every known Anarchist had been arrested; and the Anarchist book stores and printing offices of *Golos Truda* in both cities were sealed by the Tcheka. The Ukrainian Anarchists who had been arrested on the eve of the Kharkov Conference (though guaranteed immunity by the Bolsheviki under the Makhno agreement) were brought to Moscow and placed in the Butyrki; that Romanov dungeon was again serving its old purpose—even holding some of the revolutionists incarcerated there before. Presently it became known that the politicals in the Butyrki had been brutally assaulted by the Tcheka and secretly deported to unknown parts. Moscow was much agitated by this resurrection of the worst prison methods of Tsarism. Interpellation on the subject was made in the Moscow Soviet, the indignation of the deputies being so great that the Tcheka representative was shouted off the platform. Several Moscow Anarchist groups sent a vigorous protest to the authorities, which document I quote in part:

> The undersigned Anarcho-syndicalist organizations after having carefully considered the situation that has developed lately in connection with the persecution of Anarchists in Moscow, Petrograd, Kharkov, and other cities of Russia and the Ukraine, including the forcible suppression of Anarchist organizations, clubs, publications, etc., hereby express their decisive and energetic protest against this despotic crushing of not only every agitational and propagandistic activity, but

even of all purely cultural work by Anarchist organizations.

The systematic man-hunt of Anarchists in general, and of Anarcho-syndicalists in particular, with the result that every prison and jail in Soviet Russia is filled with our comrades, fully coincided in time and spirit with Lenin's speech at the Tenth Congress of the Russian Communist Party. On that occasion Lenin announced that the most merciless war must be declared against what he termed "petty bourgeois Anarchist elements" which, according to him, are developing even within the Communist Party itself owing to the "anarcho-syndicalist tendencies of the Labour Opposition." On that very day that Lenin made the above statements numbers of Anarchists were arrested all over the country, without the least cause or explanation. No charges have been preferred against any one of the imprisoned comrades, though some of them have already been condemned to long terms without hearing or trial, and in their absence. The conditions of their imprisonment are exceptionally vile and brutal. Thus one of the arrested, Comrade Maximov, after numerous vain protests against the incredibly unhygienic conditions in which he was forced to exist, was driven to the only means of protest left him—a hunger strike. Another comrade, Yarchuk, released after an imprisonment of six days, was soon rearrested without any charges being preferred against him on either occasion.

According to reliable information received by us, some of the arrested Anarchists are being sent to the prisons of Samara, far away from home and friends, and thus deprived of what little comradely assistance they might have been able to receive nearer home. A number of other comrades have been forced by the terrible conditions of their imprisonment to declare a hunger strike. One of them, after hungering twelve days, became dangerously ill.

Even physical violence is practised upon our comrades in prison. The statement of the Anarchists in the Butyrki prison in Moscow, signed by thirty-eight comrades, and sent to the Executive Committee of the All-Russian Extraordinary Commission on March 16th, contains, among other things, the following statement: "On March 15th Comrade T. Kashirin was brutally attacked and beaten in the prison of the Special Department of the Extraordinary Commission by your agent Mago and assistants, in the presence of the prison warden Dookiss."

Besides the wholesale arrests of and the physical violence toward our comrades, the Government is waging systematic war against our educational work. It has closed a number of our clubs, as well as the Moscow office of the publishing establishment of the Anarcho-syndicalist organization Golos Truda. A similar man-hunt took place in Petrograd on March 15th. Numbers of Anarchists were arrested, without cause, the printing house of Golos Truda was closed, and its workers imprisoned. No charges have been preferred against the arrested comrades, all of whom are still in prison.

These unbearably autocratic tactics of the Government towards the Anarchists are unquestionably the result of the general policy of the Bolshevik State in the exclusive control of the Communist Party in regard to Anarchism, Syndicalism, and their adherents.

This state of affairs is forcing us to raise our voices in loud protest against the panicky and brutal suppression of the Anarchist movement by the

Bolshevik Government. Here in Russia our voice is weak. It is stifled. The policy of the ruling Communist Party is designed to destroy absolutely every possibility or effort of Anarchist activity or propaganda. The Anarchists of Russia are thus forced into the condition of a complete moral hunger strike, for the Government is depriving us of the possibility to carry out even those plans and projects which it itself only recently promised to aid.

Realizing more clearly than ever before the truth of our Anarchist ideal and the imperative need of its application to life we are convinced that the revolutionary proletariat of the world is with us.

After the February Revolution Russian Anarchists returned from every land to Russia to devote themselves to revolutionary activity. The Bolsheviki had adopted the Anarchist slogan, "The factories to the workers, the land to the peasants," and thereby won the sympathies of the Anarchists. The latter saw in the Bolsheviki the spokesmen of social and economic emancipation, and joined forces with them.

Through the October period the Anarchists worked hand in hand with the Communists and fought with them side by side in the defense of the Revolution. Then came the Brest-Litovsk Treaty, which many Anarchists considered a betrayal of the Revolution. It was the first warning for them that all was not well with the Bolsheviki. But Russia was still exposed to foreign intervention, and the Anarchists felt that they must continue together to fight the common enemy.

In April, 1918, came another blow. By order of Trotsky the Anarchist headquarters in Moscow were attacked with artillery, some Anarchists wounded, a large number arrested, and all Anarchist activities "liquidated." This entirely unexpected outrage served to further to alienate the Anarchists from the ruling Party. Still the majority of them remained with the Bolsheviki: they felt that, in spite of internal persecution, to turn against the existing regime was to work into the hands of the counter-revolutionary forces. The Anarchists participated in every social, educational, and economic effort; they worked even in the military departments to aid Russia. In the Red Guards, in the volunteer regiments, and later in the Red Army; as organizers and managers of factories and shops; as chiefs of the fuel bureaus; as teachers—everywhere the Anarchists held difficult and responsible positions. Out of their ranks came some of the ablest men who worked in the foreign office with Tchicherin and Kharakan, in the various press bureaus, as Bolshevik diplomatic representatives in Turkestan, Bokhara, and the Far Eastern Republic. Throughout Russia the Anarchists worked with and for the Bolsheviki in the belief that they were advancing the cause of the Revolution. But the devotion and zeal of the Anarchists in no way deterred the Communists from relentlessly persecuting the Anarchist movement.

The peculiar general situation and the confusion of ideas created in all revolutionary circles by the Bolshevik experiment divided the Anarchist forces in Russia into several factions, thereby weakening their effect upon the course of the Revolution. There were a number of groups, each striving separately and striving vainly against the formidable machine which they themselves had helped to create. In the dense political fog many lost their sense of direction: they could not distinguish between the Bolsheviki and the Revolution. In desperation some Anarchists were driven to underground activities, even as they had been during the regime of the Tsars. But such work was more difficult and perilous under the new rulers and it also opened the door to the sinister machinations of provocators. The more mature Anarchist organizations, such as the *Nabat*, in the Ukraina, *Golos Truda* in Petrograd and Moscow, and the *Voylni Trud* group—the last two of Anarcho-syndicalist tendency—continued their work openly, as best they could.

Unfortunately, as was unavoidable under the circumstances, some evil spirits had found entry into the Anarchist ranks—debris washed ashore by the Revolutionary tide. They were types to whom the Revolution meant only destruction, occasionally even for personal advantage. They engaged in shady pursuits and, when arrested and their lives threatened, they often turned traitors and joined the Tcheka. Particularly in Kharkov and Odessa thrived this poisonous weed. The Anarchists at large were the first to take a stand against this element. The Bolsheviki, always anxious to secure the services of the Anarchist derelicts, systematically perverted the facts. They maligned, persecuted, and hounded the Anarchist movement as such. It was this Communist treachery and despotism which resulted in a bomb's being thrown during the session of the Moscow Section of the

Communist Party in September, 1919. It was an act of protest, members of the various political tendencies cooperating in it. The Anarchist organizations *Golos Truda* and *Voylni Trud* in Moscow publicly expressed their condemnation of such methods, but the Government replied with reprisals against all Anarchists. Yet, in spite of their bitter experiences and martyrdom under the Bolshevik regime, most of the Anarchists clung tenaciously to the hand that smote them. It needed the outrage upon Kronstadt to rouse them from the hypnotic spell of the Bolshevik superstition.

Power is corrupting, and Anarchists are no exception. It must in truth be admitted that a certain Anarchist element became demoralized by it; by far the largest majority retained their integrity. Neither Bolshevik persecution nor oft-attempted bribery of good position with all its special privileges succeeded in alienating the great bulk of Anarchists from their ideals. As a result they were constantly harassed and incarcerated. Their existence in the prisons was a continuous torture: in most of them still obtained the old regime and only the collective struggle of the politicals occasionally succeeded in compelling reforms and improvements. Thus it required repeated "obstructions" and hunger strikes in the Butyrki before the authorities were forced to make concessions. The politicals succeeded in establishing a sort of university, organized lectures, and received visits and food parcels. But the Tcheka frowned upon such "liberties." Suddenly, without warning, an end was put to decent treatment; the Butyrki was raided and the prisoners, numbering more than 400, and belonging to various revolutionary wings, were forcibly taken from their cells and transferred to other penal institutions. A message received at the time from one of the victims, dated April 27th, reads:

Concentration Camp, Ryazan.

On the night of April 25th we were attacked by Red soldiers and armed Tchekists and ordered to dress and get ready to leave the Butyrki. Some of the politicals, fearing that they were to be taken to execution, refused to go and were terribly beaten. The women especially were maltreated, some of them being dragged down the stairs by their hair. Many have suffered serious injury. I myself was so badly beaten that my whole body feels like one big sore. We were taken out by force in our night-clothes and thrown into wagons. The comrades in our group knew nothing of the whereabouts of the rest of the politicals, including Mensheviks, Social Revolutionists, Anarchists, and Anarcho-syndicalists.

Ten of us, among them Fanya Baron, have been brought here. Conditions in this prison are unbearable. No exercise, no fresh air; food is scarce and filthy; everywhere awful dirt, bedbugs, and lice. We mean to declare a hunger strike for better treatment. We have just been told to get ready with our things. They are going to send us away again. We do not know where to.

[Signed] T.

Upon the circumstances of the Butyrki raid becoming known the students of the Moscow University held a protest meeting and passed resolutions condemnatory of the outrage. Thereupon the student leaders were arrested and the University closed. The non-resident students were ordered to leave Moscow within three days on the pretext of lack of rations. The students volunteered to give up their *payok*, but the Government insisted on their quitting the capital. Later, when the University was re-opened, Preobrazhensky, the Dean, admonished the students to refrain from any political expressions on pain of being expelled from the University. Some of the arrested students were exiled, among them several girl students, for the sole crime of being members of a circle whose aim was to study the works of Kropotkin and other Anarchist authors. The methods of the Tsar were resurrected by his heirs to the throne in Bolshevik Russia.

After the death of Peter Kropotkin his friends and comrades decided to found a Kropotkin Museum in commemoration of the great Anarchist teacher and in furtherance of his ideas and ideals. I removed to Moscow to aid in the organization of the proposed memorial, but before long the Museum Committee concluded that for the time being the project could not be realized. Everything being under State monopoly nothing could be done without application to the authorities. To accept Government aid would have been a deliberate betrayal of the spirit of Kropotkin who throughout his life consistently refused State assistance. Once when Kropotkin was ill and in need, the Bolshevik Government offered him a large sum for the right to publish his works. Kropotkin refused. He was compelled to accept rations and medical assistance when sick, but he would neither consent to his works being published by the State nor accept any other aid from it. The Kropotkin Museum Committee took the same attitude. It accepted from the Moscow Soviet the house Kropotkin had been born in, and which was to be turned into a Kropotkin Museum; but it would ask the Government for nothing more. The house at the time was occupied by a military organization; it would require months to get it vacated and then no means would be at hand to have it renovated. Some of the Committee members felt that a Kropotkin Museum was out of place in Bolshevik Russia as long as despotism was rampant and the prisons filled with political dissenters.

While I was in Petrograd on a short visit, the Moscow apartment in which I had a room was raided by the Tcheka. I learned that the customary trap had been set and everyone arrested who called at the place during the *zassada*. I visited Ravitch to protest against such proceedings, telling her that if the object was to take me into custody I was prepared for it. Ravitch had heard nothing of the matter, but promised to get in touch with Moscow. A few days later I was informed that the Tchekists had been withdrawn from the apartment and that the arrested friends were about to be released. When I returned to my room some time later most of them had been freed. At the same time a number of Anarchists were arrested in various parts of the capital and no news of their fate or of the cause of their arrest could be learned. Several weeks later, on August 30th, the Moscow *Izvestia* published the official report of the Veh-Tcheka concerning "Anarchist banditism," announcing that ten Anarchists had been shot as "bandits" without hearing or trial.

It had become the established policy of the Bolshevik Government to mask its barbaric procedure against Anarchists with the uniform charge of banditism. This accusation was made practically against all arrested Anarchists and frequently even against sympathizers with the movement. A very convenient method of getting rid of an undesirable person: by it any one could be secretly executed and buried.

Among the ten victims were two of the best known Russian Anarchists, whose idealism and life-long devotion to the cause of humanity had stood the test of Tsarist dungeons and exile, and persecution and suffering in other countries. They were Fanya Baron, who several months before had escaped from the Ryazan prison, and Lev Tcherny who had spent many years of his life in *katorga* and exile, under the old regime. The Bolsheviki did not have the courage to say that they had shot Lev Tcherny; in the list of the executed he appeared as "Turchaninoff," which — though his real name — was unfamiliar to some even of his closest friends. Tcherny was known throughout Russia as a gifted poet and writer. In 1907 he had published an original work on "Associational Anarchism," and since his return from Siberia in 1917 he had enjoyed wide popularity among the workers of Moscow as a lecturer and founder of the "Federation of Brain Workers." He was a man of great gifts, tender and sympathetic in all his relationships. No person could be further from banditism.

The mother of Tcherny had repeatedly called at the Ossoby Otdel (Special Department of the Tcheka) to learn the fate of her son. Every time she was told to come next day; she would then be permitted to see him. As established later, Tcherny had already been shot when these promises were being made. After his death the authorities refused to turn his body over to his relatives or friends for burial. There were persistent rumours that the Tcheka had not intended to execute Tcherny, but that he died under torture.

Fanya Baron was of the type of Russian woman completely consecrated to the cause of humanity. While in America she gave all her spare time and a goodly part of her meagre earnings in a factory to further Anarchist propaganda. Years afterward, when I met her in Kharkov, her zeal and devotion had become intensified by the persecution she and her comrades had endured since their return to Russia. She possessed unbounded courage and a generous spirit. She could perform the most difficult task and deprive herself of the last piece of bread with grace and utter selflessness. Under harrowing conditions of travel, Fanya went up and down the Ukraina to spread the *Nabat*, organize the workers and peasants, or bring help and succour to her imprisoned comrades. She was one of the victims of the Butyrki raid, when she had been dragged by her hair and badly beaten. After her escape from the Ryazan prison she tramped on foot to Moscow, where she arrived in tatters and penniless. It was her desperate condition which drove her to seek shelter with her husband's brother, at whose house she was discovered by the Tcheka. This big-hearted woman, who had served the Social Revolution all her life, was done to death by the people who pretended to be the advance guard of revolution. Not content with the crime of killing Fanya Baron, the Soviet Government put the stigma of banditism on the memory of their dead victim.

Chapter 29: Traveling Salesmen Of The Revolution

Great preparations were being made by the Communists for the Third Congress of the Third International and the First Congress of the Red Trade Union International. A preliminary committee had been organized in the summer of 1920, while delegates from various countries were in Moscow. How much the Bolsheviki depended upon the First Congress of the Red Trade Union International was apparent from a remark of an old Communist. "We haven't the workers in the Third International," he said; "unless we succeed in welding together the proletariat of the world into the R. T. U. I., the Third International cannot last very long."

The Hôtel de Luxe, renovated the previous year, became the foreign guest house of the Third International and was put in festive attire. The delegates began to arrive in Moscow.

During my stay in Russia I came across three classes of visitors who came to "study the Revolution." The first category consisted of earnest idealists to whom the Bolsheviki were the symbol of the Revolution. Among them were many emigrants from America who had given up everything they possessed to return to the promised land. Most of these became bitterly disappointed after the first few months and sought to get out of Russia. Others, who did not come as

Communists, joined the Communist Party for selfish reasons and did in Rome as the Romans do. There were also the Anarchist deportees who came not of their own choice. Most of them strained every effort to leave Russia after they realized the stupendous deception that had been imposed on the world.

In the second class were journalists, newspapermen, and some adventurers. They spent from two weeks to two months in Russia, usually in Petrograd or Moscow, as the guests of the Government and in charge of Bolshevik guides. Hardly any of them knew the language and they never got further than the surface of things. Yet many of them have presumed to write and lecture authoritatively about the Russian situation. I remember my astonishment when I read in a certain London daily that the teachings of Jesus were "being realized in Russia." A preposterous falsehood of which none but a charlatan could be guilty. Other writers were not much nearer the truth. If they were at all critical of the Bolsheviki they were so at the expense of the whole Russian people, whom they charged with being "crude, primitive savages, too illiterate to grasp the meaning of the Revolution." According to these writers it was the Russian people who imposed upon the Bolsheviki their despotic and cruel methods. It did not occur to those so-called investigators that the Revolution was made by those primitive and illiterate people, and not by the present rulers in the Kremlin. Surely they must have possessed some quality which enabled them to rise to revolutionary heights-a quality which, if properly directed, would have prevented the wreck and ruin of Russia. But that quality has persistently been overlooked by Bolshevik apologists who sacrifice all truth in their determination to find extenuating circumstances for the mess made by the Bolsheviki. A few wrote with understanding of the complex problems and with sympathy for the Russian people. But their voice was ineffectual in the popular craze that Bolshevism had become.

The third category—the majority of the visitors, delegates, and members of various commissions—infested Russia to become the agents of the ruling Party. These people had every opportunity to see things as they were, to get close to the Russian people, and to learn from them the whole terrible truth. But they preferred to side with the Government, to listen to its interpretation of causes and effects. Then they went forth to misrepresent and to lie deliberately in behalf of the Bolsheviki, as the Entente agents had lied and misrepresented the Russian Revolution.

Nor did the sincere Communists realize the disgrace of the situation—not even Angelica Balabanova. Yet she had good judgment of character and knew how to appraise the people who flocked to Russia. Her experience with Mrs. Clare Sheridan was characteristic. The lady had been smuggled into Russia before Moscow realized that she was the cousin of Winston Churchill. She was obsessed by the desire "to sculp" prominent Communists. She had also begged Angelica to sit for her. "Lenin, Trotsky, and other leaders are going to; aren't you?" she pleaded. Angelica, who hated sensationalism in any form, resented the presence in Russia of these superficial visitors. "I asked her," she afterward related, "if she would have thought of 'sculpting' Lenin three years ago when the English Government denounced him as a German spy. Lenin did not make the Revolution. The Russian people made it. I told this Mrs. Sheridan that she would do better to 'sculp' Russian workingmen and women who were the real heroes of the Revolution. I know she did not like what I said. But I don't care. I can't stand people to whom the Russian struggle is mere copy for poor imitations or cheap display."

Now the new delegates were beginning to arrive. They were royally welcomed and feted. They were taken to show schools, children's homes, colonies, and model factories. It was the traditional Potemkin villages that were shown the visitors. They were graciously received and "talked to" by Lenin and Trotsky, treated to theatres, concerts, ballets, excursions, and military parades. In short, nothing was left undone to put the delegates into a frame of mind favourable to the great plan that was to be revealed to them at the Red Trade Union and the Third International Congresses. There were also continuous private conferences where the delegates were subjected to a regular third degree, Lozovsky—prominent Bolshevik labour leader—and his retinue seeking to ascertain their attitude to the Third International, the dictatorship of the proletariat, and similar subjects. Here and there was a delegate who refused to divulge the instructions of his organization on the ground that he was pledged to report only to the Congress. But such naive people reckoned without their host. They soon found themselves ostracized and at the Congress they were given no opportunity to make themselves heard effectively.

The majority of the delegates were more pliable. They learned quickly that pledges and responsibilities were considered bourgeois superstitions. To show their ultra-radicalism they quickly divested themselves of them. They became the echoes of Zinoviev, Lozovsky, and other leaders.

The American delegates to the Red Trade Union International were most conspicuous by their lack of personality. They accepted without question every proposition and suggestion of the Chair. The most flagrant intrigues and political machinations and brazen suppression of those who would not be cajoled or bullied into blind adherence found ready support by the American Communist crew and the aides they had brought with them.

The Bolsheviki know how to set the stage to produce an impression. In the staging of the two Congresses held in July, 1921, they outdid themselves. The background for the Congress of the Third International was the Kremlin. In the royal halls where once the all-powerful Romanovs had sat, the awed delegates hung with bated breath upon every word uttered by their pope, Lenin, and the other Grand Seigneurs of the Communist Church. On the eve of the Congress a great meeting was held in the big theatre to which only those whose passports had been approved by the All-Russian Tcheka were admitted. The streets leading to the theatre were turned into a veritable military camp.

Tchekists and soldiers on foot and on horseback created the proper atmosphere for the Communist conclave. At the meeting resolutions were passed extending fraternal greetings to "the revolutionists in capitalist prisons." At that very moment every Russian prison was filled with revolutionists but no greetings were sent to them. So all-pervading was Moscow hypnotism that not a single voice was raised to point out the farce of Bolshevik sympathy for political prisoners.

The Red Trade Union Congress was set on a less pretentious scale in the House of the Trade Unions. But no details were overlooked to get the proper effects. "Delegates" from Palestine and Korea—men who had not been out of Russia for years—delegates from the great industrial centres of Bokhara, Turkestan, and Adzerbeydzhan, packed the Congress to swell the Communist vote and help carry every Communist proposition. They were there to teach the workers of Europe and America how to reconstruct their respective countries and to establish Communism after the world revolution.

The plan perfected by Moscow during the year 1920-21, and which was a complete reversal of Communist principles and tactics, was very skilfully and subtly unrolled—by slow degrees—before the credulous delegates. The Red Trade Union International was to embrace all revolutionary and syndicalist organizations of the world, with Moscow as its Mecca and the Third International as its Prophet. All minor revolutionary labour organizations were to be dissolved and Communist units formed instead within the existing conservative trade union bodies. The very people who a year ago had issued the famous Bull of twenty-one points, they who had excommunicated every heretic unwilling to submit to the orders of the Holy See—the Third International—and who had applied every invective to labour in the 2nd and the 2 1/2 Internationals, were now making overtures to the most reactionary labour organizations and "resoluting" against the best efforts of the revolutionary pioneers in the Trade Union movement of every country.

Here again the American delegates proved themselves worthy of their hire. Most of them had sprung from the Industrial Workers of the World; had indeed arisen to "fame and glory" on the shoulders of that militant American labour body. Some of the delegates had valiantly escaped to safety, unselfishly preferring the Hotel de Luxe to Leavenworth Penitentiary, leaving their comrades behind in American prisons and their friends to refund the bonds they had heroically forfeited. While Industrial Workers continued to suffer persecution in capitalistic America, the renegade I.W.W.'s living in comfort and safety in Moscow maligned and attacked their former comrades and schemed to destroy their organization. Together with the Bolsheviki they were going to carry out the job begun by the American Vigilantes and the Ku Klux Klan to exterminate the I.W.W. *Les extrêmes ce touchent.*

While the Communists were passing eloquent resolutions of protest against the imprisonment of revolutionaries in foreign countries, the Anarchists in the Bolshevik prisons of Russia were being driven to desperation by their long imprisonment without opportunity for a hearing or trial. To force the hand of the Government the Anarchists incarcerated in the Taganka (Moscow) decided on a hunger strike to the death. The French, Spanish, and Italian Anarcho-syndicalists, when informed of the situation, promised to raise the question at an early session of the Labour Congress. Some, however, suggested that the Government be first approached on the matter. Thereupon a Delegate Committee was chosen, including the well-known English labour leader, Tom Mann, to call upon the Little Father in the Kremlin. The Committee visited Lenin. The latter refused to have the Anarchists released on the ground that "they were too dangerous," but the final result of the interview was a promise that they would be permitted to leave Russia; should they, however, return without permission, they would be shot. The next day Lenin's promise was substantiated by a letter of the Central Committee of the Communist Party, signed by Trotsky, reiterating what Lenin had said. Naturally the threat of shooting was omitted in the official letter.

The hunger strikers in the Taganka accepted the conditions of deportation. They had for years fought and bled for the Revolution and now they were compelled to become Ahasueruses in foreign lands or suffer slow mental and physical death in Bolshevik dungeons. The Moscow Anarchist groups chose Alexander Berkman and A. Shapiro as their representatives on the Delegates' Committee to arrange with the Government the conditions of the release and deportation of the imprisoned Anarchists.

In view of this settlement of the matter the intention of a public protest at the Congress was abandoned by the delegates. Great was their amazement when, just before the close of the Congress, Bukharin—in the name of the Central Committee of the Communist Party—launched into a scurrilous attack on the Anarchists.

Some of the foreign delegates, outraged by the dishonourable proceeding, demanded an opportunity to reply. That demand was finally granted to a representative of the French delegation after Chairman Lozovsky had exhausted every demagogic trick in a vain attempt to silence the dissenters.

At no time during the protracted negotiations on behalf of the imprisoned Anarchists and the last disgraceful proceedings at the Red Trade Union Congress did the American Communist delegates make a protest. Loudly they had shouted for political amnesty in America, but not a word had they to say in favour of the liberation of the politicals in Russia. One of the group, approached on behalf of the hunger strikers, exclaimed: "What are a few lives or even a few hundred of them as against the Revolution!" To such Communist minds the Revolution had no bearing on justice and humanity.

In the face of abject want, with men, women, and children hungrily watching the white bread baked for the Luxe Hotel in its adjoining bakery, one of the American fraternal delegates wrote to a publication at home that " the workers in Russia control the industries and are directing the affairs of the country; they get everything free and need no money." This noble delegate lived in the palatial home of the former Sugar King of Russia and enjoyed also the hospitality of the Luxe. He indeed needed no money. But he knew that the workers lacked even the basic necessities and that without money they were as helpless in Russia as in any other country, the week's *payok* not being sufficient for two days' existence. Another delegate published glowing accounts dwelling on the absence of prostitution and crime in Moscow. At the same time the Tcheka was daily executing hold-up-men, and on the Tverskaya and the Pushkin Boulevard, near the Luxe Hotel, street women mobbed the delegates with their attentions. Their best customers were the very delegates who waxed so enthusiastic about the wonders of the Bolshevik régime.

The Bolsheviki realized the value of such champions and appreciated their services. They sent them forth into the world generously equipped in every sense, to perpetuate the monstrous delusion that the Bolsheviki and the Revolution are identical and that the workers have come into their own " under the proletarian dictatorship." Woe to those who dare to tear the mask from the lying face. In Russia they are put against the wall, exiled to slow death in famine districts, or banished from the country. In Europe and America such heretics are dragged through the mire and morally lynched. Everywhere the unscrupulous tools of the great disintegrator, the Third International, spread distrust and hatred in labour and radical ranks. Formerly ideals and integrity were the impulse to revolutionary activity. Social movements were founded upon the inner needs of each country. They were maintained and supported by the interest and zeal of the workers themselves. Now all this is condemned as worthless. Instead the golden rain of Moscow is depended on to produce a rich crop of Communist organizations and publications. Even uprisings may be organized to deceive and mislead the people as to the quality and strength of the Communist Party. In reality, everything is built on a foundation that crumbles to pieces the moment Moscow withdraws its financial support.

During the two Congresses held in July, 1921, the friends and comrades of Maria Spiridonova circulated a manifesto which had been sent by them to the Central Committee of the Communist Party and to the main representatives of the Government, calling attention to the condition of Spiridonova and demanding her release for the purpose of adequate medical treatment and care.

A prominent foreign woman delegate to the Third Congress of the Communist International was approached. She promised to see Trotsky, and later it was reported that he had said that Spiridonova was "still too dangerous to be liberated." It was only after accounts of her condition had appeared in the European Socialist press that she was released, on condition that she return to prison on her recovery. Her friends in whose care she is at present face the alternative of letting Spiridonova die or turning her over to the Tcheka.

Chapter 30: Education And Culture

The proudest claims of the Bolsheviki are education, art, and culture. Communist propaganda literature and Bolshevik agents at home and abroad constantly sing the praises of these great achievements.

To the casual observer it may indeed appear that the Bolsheviki have accomplished wonders in this field. They have organized more schools than existed under the Tsar, and they have made them accessible to the masses. This is true of the larger cities. But in the provinces the existing schools met the opposition of the local Bolsheviki, who closed most of them on the alleged ground of counter-revolutionary activities, or because of lack of Communist teachers. While, then, in the large centres the percentage of children attending schools and the number of higher educational institutions is greater than in the past, the same does not apply to the rest of Russia. Still, so far as quantity is concerned, the Bolsheviki deserve credit for their educational work and the general diffusion of education.

In the case of the theatres no reservations have been made. All were permitted to continue their performances when factories were shut down for want of fuel. The opera, ballet, and Lunacharsky's plays were elaborately staged, and the *Proletcult*—organized to advance proletarian culture—was generously subsidized even when the famine was at its height. It is also true that the Government printing presses were kept busy day and night manufacturing propaganda literature and issuing the old classics. At the same time the imagists and futurists gathered unmolested in Café Domino and other places. The palaces and museums were kept up in admirable condition. In any other starved, blockaded, and attacked country all this would have been a very commendable showing.

In Russia, however, two revolutions had taken place. To be sure, the February Revolution was not far-reaching. Still, it brought about political changes without which there might not have been an October. It also released great cultural forces from the prisons and Siberia, a valuable element without which the educational work of the Bolsheviki could not have been undertaken.

It was the October Revolution which struck deepest into the vitals of Russia. It uprooted the old values and cleared the ground for new conceptions and forms of life. Inasmuch as the Bolsheviki became the sole medium of articulating and interpreting the promise of the Revolution, the earnest student will not be content merely with the increase of schools, the continuation of the ballet, or the good condition of the museums. He will want to know whether education, culture, and art in Bolshevik Russia symbolize the spirit of the Revolution, whether they serve to quicken the imagination and broaden the horizon; above all, whether they have released and helped to apply the latent qualities of the masses.

Critical inquiry in Russia is a dangerous thing. No wonder so many newcomers avoided looking beneath the surface. To them it was enough that the Montessori system, the educational ideas of Professor Dewey, and dancing by the Dalcroze method have been "adopted" by Russia. I do not contend against these innovations. But I insist that they have no bearing whatever on the Revolution; they do not prove that the Bolshevik educational experiment is superior to similar efforts in other countries, where they have been achieved without a revolution and the terrible price it involves.

State monopoly of thought is everywhere interpreting education to suit its own purpose. Similarly the Bolsheviki, to whom the State is supreme, use education to further their own ends. But while the monopoly of thought in other countries has not succeeded in entirely checking the spirit of free inquiry and critical analysis, the "proletarian dictatorship" has completely paralysed every attempt at independent investigation. The Communist criterion is dominant. The least divergence from official dogma and opinion on the part of teachers, educators, or pupils exposes them to the general charge of counter-revolution, resulting in discharge and expulsion, if nothing more drastic.

In a previous chapter I have mentioned the case of the Moscow University students expelled and exiled for protesting against Tcheka violence toward the political prisoners in the Butyrki. But it was not only such "political" offences that were punished. Offences of a purely academic nature were treated in the same manner. Thus the objection of some professors to Communist interference in the methods of instruction was sternly suppressed. Teachers and students who supported the professors were severely punished. I know a professor of sociology and literature, a brilliant scholar and a Revolutionist, who was discharged from the Moscow University because, as an Anarchist, he encouraged the critical faculty of his pupils. He is but one instance of the numerous cases of non-Communist intellectuals who, under one pretext or another, are systematically hounded and finally eliminated from Bolshevik institutions. The Communist "cells" in control of every classroom have created an atmosphere of distrust and suspicion in which real education cannot thrive.

It is true that the Bolsheviki have striven to carry education and culture into the Red Army and the villages. But here again the same conditions prevail. Communism is the State religion and, like all religions, it discourages the critical attitude and frowns upon independent inquiry. Yet without the capacity for parallelism and opportunity for verification education is valueless.

The *Proletcult* is the pet child of the Bolsheviki. Like most parents, they claim for their offspring extraordinary talents. They hold it up as the great genius who is destined to enrich the world with new values. Henceforth the masses shall no longer drink from the poisonous well of bourgeois culture. Out of their own creative impulse and through their own efforts the proletariat shall bring forth great treasures in literature, art, and music. But like most child prodigies, the *Proletcult* did not live up to its early promise. Before long it proved itself below the average, incapable of innovation, lacking originality, and without sustaining power. Already in 1920 I was told by two of the foremost foster-fathers of the *Proletcult*, Gorki and Lunacharsky, that it was a failure.

In Petrograd, Moscow, and throughout my travels I had occasion to study the efforts of the *Proletcult*. Whether expressed in printed form, on the stage, in clay or colour, they were barren of ideas or vision, and showed not a trace of the inner urge which impels creative art. They were hopelessly commonplace. I do not doubt that the masses will some day create a new culture, new art values, new forms of beauty. But these will come to life from the inner necessity of the people themselves, and not through an arbitrary will imposed upon them.

The mechanistic approach to art and culture and the *idée fixe* that nothing must express itself outside of the channels of the State have stultified the cultural and artistic expression of the Russian people. In poetry and literature, in drama, painting, and music not a single epic of the Revolution has been produced during five years. This is the more remarkable when one bears in mind how rich Russia was in works of art and how close her writers and poets were to the soul of the Russian people. Yet in the greatest upheaval in the world's history no one has come forward with pen or brush or lyre to give artistic expression to the miracle or to set to music the storm that carried the Russian people forward. Works of art, like new-born man, come in pain and travail. Verily the five years of Revolution should have proved very rich spiritually and creatively. For in those years the soul of Russia has gone through a thousand crucifixions. Yet in this regard Russia was never before so poor and desolate.

The Bolsheviki claim that a revolutionary period is not conducive to creative art. That contention is not borne out by the French Revolution. To mention only the Marseillaise, the great music of which lives and will live. The French Revolution was rich in spiritual effort, in poetry, painting, science, and in its great literature and letters. But, then, the French Revolution was never so completely in the bondage of one dogmatic idea as has been the case with Russia. The Jacobins indeed strove hard to fetter the spirit of the French Revolution and they paid dearly for it. The Bolsheviki have been copying the destructive phases of the French Revolution. But they have done nothing that can compare with the constructive achievements of that period.

I have said that nothing outstanding has been created in Russia. To be exact, I must except the great revolutionary poem, "Twelve," by Alexander Blok. But even that gifted genius, deeply inspired by the

Revolution, and imbued with the fire that had come to purify all life, soon ceased to create. His experience with the Tcheka (he was arrested in 1919), the terrorism all about him, the senseless waste of life and energy, the suffering and hopelessness of it all depressed his spirit and broke his health. Soon Alexander Blok was no more.

Even a Blok could not create with an iron band compressing his brain—the iron band of Bolshevik distrust, persecution, and censorship. How far-reaching the latter was I realized from a document the Museum Expedition had discovered in Vologda. It was a "very confidential, secret" order issued in 1920 and signed by Ulyanova, the sister of Lenin and chief of the Central Educational Department. It directed the libraries throughout Russia to "eliminate" all non-Communist literature, except the Bible, the Koran, and the classics, including even Communistic writings dealing with problems which were being "solved in a different way" by the existing régime. The condemned literature was to be sent to paper mills "because of the scarcity of paper."

Such edicts and the State monopoly of all material, printing machinery, and mediums of circulation exclude every possibility of the birth of creative work. The editor of a little coöperative paper published a brilliant poem, unsigned. It was the cry of a tortured poet's soul in protest against the continued terror. The editor was promptly arrested and his little shop closed. The author would probably have been shot had his whereabouts been known. No doubt there are many agonized cries in Russia, but they are muffled cries. No one may hear them or interpret their meaning. The future alone has the key to the cultural and artistic treasures now hidden from the Argus eyes of the Department of Education and the numerous other censorial institutions.

Russia is now the dumping ground for mediocrities in art and culture. They fit into the narrow groove, they dance attendance on the all-powerful political commissars. They live in the Kremlin and skim the cream of life, while the real poets—like Blok and others—die of want and despair.

The void in literature, poetry, and art is felt most in the theatres, the State theatres especially. I once sat through five hours of acting in the Alexandrovsky Theatre in Petrograd when "Othello" was staged, with Andreyeva, Gorki's wife, as Desdemona. It is hard to imagine a play more atrociously presented. I saw most of the other plays in the

State theatre and not one of them gave any hint of the earthquake that had shaken Russia. There was no new note in interpretation, scenery, or method. It was all commonplace and inadequate, innocent even of the advancement made in dramatic art in bourgeois countries, and utterly inconsequential in the light of the Revolution.

The only exception was the Moscow Art Theatre. Its performance of Gorki's "Night's Lodging" was especially powerful. Real art was also presented in the Stanislavsky Studio. These were the only oases in the art desert of Russia. But even the Art Theatre showed no trace of the great revolutionary events Russia was living through. The repertoire which had made the Art Theatre famous a quarter of a century before still continued night after night. There were no new Ibsens, Tolstois, or Tchekovs to thunder their protest against the new evils, and if there had been no theatre could have staged them. It was safer to interpret the past than to voice the present. Yet, though the Art Theatre kept strictly within the past, Stanislavsky was often in difficulties with the authorities. He had suffered arrest and was once evicted from his studio. He had just moved into a new place when I visited him with Louise Bryant who had asked me to act as her interpreter. Stanislavsky looked forlorn and discouraged among his still unpacked boxes of stage property. I saw him also on several other occasions and found him almost hopeless about the future of the theatre in Russia. "The theatre can grow only through inspiration from new works of art," he would say; "without it the interpretive artist must stagnate and the theatre deteriorate." But Stanislavsky himself was top much the creative artist to stagnate. He sought other forms of interpretation. His newest venture was an attempt to bring singing and dramatic acting into coöperative harmony. I attended a dress rehearsal of such a performance and found it very impressive. The effect of the voice was greatly enhanced by the realistic finesse which Stanislavsky achieved in dramatic art. But these efforts were entirely the work of himself and his little circle of art students; they had nothing to do with the Bolsheviki of the *Proletcult*.

There are some other innovations, begun long before the advent of the Bolsheviki and permitted by them to continue because they have no bearing on the Russian actuality. The Kamerney Theatre registers its revolt against the imposition of the play upon the acting, against the limitation of expression involved in the orthodox interpretation of dramatic art. It achieves noteworthy results by the new mode of acting, complemented by original scenery and music, but mostly in plays of a lighter genre.

Another unique attempt is essayed by the Semperante Theatre. It is based on the conception that the written drama checks the growth and diversity of the interpretive artist. Plays should therefore be improvised, thereby affording greater scope to spontaneity, inspiration, and mood of the artist. It is a novel experiment, but as the improvised plays must also keep within the limits of the State censorship, the work of the Semperantists suffers from a lack of ideas.

The most interesting cultural endeavour I met in Kiev was the work of the Jewish *Kulturliga*. Its nucleus was organized in 1918 to minister to the needs of pogrom victims. They had to be provided for, sheltered, fed, and clothed. Young Jewish literary men and an able organizer brought the *Kulturliga* to life. They did not content themselves with ministering only to the physical needs of the unfortunates. They organized children's homes, public schools, high schools, evening classes; later a seminary and art school were added. When we visited Kiev the *Kulturliga* owned a printing plant and a studio, besides its other educational institutions, and had succeeded in organizing 230 branches in the Ukraina. At a literary evening and a special performance arranged in honour of the Expedition we were able to witness the extraordinary achievements of the, *Kulturliga*.

At the literary evening Perez's poem "The Four Seasons" was rendered by recitative group singing. The effect was striking. Nature at the birth of spring, birds sending forth their joyous song of love, the mystery and romance of mating, the ecstasy of renewing and becoming, the rumbling of the approaching storm, the crash of the mighty giants struck by lightning, rain softly falling, the leaves fluttering to earth, the somberness and pathos of autumn, the last desperate resistance of Nature against death, the trees shrouded in white—all were made vivid and alive by the new form of collective recitative. Every nuance of Nature was brought out by the group of artists on the improvised little stage of the *Kulturliga*.

The next day we visited the art school. The children's classes were the more interesting. There was no discipline, no rigid rules, no mechanistic control of their art impulses. The children did drawing, painting, and modeling—mostly Jewish motifs: a pogromed city, by a boy of fourteen; a devout Jew in his tales praying in the synagogue, mortal fear of the pogrom savages written in his every feature; an old

Jewish woman, the tragic remnant of a whole family slaughtered; and similar scenes from the life of the Russian Jew. The efforts were often crude, but there was about them nothing of the stilted manner characteristic of the *Proletcult*. There was no attempt to impose a definite formula on art expression.

Later we attended the studio. In a bare room, without scenery, lighting, costumes, or make-up, the artists of the *Kulturliga* gave several one-act plays and presented also an unpublished work found among the effects of a playwright. The performance had an artistic touch and finish I had rarely seen before. The play is called "The End of the World." The wrath of God rolls like thunder across the world, commanding man to prepare for the end. Yet man heeds not. Then all the elements are let loose, pursuing one another in wild fury; the storm rages and shrieks, and man's groans are drowned in the terrific hour of judgment. The world goes under, and all is dead.

Then something begins to move again. Black shadows symbolizing half beast, half man, with distorted faces and hesitating movements, crouch out of their caves. In awe and fear they stretch their trembling hands toward one another. Haltingly at first, then with growing confidence, man attempts in common effort with his follows to lift himself out of the black void. Light begins to break. Again a thunderous voice rolls over the earth. It is the voice of fulfillment.

It was a stirring artistic achievement.

When the Liga was first organized the Bolsheviki subsidized its work. Later, when they returned to Kiev after its evacuation by Denikin, they gave very scanty support to the educational institutions of the *Kulturliga*. This unfriendly attitude was due to the *Yevkom*, the Jewish Communist Section, which intrigues against every independent Jewish cultural endeavour. When we left Kiev the ardent workers of the Liga were much worried about the future of the organization. I am not in a position to say at this writing whether the *Liga* was able to continue its work or was closed altogether. However, laudable as were the innovations of the *Kulturliga* and the attempts of the Kamerney and Semperante at new modes of expression, they could not be considered as having any bearing on the Revolution.

State support to so-called art is given mostly to Lunacharsky's dramatic ventures and other Communist interpretations of culture.

When I first met Lunacharsky I thought him much less the politician than the artist. I heard him lecture at the Sverdlov University before a large audience of workingmen and women, popularizing the origin and development of art. It was done splendidly. When I met him again he was so thoroughly in the meshes of Party discipline and so completely shorn of his power that every effort of his was frustrated. Then he began to write plays. That was his undoing. He could not employ the material of the actual reality, and the February Revolution, Kerensky, and the Constituent Assembly had already been caricatured to a thread. Lunacharsky turned to the German Revolution. He wrote "The Smith and the Councillor," a sort of burlesque. The play is so amateurish and commonplace that no theatre outside of Russia would have cared to present it. But Lunacharsky was in control of the theatres — why not exploit them for his own works? The play was staged at great cost, at a time when millions on the Volga were starving. But even that could have been forgiven if the play had any meaning or contained anything suggestive of the tragedy of Russia. Instead, it lacked all life and was rich only in vulgar scenes portraying Ludendorff, the renegade Social Democratic President, a degenerate aristocrat, and a princess of the demimonde. The drunken men frantically scramble for the possession of the woman, literally tearing her clothing off her back. A revolting scene, yet in the whole audience of teachers and members of the Department of Education not a single protest was voiced against the affront to the taste and intelligence of revolutionary Russia. On the contrary, they applauded the playwright, for those sycophants depended on Lunacharsky for their rations. They could not afford to be critical.

Vanity and power break the strongest character, and Lunacharsky is not strong. It is his lack of will which makes him submit against his better judgment, to the galling discipline and espionage placed over him. Perhaps he avenges himself by forcing upon the public at large and the actors under his charge his dramatic works.

After a careful analysis of the educational and cultural efforts of the Bolsheviki the earnest student will come to the following conclusions: first, there is quantity rather than substance in the education of Russia to-day; secondly, the theatres, the ballet, and the museums receive generous support from the Government, but the reason for it is not so much love of art as the necessity of finding some outlet for the checked and stifled aspirations of the people.

The political dictatorship of the Bolsheviki with one stroke suppressed the social phase of life in Russia. There was no forum even for the most inoffensive social intercourse, no clubs, no meeting places, no restaurants, not even a dance hall. I remember the shocked expression of Zorin when I asked him if the young people could not occasionally meet for a dance free from Communist supervision. "Dance halls are gathering places for counter-revolutionists; we closed them," he informed me. The emotional and human needs of the people were considered dangerous to the régime.

On the other hand, the dreadful existence—hunger, cold, and darkness—was sapping the life of the people. Gloom and despair by day, congestion, lack of light and heat at night, and no escape from it all. There was, of course, the political life of the Communist Party—a life stern and forbidding, a life without colour or warmth. The masses had no contact with or interest in that life, and they were not permitted to have anything of their own. A people bottled up is a menace. Some outlet had to be provided, some relief from the black despair. The theatre, the opera, and the museum were that relief. What if the theatres gave nothing new? What if the opera had bad singing? And the ballet continued to move in the old toe circles? The places were warm; they had light. They furnished the opportunity for human association and one could forget the misery and loneliness— one might even forget the Tcheka. The theatre, the opera, the ballet, and the museum became the safety valve of the Bolshevik régime. And as the theatres gave nothing of protest, nothing new or vital, they were permitted to continue. They solved a great and difficult problem and furnished excellent copy for foreign propaganda.

Chapter 31: Exploiting The Famine

Late in the summer of 1921 there came the harrowing news of the famine. To those who had kept in touch with inner affairs the information was not quite unexpected. We had learned during the early part of the summer that a large proportion of the population was doomed to death from starvation. At that time a group of scientific agriculturists had assembled in Moscow. Their report showed that, owing to bureaucratic centralization, and corruption and delay in seed distribution, timely and sufficient sowing had been prevented. The Soviet press kept the report of the agricultural conference from the public. But in July items began to appear in the *Pravda* and the *Izvestia* telling of the terrible drought in the Volga region and the fearful conditions in the famine-stricken districts.

Immediately various groups and individuals came forward ready to coöperate with the Government in coping with the calamity. The Left Wing elements — Anarchists, Social Revolutionists, and Maximalists — offered to organize relief work and to collect funds. But they received no encouragement from the Soviet authorities. On the other hand, elements of the Right, the Cadets (Constitutional Democrats), were received with open arms. Kishkin, Minister of Finance under Kerensky, Kuskova, Prokopovitch, and other prominent Conservatives, who had bitterly fought the Revolution, were accepted by the Bolsheviki. These people had been denounced as counter-revolutionists and repeatedly arrested and imprisoned, yet they were given preference and permitted to organize the group known as the Citizens' Committee. When the latter refused to work under the guardianship of the Moscow Soviet, insisting upon complete autonomy and the right to publish its own paper, the Government consented. Such discrimination in favour of reactionaries as against those who had faithfully stood by the Revolution could be explained only in two ways. First, the Bolsheviki considered it dangerous to grant the Left elements free access to the peasantry; secondly, it was necessary to make an impression on Europe, which could be effectively done by means of the conservative group. This became clear before the Citizens' Committee began its relief work.

In the beginning the Committee received the entire support of the Government. A special building was assigned for its headquarters and it was granted the right to issue its own paper, called *Pomoshtch* (Succour). Members of the Committee were also promised permission to go to Western Europe for the purpose of arousing interest and getting support for the famine stricken. Two numbers of the paper were issued. Its appearance caused significant comment: it was an exact reproduction, in size, type, and general form, of the old *Vyedomosti*, the most reactionary sheet under the former regime. The publication was, of course, very guarded in its tone.; But between the lines one could read its antagonism to the ruling Party. Its first issue contained a letter from the Metropolitan *Tikhon*, wherein he commanded the faithful to send their contributions to him. He assured his flock that he was to have complete control of the distribution of the donations. The Citizens' Committee was, given carte blanche in carrying on its work, and the fact was heralded by the Bolsheviki as proof of their liberality and willingness to coöperate with all elements in famine relief.

Presently the Soviet Government entered into an agreement with the American Relief Administration and other European organizations regarding aid for the Volga sufferers, and then the headquarters of the Citizens' Committee were raided, the paper suppressed, and the leading members of the Committee thrown into the Tcheka on the usual charge of counterrevolution. Now it was reasonably certain that Mme. Kuskova and her co-workers were no more counter-revolutionary when they were permitted to organize Volga relief than they had been at any time since 1917. Why, then, did the Communist State accept them while rejecting the assistance of true revolutionists? For no other reason than propaganda purposes. When the Citizens' Committee had served that purpose it was kicked overboard in true Bolshevik fashion. Only one person the Tcheka dared not touch—Vera Nikolayevna Figner, the venerable revolutionist. Great humanitarian that she is, she joined the Citizens' Committee and devoted herself to its work with the same zeal that had made her so effective as one of the leading spirits of the Narodnaya Volya. Twenty-two years of living death in Schlüsselburg had failed to destroy her ardour. When the Citizens' Committee was arrested, Vera Nikolayevna demanded to share the same fate, but the Tcheka knew the spiritual influence of this woman in Russia and abroad, and she was left in peace. The other members of the Citizens' Committee were kept in prison for a long time, then exiled to remote parts of Russia and finally deported.

Except for the foreign organizations doing relief work in Russia, the Soviet Government could now stand before the world as the sole dispenser of support to the starving in the famine district. Kalinin, the marionette President of the Socialist Republic, equipped with much propaganda literature and surrounded by a large staff of Soviet officials and foreign correspondents, made his triumphal march through the stricken territory. It was widely heralded throughout the world, and the desired effect was achieved. But the real work in the famine region was carried on not so much by the official machine as by the great host of unknown men and women from the ranks of the proletariat and the intelligentsia. Most devotedly and with utter consecration they gave of their own depleted energies. Many of them perished from typhus, exposure, and exhaustion; some were slain by the power of darkness which now, even more than in Tolstoi's time, holds many sections of Russia in its grip. Doctors, nurses, and relief workers were often killed by the unfortunates they had come to aid, as evil spirits who had willed the famine and the misfortunes of Russia. These were the real heroes and martyrs, unknown and unsung.

Chapter 32: The Socialist Republic Resorts To Deportation

The Tcheka had succeeded in terrorizing the whole people. The only exceptions were the politicals, whose courage and devotion to their ideals defied the Bolsheviki as it had the Romanovs. I knew many of those brave spirits, and I saw in them the only hope to sustain one amid the general wreckage. They were the living proof of the powerlessness of terror against an Ideal.

Typical of this class was a certain Anarchist who had long been sought for by the Tcheka as an important Makhnovetz. He was a member of the military staff of the revolutionary *povstantsi* of the Ukraina and the close friend and counsellor of Makhno. He had already known him intimately when they were together in *katorga* in the days of the Tsar. He had shared all the hardships and danger of the *povstantsi* life and participated in their campaigns against the enemies of the Revolution. After the defeat of Wrangel and the last treachery of the Bolsheviki toward Makhno, when the latter's army had become scattered and many of its members killed, this man succeeded in escaping the Bolshevik net. He determined to come to Moscow, there to write a history of *Makhnovstchina*. It was a perilous journey, made under most difficult conditions, with death constantly treading his footsteps. Under an assumed name he secured a tiny room in the environs of the capital. He lived in most abject poverty, always in danger of his life, visiting his wife in the city only under cover of darkness. Once in every twenty four hours he would come to the appointed place for a little respite and his sole meal of the day, consisting of potatoes, herring, and tea. Every moment he risked being recognized, for he was well known in Moscow, and recognition meant summary execution. His wife also, if discovered, would have met the same fate — the devoted woman who, though with child at the time, had followed him to Moscow. After a desperate hunt for employment she found a position in a créche, but as pregnant women were not accepted in such institutions, she had to disguise her condition. All day long she had to be on her feet, attending to her duties, and living in constant fear for the safety of her husband.

When the baby was born the situation became more aggravated. The woman was harassed by her superiors because she had obtained the position without their knowledge of her condition. Petty officialdom and hard work exhausted her energies and the daily anxiety about the man she loved nearly drove her frantic. Yet never a sign of all that troubled her when the man would visit her.

Many evenings I spent with this couple. They were entirely cut off from the outside world and former friends, all alone save for the fear of discovery and death which was their constant companion. In the dreary, damp room, the baby asleep, we passed many hours talking in subdued voices about the Ukrainian peasantry and the Makhno movement. My friend was familiar with every phase of it from personal experience, which he was now incorporating into his book on Makhno. He was absorbed in that work, which was for the first time to give to the world the truth about Makhno and the *povstantsi*. Deeply concerned about his wife and child, he was entirely oblivious to his own safety, though knowing that every day the Tcheka net was drawn closer about him. With great difficulty he was finally prevailed upon to leave his beloved Russia, as the only way of saving his family. What a commentary on the Socialist Republic, whose bravest and truest sons must keep in hiding or forsake their native soil!

Life in Russia had become to me a constant torture; the need of breaking my two years' silence was imperative. During all the summer I was in the throes of a bitter conflict between the necessity of leaving and my inability to tear myself away from what had been an ideal to me. It was like the tragic end of a great love to which one clings long after it is no more.

In the midst of my struggle there happened an event which further served to demonstrate the complete collapse of the Bolsheviki as revolutionists. It was the announcement of the return to Russia of the Tsarist General Slastchev, one of the most reactionary and brutal militarists of the old régime. He had fought against the Revolution from its very beginning and had led some of the Wrangel forces in the Crimea. He was guilty of fiendish barbarities to war prisoners and infamous as a maker of pogroms. Now Slastchev recanted and was returning to "his Fatherland." This arch counter-revolutionist and Jew-baiter, together with several other Tsarist generals and White guardists, was received by the Bolsheviki with military honours. No doubt it was just retribution that the anti-Semite had to salute the Jew Trotsky, his military superior. But to the Revolution and the Russian people the triumphal return of the imperialists was an outrage.

The old general had changed his colours but not his nature. In his letter to the officers and men of the Wrangel Army he delivered himself of the following:

> I, Slastchev Krimsky, command you to return to your Fatherland and into the fold of the Red Army. Our country needs our defense against her enemies. I command you to return.

As a reward for his newly fledged love of the Socialist Fatherland, Slastchev Krimsky was commissioned to quell the Karelian peasants who demanded self-determination, and Slastchev had the opportunity of giving full play to the autocratic powers he was vested with.

Military receptions and honours for the man who had been foremost in the attempt to crush the Revolution, and imprisonment or death for the lovers of liberty. At the same time the true sons of Russia, who had defended the Revolution against every attack and had aided the Bolsheviki to political power, were made homeless by deportation to foreign lands. A more tragic débâcle history has never before witnessed. The first to be deported by the "revolutionary" Government were ten Anarchists, most of them known in the international revolutionary movement as tried idealists and martyrs for their cause. Among them was Volin, a highly cultured man, a gifted writer and lecturer, who had been editor of various Anarchist publications in Europe and America. In Russia, where he returned in 1917, he helped to organize the Ukrainian Confederation of *Nabat* and was for a time lecturer for the Soviet Department of Education in Kharkov. Volin had been a member of an Anarchist partisan military unit that fought against Austro-German occupation, and for a considerable time he also conducted educational and cultural work in the Makhno Army. During the year 1921 he was imprisoned by the Bolsheviki and deported after the hunger strike of the Taganka Anarchists which lasted ten and a half days.

In the same group was G. Maximoff, an Anarchist of many years' standing. Before the Revolution he had been active among the students of the Petrograd University and also among the peasants. He participated in all the revolutionary struggles beginning with the February Revolution, was one of the editors of *Golos Truda* and member of the All-Russian Secretariat of Anarcho-syndicalists. He is an able and popular writer and lecturer.

Mark Mratchny, another of the deported, has been an Anarchist since 1907. At the time when Hetman Skoropadsky ruled Ukraina with the help of German bayonets, Mratchny was a member of the Revolutionary Bureau of the students of Kharkov. He held the position of instructor in the Soviet School Department of Kharkov, and later in Siberia. He edited the *Nabat* during the period of agreement between Makhno and the Bolsheviki, and was later arrested together with the other Anarchists who had come to Kharkov for the Anarchist Conference.

Among the deported was also Yartchuk, famous as one of the leaders of the Kronstadt sailors in the uprising of July, 1917, a man who enjoyed exceptional influence among the sailors and workers and whose idealism and devotion are matters of historic record. In the group there were also several students — mere youths who had participated in the Anarchist hunger strike in the Taganka prison.

To remain longer in Bolshevik Russia had become unbearable. I was compelled to speak out, and decided to leave the country. Friends were making arrangements to open a sub rosa passage abroad, but just as all preparations were completed we were informed of new developments. Berlin Anarchists had made a demand upon the Soviet Government that passports be issued for Alexander

Berkman, A. Shapiro, and myself, to enable us to attend the International Anarchist Congress which was to convene in Berlin in December, 1921. Whether due to that demand or for other reasons, the Soviet Government finally issued the required papers and on December 1, 1921, I left Russia in the company of Alexander Berkman and A. Shapiro. It was just one year and eleven months since I had set foot on what I believed to be the promised land. My heart was heavy with the tragedy of Russia. One thought stood out in bold relief: I must raise my voice against the crimes committed in the name of the Revolution. I would be heard regardless of friend or foe.

Afterword

Non-Bolshevik Socialist critics of the Russian failure contend that the Revolution could not have succeeded in Russia because industrial conditions had not reached the necessary climax in that country. They point to Marx, who taught that a social revolution is possible only in countries with a highly developed industrial system and its attendant social antagonisms. They therefore claim that the Russian Revolution could not be a social revolution, and that historically it had to evolve along constitutional, democratic lines, complemented by a growing industry, in order to ripen the country economically for the basic change.

This orthodox Marxian view leaves an important factor out of consideration—a factor perhaps more vital to the possibility and success of a social revolution than even the industrial element. That is the psychology of the masses at a given period. Why is there, for instance, no social revolution in the United States, France, or even in Germany? Surely these countries have reached the industrial development set by Marx as the culminating stage. The truth is that industrial development and sharp social contrasts are of themselves by no means sufficient to give birth to a new society or to call forth a social revolution. The necessary social consciousness, the required mass psychology, is missing in such countries as the United States and the others mentioned. That explains why no social revolution has taken place there.

In this regard Russia had the advantage of other more industrialized and "civilized" lands. It is true that Russia was not as advanced industrially as her Western neighbours. But the Russian mass psychology, inspired and intensified by the February Revolution, was ripening at so fast a pace that within a few months the people were ready for such ultra-revolutionary slogans as "All power to the Soviets" and "The land to the peasants, the factories to the workers."

The significance of these slogans should not be under-estimated. Expressing in a large degree the instinctive and semi-conscious will of the people, they yet signified the complete social, economic, and industrial reorganization of Russia. What country in Europe or America is prepared to interpret such revolutionary mottoes into life? Yet in Russia, in the months of June and July, 1917, these slogans became popular and were enthusiastically and actively taken up, in. the form of direct action, by the bulk of the industrial and agrarian population of more than 150 millions. That was sufficient proof of the "ripeness" of the Russian people for the social revolution.

As to economic "preparedness" in the Marxian sense, it must not be forgotten that Russia is preëminently an agrarian country. Marx's dictum presupposes the industrialization of the peasant and farmer population in every highly developed society, as a step toward social fitness for revolution. But events in Russia, in 1917, demonstrated that revolution does not await this process of industrialization and — what is more important — cannot be made to wait. The Russian peasants began to expropriate the landlords and the workers took possession of the factories without taking cognizance of Marxian dicta. This popular action, by virtue of its own logic, ushered in the social revolution in Russia, upsetting all Marxian calculations. The psychology of the Slav proved stronger than social democratic theories.

That psychology involved the passionate yearning for liberty nurtured by a century of revolutionary agitation among all classes of society. The Russian people had fortunately remained politically unsophisticated and untouched by the corruption and confusion created among the proletariat of other countries by "democratic" liberty and self-government. The Russian remained, in this sense, natural and simple, unfamiliar with the subtleties of politics, of parliamentary trickery, and legal makeshifts. On the other hand, his primitive sense of justice and right was strong and vital, without the disintegrating finesse of pseudo-civilization. He knew what he wanted and he did not wait for "historic inevitability" to bring it to him: he employed direct action. The Revolution to him was a fact of life, not a mere theory for discussion.

Thus the social revolution took place in Russia in spite of the industrial backwardness of the country. But to make the Revolution was not enough. It was necessary for it to advance and broaden, to develop into economic and social reconstruction. That phase of the Revolution necessitated fullest play of personal initiative and collective effort. The development and success of the Revolution depended on the broadest exercise of the creative genius of the people, on the coöperation of the intellectual and manual proletariat. Common interest is the leit motif of all revolutionary endeavour, especially on its constructive side. This spirit of mutual purpose and solidarity swept Russia with a mighty wave in the first days of the October-November Revolution. Inherent in that enthusiasm were forces that could have moved mountains if intelligently guided by exclusive consideration for the well-being of the whole people. The medium for such effective guidance was on hand: the labour organizations and the coöperatives with which Russia was covered as with a network of bridges combining the city with the country; the Soviets which sprang into being responsive to the needs of the Russian people; and, finally, the intelligentsia whose traditions for a century expressed heroic devotion to the cause of Russia's emancipation.

But such a development was by no means within the programme of the Bolsheviki. For several months following October they suffered the popular forces to manifest themselves, the people carrying the Revolution into ever-widening channels. But as soon as the Communist Party felt itself sufficiently strong in the government saddle, it began to limit the scope of popular activity. All the succeeding acts of the Bolsheviki, all their following policies, changes of policies, their compromises and retreats, their methods of suppression and persecution, their terrorism and extermination of all other political views — all were but the means to an end: the retaining of the State power in the hands of the Communist Party. Indeed, the Bolsheviki themselves (in Russia) made no secret of it. The

Communist Party, they contended, is the advance guard of the proletariat, and the dictatorship must rest in its hands. Alas, the Bolsheviki reckoned without their host—without the peasantry, whom neither the *razvyoriska*, the Tcheka, nor the wholesale shooting could persuade to support the Bolshevik régime. The peasantry became the rock upon which the best-laid plans and schemes of Lenin were wrecked. But Lenin, a nimble acrobat, was skilled in performing within the narrowest margin. The new economic policy was introduced just in time to ward off the disaster which was slowly but surely overtaking the whole Communist edifice.

II

The "new economic policy" came as a surprise and a shock to most Communists. They saw in it a reversal of everything that their Party had been proclaiming—a reversal of Communism itself. In protest some of the oldest members of the Party, men who had faced danger and persecution under the old régime while Lenin and Trotsky lived abroad in safety, left the Communist Party embittered and disappointed. The leaders then declared a lockout. They ordered the clearing of the Party ranks of all "doubtful " elements. Everybody suspected of an independent attitude and those who did not accept the new economic policy as the last word in revolutionary wisdom were expelled. Among them were Communists who for years had rendered most devoted service. Some of them, hurt to the quick by the unjust and brutal procedure, and shaken to their depths by the collapse of what they held most high, even resorted to suicide. But the smooth sailing of Lenin's new gospel had to be assured, the gospel of the sanctity of private property and the freedom of cutthroat competition erected upon the ruins of four years of revolution.

However, Communist indignation over the new economic policy merely indicated the confusion of mind on the part of Lenin's opponents. What else but mental confusion could approve of the numerous acrobatic political stunts of Lenin and yet grow indignant at the final somersault, its logical culmination? The trouble with the devout Communists was that they clung to the Immaculate Conception of the Communist State which by the aid of the Revolution was to redeem the world. But most of the leading Communists never entertained such a delusion. Least of all Lenin.

During my first interview I received the impression that he was a shrewd politician who knew exactly what he was about and that he would stop at nothing to achieve his ends. After hearing him speak on several occasions and reading his works I became convinced that Lenin had very little concern in the Revolution and that Communism to him was a very remote thing. The centralized political State was Lenin's deity, to which everything else was to be sacrificed. Someone said that Lenin would sacrifice the Revolution to save Russia. Lenin's policies, however, have proven that he was willing to sacrifice both the Revolution and the country, or at least part of the latter, in order to realize his political scheme with what was left of Russia.

Lenin was the most pliable politician in history. He could be an ultra-revolutionary, a compromiser and conservative at the same time. When like a mighty wave the cry swept over Russia, "All power to the Soviets! " Lenin swam with the tide. When the peasants took possession of the land and the workers of the factories, Lenin not only approved of those direct methods but went further. He issued the famous motto, "Rob the robbers," a slogan which served to confuse the minds of the people and caused untold injury to revolutionary idealism. Never before did any real revolutionist interpret social expropriation as the transfer of wealth from one set of individuals to another. Yet that was exactly what Lenin's slogan meant. The indiscriminate and irresponsible raids, the accumulation of the wealth of the former bourgeoisie by the new Soviet bureaucracy, the chicanery practised toward those whose only crime was their former status, were all the results of Lenin's "Rob the robbers" policy. The whole subsequent history of the Revolution is a kaleidoscope of Lenin's compromises and betrayal of his own slogans.

Bolshevik acts and methods since the October days may seem to contradict the new economic policy. But in reality they are links in the chain which was to forge the all-powerful, centralized Government with State Capitalism as its economic expression. Lenin possessed clarity of vision and an iron will. He knew how to make his comrades in Russia and outside of it believe that his scheme was true Socialism and his methods the revolution. No wonder that Lenin felt such contempt for his flock, which he never hesitated to fling into their faces. "Only fools can believe that Communism is possible in Russia now," was Lenin's reply to the opponents of the new economic policy.

As a matter of fact, Lenin was right. True Communism was never attempted in Russia, unless one considers thirty-three categories of pay, different food rations, privileges to some and indifference to the great mass as Communism.

In the early period of the Revolution it was comparatively easy for the Communist Party to possess itself of power. All the revolutionary elements, carried away by the ultra-revolutionary promises of the Bolsheviki, helped the latter to power. Once in possession of the State the Communists began their process of elimination. All the political parties and groups which refused to submit to the new dictatorship had to go. First the Anarchists and Left Social Revolutionists, then the Mensheviki and other opponents from the Right, and finally everybody who dared aspire to an opinion of his own. Similar was the fate of all independent organizations. They were either subordinated to the needs of the new State or destroyed altogether, as were the Soviets, the trade unions and the coöperatives — three great factors for the realization of the hopes of the Revolution.

The Soviets first manifested themselves in the revolution of 1905 They played an important part during that brief but significant period. Though the revolution was crushed, the Soviet idea remained rooted in the minds and hearts of the Russian masses. At the first dawn which illuminated Russia in February, 1917, the Soviets revived again and came into bloom in a very short time. To the people the Soviets by no means represented a curtailment of the spirit of the Revolution. On the contrary, the Revolution was to find its highest, freest practical expression through the Soviets. That was why the Soviets so spontaneously and rapidly spread throughout Russia. The Bolsheviki realized the significance of the popular trend and joined the cry. But once in control of the Government the Communists saw that the Soviets threatened the supremacy of the State. At the same time they could not destroy them arbitrarily without undermining their own prestige at home and abroad as the sponsors of the Soviet system. They began to shear them gradually of their powers and finally to subordinate them to their own needs.

The Russian trade unions were much more amenable to emasculation. Numerically and in point of revolutionary fibre they were still in their childhood. By declaring adherence to the trade unions obligatory the Russian labour organizations gained in physical stature, but mentally they remained in the infant stage. The

Communist State became the wet nurse of the trade unions. In return, the organizations served as the flunkeys of the State. "A school for Communism," said Lenin in the famous controversy on the functions of the trade unions. Quite right. But an antiquated school where the spirit of the child is fettered and crushed. Nowhere in the world are labour organizations as subservient to the will and the dictates of the State as they are in Bolshevik Russia.

The fate of the coöperatives is too well known to require elucidation. The coöperatives were the most essential link between the city and the country. Their value to the Revolution as a popular and successful medium of exchange and distribution and to the reconstruction of Russia was incalculable. The Bolsheviki transformed them into cogs of the Government machine and thereby destroyed their usefulness and efficiency.

III

It is now clear why the Russian Revolution, as conducted by the Communist Party, was a failure. The political power of the Party, organized and centralized in the State, sought to maintain itself by all means at hand. The central authorities attempted to force the activities of the people into forms corresponding with the purposes of the Party. The sole aim of the latter was to strengthen the State and monopolize all economical, political, and social activities — even all cultural manifestations. The Revolution had an entirely different object, and in its very character it was the negation of authority and centralization. It strove to open ever-larger fields for proletarian expression and to multiply the phases of individual and collective effort. The aims and tendencies of the Revolution were diametrically opposed to those of the ruling political party.

Just as diametrically opposed were the methods of the Revolution and of the State. Those of the former were inspired by the spirit of the Revolution itself: that is to say, by emancipation from all oppressive and limiting forces; in short; by libertarian principles. The methods of the State, on the contrary — of the Bolshevik State as of every government — were based on coercion, which in the course of things necessarily developed into systematic violence, oppression, and terrorism. Thus two opposing tendencies struggled for supremacy:

the Bolshevik State against the Revolution. That struggle was a life-and-death struggle. The two tendencies, contradictory in aims and methods, could not work harmoniously: the triumph of the State meant the defeat of the Revolution.

It would be an error to assume that the failure of the Revolution was due entirely to the character of the Bolsheviki. Fundamentally, it was the result of the principles and methods of Bolshevism. It was the authoritarian spirit and principles of the State which stifled the libertarian and liberating aspirations. Were any other political party in control of the government in Russia the result would have been essentially the same. It is not so much the Bolsheviki who killed the Russian Revolution as the Bolshevik idea. It was Marxism, however modified; in short, fanatical governmentalism. Only this understanding of the underlying forces that crushed the Revolution can present the true lesson of that world-stirring event. The Russian Revolution reflects on a small scale the century-old struggle of the libertarian principle against the authoritarian. For what is progress if not the more general acceptance of the principles of liberty as against those of coercion? The Russian Revolution was a libertarian step defeated by the Bolshevik State, by the temporary victory of the reactionary, the governmental idea.

That victory was due to a number of causes. Most of them have already been dealt with in the preceding chapters. The main cause, however, was not the industrial backwardness of Russia, as claimed by many writers on the subject. That cause was cultural which, though giving the Russian people certain advantages over their more sophisticated neighbours, also had some fatal disadvantages. The Russian was "culturally backward" in the sense of being unspoiled by political and parliamentary corruption. On the other hand, that very condition involved inexperience in the political game and a naive faith in the miraculous power of the party that talked the loudest and made the most promises. This faith in the power of government served to enslave the Russian people to the Communist Party even before the great masses realized that the yoke had been put around their necks.

The libertarian principle was strong in the initial days of the Revolution, the need for free expression all-absorbing. But when the first wave of enthusiasm receded into the ebb of everyday prosaic life, a firm conviction was needed to keep the fires of liberty burning.

There was only a comparative handful in the great vastness of Russia to keep those fires lit—the Anarchists, whose number was small and whose efforts, absolutely suppressed under the Tsar, had had no time to bear fruit. The Russian people, to some extent instinctive Anarchists, were yet too unfamiliar with true libertarian principles and methods to apply them effectively to life. Most of the Russian Anarchists themselves were unfortunately still in the meshes of limited group activities and of individualistic endeavour as against the more important social and collective efforts. The Anarchists, the future unbiased historian will admit, have played a very important role in the Russian Revolution—a role far more significant and fruitful than their comparatively small number would have led one to expect. Yet honesty and sincerity compel me to state that their work would have been of infinitely greater practical value had they been better organized and equipped to guide the released energies of the people toward the reorganization of life on a libertarian foundation.

But the failure of the Anarchists in the Russian Revolution—in the sense just indicated—does by no means argue the defeat of the libertarian idea. On the contrary, the Russian Revolution has demonstrated beyond doubt that the State idea, State Socialism, in all its manifestations (economic, political, social, educational) is entirely and hopelessly bankrupt. Never before in all history has authority, government, the State, proved so inherently static, reactionary, and even counter-revolutionary in effect. In short, the very antithesis of revolution.

It remains true, as it has through all progress, that only the libertarian spirit and method can bring man a step further in his eternal striving for the better, finer, and freer life. Applied to the great social upheavals known as revolutions, this tendency is as potent as in the ordinary evolutionary process. The authoritarian method has been a failure all through history and now it has again failed in the Russian Revolution. So far human ingenuity has discovered no other principle except the libertarian, for man has indeed uttered the highest wisdom when he said that liberty is the mother of order, not its daughter. All political tenets and parties notwithstanding, no revolution can be truly and permanently successful unless it puts its emphatic veto upon all tyranny and centralization, and determinedly strives to make the revolution a real revaluation of all economic, social, and cultural values. Not mere substitution of one political party for another in the control of the Government, not the masking of autocracy by proletarian slogans, not the dictatorship of a new class over an old one, not political scene shifting of any kind, but the complete reversal of all these authoritarian principles will alone serve the revolution.

In the economic field this transformation must be in the hands of the industrial masses: the latter have the choice between an industrial State and anarcho-syndicalism. In the case of the former the menace to the constructive development of the new social structure would be as great as from the political State. It would become a dead weight upon the growth of the new forms of life. For that very reason syndicalism (or industrialism) alone is not, as its exponents claim, sufficient unto itself. It is only when the libertarian spirit permeates the economic organizations of the workers that the manifold creative energies of the people can manifest themselves. and the revolution be safeguarded and defended. Only free initiative and popular participation in the affairs of the revolution can prevent the terrible blunders committed in Russia. For instance, with fuel only a hundred *versts* [about sixty-six miles] from Petrograd there would have been no necessity for that city to suffer from cold had the workers' economic organizations of Petrograd been free to exercise their initiative for the common good. The peasants of the Ukraina would not have been hampered in the cultivation of their land had they had access to the farm implements stacked up in the warehouses of Kharkov and other industrial centres awaiting orders from Moscow for their distribution. These are characteristic examples of Bolshevik governmentalism and centralization, which should serve as a warning to the workers of Europe and America of the destructive effects of Statism.

The industrial power of the masses, expressed through their libertarian associations—Anarcho-syndicalism—is alone able to organize successfully the economic life and carry on production. On the other hand, the coöperatives, working in harmony with the industrial bodies, serve as the distributing and exchange media between city and country, and at the same time link in fraternal bond the industrial and agrarian masses. A common tie of mutual service and aid is created which is the strongest bulwark of the revolution— far more effective then compulsory labour, the Red Army, or terrorism. In that way alone can revolution act as a leaven to quicken the development of new social forms and inspire the masses to greater achievements.

But libertarian industrial organizations and the coöperatives are not the only media in the interplay of the complex phases of social life. There are the cultural forces which, though closely related to the economic activities, have yet their own functions to perform. In Russia the Communist State became the sole arbiter of all the needs of the social body. The result, as already described, was complete cultural stagnation and the paralysis of all creative endeavour. If such a débâcle is to be avoided in the future, the cultural forces, while remaining rooted in the economic soil, must yet retain independent scope and freedom of expression. Not adher- ence to the dominant political party but devotion to the revolution, knowledge, ability, and — above all — the creative impulse should be the criterion of fitness for cultural work. In Russia this was made impossible almost from the beginning of the October Revolution, by the violent separation of the intelligentsia and the masses. It is true that the original offender in this case was the intelligentsia, especially the technical intelligentsia, which in Russia tenaciously clung — as it does in other countries — to the coat-tails of the bourgeoisie. This element, unable to comprehend the significance of revolutionary events, strove to stem the tide by wholesale sabotage. But in Russia there was also another kind of intelligentsia — one with a glorious revolutionary past of a hundred years. That part of the intelligentsia kept faith with the people, though it could not unreservedly accept the new dictatorship. The fatal error of the Bolsheviki was that they made no distinction between the two elements. They met sabotage with wholesale terror against the intelligentsia as a class, and inaugurated a campaign of hatred more intensive than the persecution of the bourgeoisie itself — a method which created an abyss between the intelligentsia and the proletariat and reared a barrier against constructive work.

Lenin was the first to realize that criminal blunder. He pointed out that it was a grave error to lead the workers to believe that they could build up the industries and engage in cultural work without the aid and coöperation of the intelligentsia. The proletariat had neither the knowledge nor the training for the task, and the intelligentsia had to be restored in the direction of the industrial life. But the recognition of one error never safeguarded Lenin and his Party from immediately committing another. The technical intelligentsia was called back on terms which added disintegration to the antagonism against the régime.

While the workers continued to starve, engineers, industrial experts, and technicians received high salaries, special privileges, and the best rations. They became the pampered employees of the State and the new slave drivers of the masses. The latter, fed for years on the fallacious teachings that muscle alone is necessary for a successful revolution and that only physical labour is productive, and incited by the campaign of hatred which stamped every intellectual a counter-revolutionist and speculator, could not make peace with those they had been taught to scorn and distrust.

Unfortunately Russia is not the only country where this proletarian attitude against the intelligentsia prevails. Everywhere political demagogues play upon the ignorance of the masses, teach them that education and culture are bourgeois prejudices, that the workers can do without them, and that they alone are able to rebuild society. The Russian Revolution has made it very clear that both brain and muscle are indispensable to the work of social regeneration. Intellectual and physical labour are as closely related in the social body as brain and hand in the human organism. One cannot function without the other.

It is true that most intellectuals consider themselves a class apart from and superior to the workers, but social conditions everywhere are fast demolishing the high pedestal of the intelligentsia. They are made to see that they, too, are proletarians, even more dependent upon the economic master than the manual worker. Unlike the physicial proletarian, who can pick up his tools and tramp the world in search of a change from a galling situation, the intellectual proletarians have their roots more firmly in their particular social environment and cannot so easily change their occupation or mode of living. It is therefore of utmost importance to bring home to the workers the rapid proletarization of the intellectuals and the common tie thus created between them. If the Western world is to profit by the lessons of Russia, the demagogic flattery of the masses and blind antagonism toward the intelligentsia must cease. That does not mean, however, that the toilers should depend entirely upon the intellectual element. On the contrary, the masses must begin right now to prepare and equip themselves for the great task the revolution will put upon them. They should acquire the knowledge and technical skill necessary for managing and directing the intricate mechanism of the industrial and social structure of their respective countries. But even at best the workers will need the coöperation of the professional and cultural elements. Similarly the latter must realize that their true interests are identical with those of the masses. Once the two social forces learn to blend into one harmonious whole, the tragic aspects of the Russian Revolution would to a great extent be eliminated. No one would be shot because he "once acquired an education." The scientist, the engineer, the specialist, the investigator, the educator, and the creative artist, as well as the carpenter, machinist, and the rest, are all part and parcel of the collective force which is to shape the revolution into the great architect of the new social edifice. Not hatred, but unity; not antagonism, but fellowship; not shooting, but sympathy — that is the lesson of the great Russian débâcle for the intelligentsia as well as the workers. All must learn the value of mutual aid and libertarian cooperation. Yet each must be able to remain independent in his own sphere and in harmony with the best he can yield to society. Only in that way will productive labour and educational and cultural endeavour express themselves in ever newer and richer forms. That is to me the all-embracing and vital moral taught by the Russian Revolution.

IV

In the previous pages I have tried to point out why Bolshevik principles, methods, and tactics failed, and that similar principles and methods applied in any other country, even of the highest industrial development, must also fail. I have further shown that it is not only Bolshevism that failed, but Marxism itself. That is to say, the *state idea*, the authoritarian principle, has been proven bankrupt by the experience of the Russian Revolution. If I were to sum up my whole argument in one sentence I should say: The inherent tendency of the State is to concentrate, to narrow, and monopolize all social activities; the nature of revolution is, on the contrary, to grow, to broaden, and disseminate itself in ever-wider circles. In other words, the State is institutional and static; revolution is fluent, dynamic. These two tendencies are incompatible and mutually destructive. The State idea killed the Russian Revolution and it must have the same result in all other revolutions, unless the libertarian ideas prevail.

Yet I go much further. It is not only Bolshevism, Marxism, and Governmentalism which are fatal to revolution as well as to all vital human progress. The main cause of the defeat of the Russian Revolution lies much deeper. It is to be found in the whole Socialist conception of revolution itself.

The dominant, almost general, idea of revolution—particularly the Socialist idea—is that revolution is a violent change of social conditions through which one social class, the working class, becomes dominant over another class, the capitalist class. It is the conception of a purely physical change, and as such it involves only political scene shifting and institutional rearrangements. Bourgeois dictatorship is replaced by the "dictatorship of the proletariat "—or by that of its "advance guard," the Communist Party; Lenin takes the seat of the Romanovs, the Imperial Cabinet is rechristened Soviet of People's Commissars, Trotsky is appointed Minister of War, and a labourer becomes the Military Governor General of Moscow. That is, in essence, the Bolshevik conception of revolution, as translated into actual practice. And with a few minor alterations it is also the idea of revolution held by all other Socialist parties.

This conception is inherently and fatally false. Revolution is indeed a violent process. But if it is to result only in a change of dictatorship, in a shifting of names and political personalities, then it is hardly worth while. It is surely not worth all the struggle and sacrifice, the stupendous loss in human life and cultural values that result from every revolution. If such a revolution were even to bring greater social well being (which has not been the case in Russia) then it would also not be worth the terrific price paid: mere improvement can be brought about without bloody revolution. It is not palliatives or reforms that are the real aim and purpose of revolution, as I conceive it.

In my opinion—a thousandfold strengthened by the Russian experience—the great mission of revolution, of the *social revolution*, is a fundamental transvaluation of values. A transvaluation not only of social, but also of human values. The latter are even preëminent, for they are the basis of all social values. Our institutions and conditions rest upon deep-seated ideas. To change those conditions and at the same time leave the underlying ideas and values intact means only a superficial transformation, one that cannot be permanent or bring real betterment. It is a change of form only, not of substance, as so tragically proven by Russia.

It is at once the great failure and the great tragedy of the Russian Revolution that it attempted (in the leadership of the ruling political party) to change only institutions and conditions while ignoring entirely the human and social values involved in the Revolution. Worse yet, in its mad passion for power, the Communist State even sought to strengthen and deepen the very ideas and conceptions which the Revolution had come to destroy. It supported and encouraged all the worst anti-social qualities and systematically destroyed the already awakened conception of the new revolutionary values. The sense of justice and equality, the love of liberty and of human brotherhood — these fundamentals of the real regeneration of society — the Communist State suppressed to the point of extermination. Man's instinctive sense of equity was branded as weak sentimentality; human dignity and liberty became a bourgeois superstition; the sanctity of life, which is the very essence of social reconstruction, was condemned as anrevolutionary, almost counter-revolutionary. This fearful perversion of fundamental values bore within itself the seed of destruction. With the conception that the Revolution was only a means of securing political power, it was inevitable that all revolutionary values should be subordinated to the needs of the Socialist State; indeed, exploited to further the security of the newly acquired governmental power. "Reasons of State," masked as the "interests of the Revolution and of the People," became the sole criterion of action, even of feeling. Violence, the tragic inevitability of revolutionary upheavals, became an established custom, a habit, and was presently enthroned as the most powerful and "ideal" institution. Did not Zinoviev himself canonize Dzerzhinsky, the head of the bloody Tcheka, as the "saint of the Revolution"? Were not the greatest public honours paid by the State to Uritsky, the founder and sadistic chief of the Petrograd Tcheka?

This perversion of the ethical values soon crystallized into the all-dominating slogan of the Communist Party: *the end justifies all means.* Similarly in the past the Inquisition and the Jesuits adopted this motto and subordinated to it all morality. It avenged itself upon the Jesuits as it did upon the Russian Revolution. In the wake of this slogan followed lying, deceit, hypocrisy and treachery, murder, open and secret. It should be of utmost interest to students of social psychology that two movements as widely separated in time and ideas as Jesuitism and Bolshevism reached exactly similar results in the evolution of the principle that the end justifies all means. The historic parallel, almost entirely ignored so far, contains a most important lesson for all coming revolutions and for the whole future of mankind.

There is no greater fallacy than the belief that aims and purposes are one thing, while methods and tactics are another. This conception is a potent menace to social regeneration. All human experience teaches that methods and means cannot be separated from the ultimate aim. The means employed become, through individual habit and social practice, part and parcel of the final purpose; they influence it, modify it, and presently the aims and means become identical. From the day of my arrival in Russia I felt it, at first vaguely, then ever more consciously and clearly. The great and inspiring aims of the Revolution became so clouded with and obscured by the methods used by the ruling political power that it was hard to distinguish what was temporary means and what final purpose. Psychologically and socially the means necessarily influence and alter the aims. The whole history of man is continuous proof of the maxim that to divest one's methods of ethical concepts means to sink into the depths of utter demoralization. In that lies the real tragedy of the Bolshevik philosophy as applied to the Russian Revolution. May this lesson not be in vain.

No revolution can ever succeed as a factor of liberation unless the *means* used to further it be identical in spirit and tendency with the *purposes* to be achieved. Revolution is the negation of the existing, a violent protest against man's inhumanity to man with all the thousand and one slaveries it involves. It is the destroyer of dominant values upon which a complex system of injustice, oppression, and wrong has been built up by ignorance and brutality. It is the herald of *new values*, ushering in a transformation of the basic relations of man to man, and of man to society. It is not a mere reformer, patching up some social evils; not a mere changer of forms and institutions; not only a re-distributor of social well-being. It is all that, yet more, much more. It is, first and foremost, the *transvaluator*, the bearer of new values. It is the great *teacher of the new ethics*, inspiring man with a new concept of life and its manifestations in social relationships. It is the mental and spiritual regenerator.

Its first ethical precept is the identity of means used and aims sought. The ultimate end of all revolutionary social change is to establish the sanctity of human life, the dignity of man, the right of every human being to liberty and well being. Unless this be the essential aim of revolution, violent social changes would have no justification. For external social alterations can be, and have been, accomplished by the normal processes of evolution. Revolution, on the contrary, signifies not mere external change, but internal, basic, fundamental change. That internal change of concepts and ideas, permeating ever-larger social strata, finally culminates in the violent upheaval known as revolution. Shall that climax reverse the process of transvaluation, turn against it, betray it? That is what happened in Russia. On the contrary, the revolution itself must quicken and further the process of which it is the cumulative expression; its main mission is to inspire it, to carry it to greater heights, give it fullest scope for expression. Only thus is revolution true to itself.

Applied in practice it means that the period of the actual revolution, the so-called transitory stage, must be the introduction, the prelude to the new social conditions. It is the threshold to the *new life*, the new *house of man and humanity.* As such it must be of the spirit of the new life, harmonious with the construction of the new edifice.

To-day is the parent of to-morrow. The present casts its shadow far into the future. That is the law of life, individual and social. Revolution that divests itself of ethical values—thereby lays the foundation of injustice, deceit, and oppression for the future society. The means used to prepare the future become its cornerstone. Witness the tragic condition of Russia. The methods of State centralization have paralysed individual initiative and effort; the tyranny of the dictatorship has cowed the people into slavish submission and all but extinguished the fires of liberty; organized terrorism has depraved and brutalized the masses and stifled every idealistic aspiration; institutionalized murder has cheapened human life, and all sense of the dignity of man and the value of life has been eliminated; coercion at every step has made effort bitter, labour a punishment, has turned the whole of existence into a scheme of mutual deceit, and has revived the lowest and most brutal instincts of man. A sorry heritage to begin a new life of freedom and brotherhood.

It cannot be sufficiently emphasized that revolution is in vain unless inspired by its ultimate ideal. Revolutionary methods must be in tune with revolutionary aims. The means used to further the revolution must harmonize with its purposes. In short, the ethical values which the revolution is to establish in the new society must be initiated with the revolutionary activities of the so-called transitional period. The latter can serve as a real and dependable bridge to the better life only if built of the same material as the life to be achieved. Revolution is the mirror of the coming day; it is the child that is to be the Man of To-morrow.